T0269431

HARRY DEE
MEMOIRS

Harry Dee

authorHOUSE®

AuthorHouse™
1663 Liberty Drive
Bloomington, IN 47403
www.authorhouse.com
Phone: 1 (800) 839-8640

© 2016 Christopher Dee. All rights reserved.

No part of this book may be reproduced, stored in a retrieval system, or
transmitted by any means without the written permission of the author.

Published by AuthorHouse   07/05/2016

ISBN: 978-1-5246-0442-4 (sc)
ISBN: 978-1-5246-0441-7 (e)

Print information available on the last page.

Any people depicted in stock imagery provided by Thinkstock are models,
and such images are being used for illustrative purposes only.
Certain stock imagery © Thinkstock.

This book is printed on acid-free paper.

Because of the dynamic nature of the Internet, any web addresses or links contained in
this book may have changed since publication and may no longer be valid. The views
expressed in this work are solely those of the author and do not necessarily reflect the
views of the publisher, and the publisher hereby disclaims any responsibility for them.

April 15, 2016

In the spring of 1997, just before my father went into the hospital, he gave me four black and white marble composition books. From February 15, 1990 to September 21, 1996, my father had been writing his memoirs upstairs at his desk. He celebrated his 80th birthday in the hospital and shortly after that he was able to come home. I did some more family history research and I found some death certificates and cemetery information. My father and I talked about his memoirs and he added a few more thoughts and some more information.

He wasn't able to write any more chapters. His memoirs are the first half of his life.

This book is dedicated to my father and also to our dear friend Katherine Evancie.

Katherine was an editor at a book publishing company in New York. She read the memoirs and we talked about getting them published. She is buried very close to my father in St. Philip's Cemetery.

May they rest in peace.

Christopher Dee

For Christopher, Clare, and Patricia, our dear children, and, God willing, their children.

"Y'know - Babylon once had 2 million people in it, and all we know about 'em is the names of the kings and some copies of wheat contracts. . . and contracts for the sale of slaves. Yet every night all those families sat down to supper, and the father came home from his work, and the smoke went up the chimney,-same as here. And even in Greece and Rome, all we know about the <u>real</u> life of the people is what we can piece together out of the joking palms and the comedies they wrote for the theatre back then. So I am going to have a copy of this play in the cornerstone and the people of the thousand years from now'll know a few simple facts about us. . . This is the way we were: in our growing up and in our marrying and in our living and in our dying. . ."

Stage manager Our Town, Act one.

Thornton Wilder 1938.

Thursday, February 15, 1990

Among childhood's most happy memories were visits to Grandma and Grandpa Foley in Philadelphia. The Pennsylvania Railroad in the 1920's used to offer inexpensive Sunday excursions. The run from Manhattan to 30th Street took only about an hour and a half. Thus we went often. Mother hustled Lillian and me early enough to get to Mass at St. Clement's, after which we sometimes met Kelly and the McLaughlin cousins.

Unlike New York City subway cars, Pensie coaches had doors at the end only, lamps with glass globes down the middle of the arched ceiling, luggage racks of metal rods, and double seats, in stuffy velvet, whose backs could be flipped so that riders could face forward or backward. At each end a toilet, unlocked only when the train was running in open country, for there were no holding tanks. Drinking water and folded paper cups.

Over in New Jersey, just beyond the tunnels, at a clearing called Manhattan Transfer, the electric engine was exchanged for a mammoth steam locomotive that hurled us alone at a mile a minute. Lillian and I took turns at the window, fascinated by so much so different from Brooklyn.

Before the present 30th Street station was built, passengers for West Philadelphia stepped down to the ground. That wheezing black giant, whose wheels were taller than many grown-ups, snorted puffs of smoke and steam and an odor all its own that we called coal gas. Mindful of the soot, we hurried to the station, heads down, though sometimes I managed a glance at the engineer high in his window.

The P.R. T. (Philadelphia Rapid Transit) trolley car marked "Darby 11" soon rattled out to the University of Pennsylvania, and along Woodland Avenue down whose side streets one could glimpse two story brick single-family houses, shoulder-to-shoulder, row upon row, flat roofs, wooden porches, and all of the same design.

Philadelphia Rapid Transit had an unusual practice in collecting fares on that line. In traveling from downtown west toward Darby, the fare was paid upon entering the trolley car, but on the return trip upon leaving. Until steel bars were installed, we sometimes saw young men climb out the back windows.

While most were row houses, many shared only one wall and a symmetrical plan, so that each was a mirror image of the other. Such was the Foleys' at 7214 Greenway Avenue; the Bob Walkers on the left. Red brick, gabled roof, three stories, the ridge from side to side, screened porch, the last house on the street. Father to the west stretched open fields right and left down to Cobbs Creek Parkway, the park, creek and Darby, in Delaware County. An unbroken view extended on the left to the Blue Bell Tavern on the corner of Woodland Avenue.

I must have been about six or seven years old when grandpa Foley had occasion to fetch something in a wheelbarrow, manure perhaps for his garden. When we reached the Blue Bell, he asked me to stay with the wheelbarrow. A few minutes later he was minding the barrow, and I was crossing a white tiled floor, and looking up at a man in a white shirt who stretched over the bar, and handed down a glass of ginger ale.

Except for a red- brick walk that sloped alongside Quigley's on the corner down to Foley's, there was no pavement nor other house west of 72nd Street. Antique working gas lamps lent a Victorian charm, especially at night, with their soft light and no glare.

Dense ivy climbed the side wall all the way to the peak. In summer Uncle Eddie had to prune it off the screens. A concrete walk lay from the iron front gate to the back porch, a wooden lean-to screened by a lattice of weathered cedar. No one used the front door. My mother used to reach up in passing and tap on a living room window. By the time we got to the porch, Grandma would be opening the kitchen door. Even Mr. Mc Ann, the mailman, would come in that way and chat, having ignored the mail slot in the front door.

The kitchen was a lean-to with no cellar, as broad as the rest of the house, and half as deep, a place of unique aromas. Indeed every room in that house had its own peculiar scent. Standing in the doorway, one could see through the kitchen, living room, and hall to the front door, except in winter when the hall door was kept shut. Door locks, by the way, were square boxes held by screws in the corners. Thus keys were long enough to reach through the doors. Knobs were dark brown porcelain.

In the middle of the kitchen: a large oaken table and six high-back chairs. White table cloth. A built-in cupboard, white, in the far right corner. At its left, an old fashioned one-piece couch, with no arms or back, but a kind of built-in pillow sloping up to the right. Grandchildren like to sit there reading the Sunday funnies. An oaken buffet just fit between the side windows. A steeple mantel clock counted the hours and gonged once on the half-hour. What became of that treasure, I don't know. I do recall cousin Eddie Kelly's sharing the hope of inheriting it.

A Morris chair, every one's favorite, in the left far corner beyond the window. He's been gone 64 years, but I still see Grandpa Foley there at the window reading The Bulletin or The Philadelphia Inquirer, gray woolen cardigan, baggy pants, leather slippers with knitted gussets over the ankles, and finger-hold loops over the heels. After supper he'd sit alone in the dark, the only sound the ticking of the clock, and dangling from his left hand a black rosary. Then some nights he'd make tea. The kettle was usually steaming on the coal stove.

First he'd spread a few pages of newspaper over his place at the table. If there were left-over boiled potatoes, he'd peel one and sprinkle salt, while the tea cooled in the saucer. Children were not served tea or coffee, milk being preferred, milk occasionally flavored with Bosco chocolate syrup, but sharing cold potatoes was a novel treat.

Opposite the buffet, and behind Grandpa's place at table: a wide sink against the wall shared with the Walkers. One had to be thirsty to drink plain Philadelphia water. It tasted as bad as that in the Flatbush section of Brooklyn. When Lillian and I were very young, we spent part of the summer at Grandma's. Mother joined us on Saturday afternoon. Before supper Grandma would draw a chair up to the sink, and with a bar of Fels Naptha laundry soap, made sure our hands, face, neck, and arms were shining.

Against the back wall, near the door, an antique oaken ice box, the kind with a thick lid over the ice chamber, shiny brass hardware, and a porcelain pan underneath to catch the runoff.

Just left of the coal stove, a wide window affording a view through the porch and Concord grape arbor to the back gate.

At the right of the Morris chair: the door to the living room, a warm cozy retreat where Grandma listened to her Philco radio, or read The Saturday Evening Post, Ladies Home Journal, Country Gentleman, or The Messenger of the Sacred Heart. I don't recall ever seeing her use it but next to her easy chair stood a rectangular footstool upholstered in a bright print. The top was hinged over a cavity usually holding a box of Whitman's chocolates or Frahlinger's salt-water taffy from the Atlantic City. The latter were sticks about 3 in. long, as thick as a pencil, and wrapped in waxed paper. The boxes were full or nearly full, until grandchildren yielded to temptation.

I said Grandma listened to the radio. Poor Grandpa was too deaf, after many years as a steamfitter with Baldwin Locomotive. Oh, he could hear if you shouted loud enough, but normal speech, the radio and phonograph were too soft. But, by the grace of God, he could read without glasses.

Also in the living room: a phonograph, "Victrola", of reddish brown mahogany veneers. When you raised the square lid, hinged at the back, a latch held it open until you were ready to listen. The turntable ran by a spring wound by a crank on the right side. After you flipped a lever under the table, and waited for full speed, care had to be taken not to scratch the record as the needle was lowered onto the outermost grooves.

All the 78 r.p.m. records were "R.C.A. Victor Red Seal", each in a protective paper envelope with holes in the center exposing the labels, and stored on edge in the partitioned cabinet below. As the spring unwound, the speed got slower and slower, thus distorting the sound. Working the crank, and flipping the records, kept one alert. The reward was great, however, for there were such eminent talents as Enrico Caruso, Fritz Kreisler, John McCormick, and vaudeville comedians Gallagher and Sheen, among others.

After Grandma died on February 1, 1939, Uncle Eddie married his long time sweetheart, Frances, sold the house, and moved to Camden, New Jersey, just across the Delaware. The Victrola and records passed to the Kelly's, who offered them to me. Uncle Ed Kelly was to ship them from Darby to Brooklyn, or so I understood, but as with all Foley treasures, I never knew what became of them, nor did I choose to ask.

Edward Bernard Foley, (Uncle Eddie) born in 1892, supported his mother – his father having died in 1926 – until she died in 1939.

His wife, Frances Foley lived only a few years and they had no children.

In early 1947, Uncle Eddie became quite ill. Katie, his sister, nursed him in her Darby home, just as she had done in 1937 for my sister, Lillian. Eddie died on June 18, 1947, a son who devoted most of his life to taking care in their old age of his father and mother. May he and they rest in peace.

In the center of the room: a round dark brown table, perhaps walnut, covered by a white doily, and decorated by a vase of seasonal flowers from the side yard, daisies, gladiolas, whatever. On Easter Sunday mornings Lillian and I'd come down to discover on it baskets left by the Easter Bunny. Jelly beans, solid chocolate eggs, hollow bunnies, and hard-boiled eggs tinted in pastel shades. Afterwards we'd be prompted to search the back yard for still more colored eggs.

Lillian and I helped with chores: sweeping the sidewalk, "redding" the table after meals, drying dishes, dusting, fetching jelly or preserves from the cellar cabinet, or a loaf of bread from the Acme on Woodland Avenue, across from St. Clement's. Then there was polishing that living room table.

At home we polished furniture with crude oil from Scharf's Hardware on Washington Avenue. He filled your bottle from a barrel, as was the custom with kerosene also. Grandma, however, favored "lemon oil", well applied and buffed. I was done only when Grandma said it was done. "Here, look; you missed a spot, and there."

Enclosed stairs separated the living room from the parlor, that seldom-used guardian of dark Victorian velvet-covered chairs, corner shelves, and fragile knickknacks. Here the Foley daughters had received gentlemen callers. Grandpa (obit. September 12, 1926) was laid out there. The hall being so narrow, the coffin was passed through the front window. The undertaker, Bart Cavanaugh, hung the traditional sign at the front door, a rosette and streamers of black ribbon. Men mourners clustered in the kitchen; woman in the living room.

The front door, held open on hot days by a cast iron alligator, had a round mechanical bell in the middle that clanged when the flat handle was twisted a half turn. On its upper half: two vertical panes of beveled clear glass screened by white lace. The sill of white marble.

Rocking chairs on the porch, also a wicker table holding magazines and cardboard fans with flat wooden handles and advertisements for Bart Cavanaugh's services.

Across Greenway, and closer to 72nd Street, a church with a black congregation. In those days the usage was "colored" or "negro", at which no offense was intended nor taken. Now the church building was unusual, in that services were held below ground level, in what would have been called the basement, if construction had been completed. Passersby could have missed seeing it, unless they heard the hymn singing.

Seldom during the week did we see blacks in the neighborhood – the section may have been called Paschall – but on Sunday afternoon the small congregation gathered, dressed up in "Sunday best".

From the porch we could see about a quarter mile away a Baltimore and Ohio railroad bridge across the parkway and creek to Darby. Lillian and I liked to count freight cars lumbering over, sometimes as many as one hundred.

One afternoon Uncle Eddie took Billy McLaughlin and me for a walk to Yeadon, perhaps to visit Holy Cross Cemetery. We may have been nine or ten years old. Whatever the plan, Uncle Eddie led us across that bridge. There being no gravel nor other roadbed, we had to step deliberately from tie to tie. Billy gave no hint of fear, but though I said nothing, at every step I dreaded falling through.

Just inside the front door, a ceramic umbrella stand, empty except for a black- thorn walking stick. Close to the ceiling, a cluster of thin rectangular glass pendants that tinkled in a draft, as they jostled one another.

Stairs were boxed in between partitions, but there was no door, below or above. As we climbed, we'd see St. Joseph peering back at us from a black oval frame hung in the hall. Turn left into the master bedroom.

Dresser and mirror. Arrayed across the scarf: round hand held mirror, tortoise shell comb and hair pin box, hairbrush, hat pins, and milky-glass bottles. Dark brown armoire, tall and wide. On a windowsill, almost hidden by the curtain, a wooden box with wires, handles, dials, a device that Grandpa had hoped would relieve his "rheumatism". Between the front windows, a framed illuminated Papal blessing, probably on the occasion of a wedding anniversary. It would have been helpful in researching family history a few years ago, but it too had vanished. On the far side of the high double bed, up near the head board, what appeared to be an oaken armchair, but whose lid covered a white porcelain chamber pot, relics of days long gone. My mother once told us of having as a child to walk a line of planks to an outhouse. Still another relic, a wash stand with rods on the sides for towels, and holding a large ornate ceramic bowl and matching pitcher. A crucifix over the head board.

Beyond the stairs, a smaller bedroom over the living room, the one that Lillian and I slept in as toddlers. A huge framed picture of St. Anthony of Padua holding the Christ child. A single window allowed a view of the back yard, beyond the kitchen roof and porch, and the lot fronting on Yokum Street, which too was unpaved west of 72nd Street, nor did it have a brick walk.

A family named Flynn lived there in an isolated house on the edge of the fields. Their rooster chanting Matins added proof that Lillian and I had been transposed to a new, more charming world.

On New Year's Eve we asked to be awakened so we could join in the noisemaking with pots and wooden spoons. I recall being peeved one morning because, as I believed, no one had roused us. Of course, I was mistaken; evidently I had been only half awake.

Originally that bedroom was almost the size of the living room below, the hall making the difference. Then the only water in the house was hand-pumped from a well in the kitchen. My mother told of drawing water for ballplayers from the field behind the Blue Bell. With the coming of city water and indoor plumbing, the well was capped – surely a regrettable move – and a narrow bathroom was fashioned by a partition parallel to the side wall. It may have been Uncle Will McLaughlin, a plumbing contractor, who did the work.

The bathtub stood on four iron feet shaped like cats' paws. Faucets had white porcelain handles. An oaken tank close to the ceiling held water that flushed the toilet when a wooden handle hanging on a chain at the left was pulled. Lifebuoy soap with its peculiar salmon color and medicinal odor. Chrome-plated safety razor. Gillette blue blades, double edged. An ashtray of green glass shaped like a canoe. Uncle Eddie smoked Chesterfield brand cigarettes. Linoleum wall-to-wall. Incidentally, there was another toilet off the back porch, nestled in the corner near Walkers'. The bowl was cast iron, painted green. The door was of tongue-in-groove boards with a latch like those on the kitchen cupboard and the tool shed.

The rear bedroom on the third floor was Uncle Eddie's. Hanging near the door, a framed high-school diploma awarded to "Elizabeth G. Foley". Only after many years did it dawn on me who that was. In the closet, a World War One American helmet and gas mask, solitary reminder of Uncle Eddie's service in France with the Kentucky engineers. He had been operating a linotype in Louisville. I say solitary because he never spoke of the war, nor did anyone else. He was active in the Elks, whose monogram he interpreted for a nephew as "Best People On Earth".

After the war he worked for Curtis Publishing in Philadelphia, not far from Independence Hall, leaving home after supper, and creeping back in the middle of the night. Grandchildren, therefore, learned to keep quiet lest we wake him up, even though his snoring could be heard on the floor below.

The front third-floor bedroom was memorable for its feather mattress, down comforter, and ancient wooden trunk with leather straps and convex lid.

Though Lillian and I were first to go to bed, we were never first to get up. One summer morning Grandpa was attaching a latch to the front gate post, one he had fashioned from a thin sheet of steel, and painted green, his favorite.

He found a cap pistol once, rusted and unworkable. On our next visit he presented it to me, cleaned and painted green. What boy could have had a more lovable grandfather?

Neither he nor Grandma nor any other Foley could have been described as affectionate. Never did I hear anyone say to anyone else "I love you", or other terms of endearment. Never did I see anyone hug anyone else. Ethnic-cultured conditioning perhaps. Shaking hands and a pat on the head with "My, how you've grown" were what a small boy came to expect. But then there were the cap pistol, and the glass of ginger ale and the Easter baskets and the walk to Darby and the un-roasted peanuts to plant in the yard and the quarter that Grandma gave me when Billy McLaughlin and I were leaving for a public swimming pool, and the five dollar gold pieces at Christmas.

Most mornings we'd come down to find Grandpa cultivating his flowers or vegetables, tomatoes, peppers, beans, scallions, carrots, all in neat rows near the back fence, and beyond the tiny white-washed tool shed that my mother dubbed "Pop's garage". She recalled how once in a while he'd come home from work and immediately hurry out with the coal scuttle and shovel. He had passed horse manure on the way from the trolley.

Lucky was the youngster who happened to be close when Grandpa was washing scallions or carrots at the garden faucet. A blue bandana dried his hands.

A small plot of grass and white clover lay between the wire fence and the concord-grape arbor, and just behind the latticed porch. An arbor of white grapes shaded the sidewalk on the other side of the porch. On Mondays Grandma dried the laundry over the lawn, propping up sagging lines with poles having matched ends. One day while Lillian and I were searching for a four leaf clover, Uncle Eddie happened by, and announced that if we" prefer to catch a robin, we need only sprinkle salt on its tail, a tactic that proved as futile as hunting for a lucky clover, for we had neglected to ask how to get birds to stand still long enough.

Those same laundry lines served on other days to hold rugs draped over while dust was beaten out with a broom stick or wire loops on a long handle. Though this chore was reserved for grownups, small fry could shop at the Acme, given a written note and a coin purse.

Back in Brooklyn, groceries were assembled on the counter, wrapped in brown paper, and tied with a string from a wire ball hung from the ceiling. Heavy bundles were carried out with a handle formed from a cardboard tube and wire looped at the ends. In Philadelphia, however, the customer brought from home a basket hung under his arm. In those days perishable foods didn't last long in the ice box, and so butter, milk, meat and such were bought in small quantities. Almost every day something was needed from the store. Thus the basket need not be huge, nor the load heavy.

A popular dish in Grandma's was dried beef in a thick cream sauce. Another was sliced tomatoes fried in a little milk. Potatoes were boiled with the skins on. At breakfast soft-boiled eggs were served standing in a small china cup. The top of the shell was then cracked and then lifted off so that the egg could be scooped out. Breakfast after Sunday Mass was often fried eggs and Philadelphia's own spicy, crisp, fried scrapple. Heavenly!

The Foley table was always set with bread, butter, milk, sugar, extra spoons in a cut glass jar, black pepper, coarse red pepper, napkins in rings, and salt in tiny shallow dishes that one dipped the tip of his knife into.

At dinner Lillian and I were required to eat at least two slices of bread, and to clean our plates if we hoped to get dessert. First and last slices of bread, the "crusts", we were assured would guarantee our growing up to have curly hair. In my view one slice was as good as another when plastered with Grandma's own homemade grape jelly or that old style peanut butter: only ground salted peanuts. By the way, except for sparse hair on the sides, Grandpa was bald.

Dessert could have been rice or tapioca or bread pudding, junket, pie, cake, cookies, or, as a special treat ice cream. Some of us would take the short cut out back and up Yokum Street to a nearby shop on Woodland Avenue, where we had carried a large bowl. Care had to be taken on the way back lest the wind rip away the waxed-paper cover.

A local treat was served by a peddler from a hand cart holding a block of ice and bottles of syrups. A hand tool like an inverted metal cup with fine teeth was scraped across the ice forming inside a ball of crystals and chips. This was dropped onto a square of waxed paper, and then sprinkled with the chosen flavor, grape, lemon, etc.

After Sunday dinner Lillian and I often visited the Kellys, in Darby. A path through the fields stretched diagonally toward the Woodland Avenue bridge that crosses narrow Cobbs Creek at the southern end of the slender park. A common sight in the park on Sundays was a small group singing hymns to the accompaniment of a small harmonium. "Rock of Ages" or "In the Sweet By and By" or "The Old Rugged Cross" etc.

Cobbs Creek as viewed from the bridge looked more like a long pond, hardly a ripple, and narrow enough that everyone could have thrown a stone across.

Beyond the bridge the avenue becomes Darby's Main Street. Philadelphia law against selling fireworks did not apply in Delaware County. Billy McLaughlin used to cross over to buy "salutes" and sparklers set out on tables along the sidewalk. The smallest firecrackers came in clusters so that they'd explode in rapid succession, or they could be detached, which Billy did, and fired one at a time from a smoldering punk.

A few doors up was a tavern with a sign over a side door, "Family Entrance". My mother and Aunt Katie went in there once for a private chat and a glass of Schmidt's beer.

Across the street, alongside the creek, stood the massive red-brick Fels soap factory. Aunt Katie may have worked there while she was single. If the work day started at 8 AM, the gate was locked at 8 AM, and not re-opened until noon. Similarly at 1 PM, after lunch. Thus to be late was to miss a half days pay. Incidentally, my mother said that Grandma used to call her children just once in the morning, whether for school or later for work. I myself remember her calling Uncle Eddie in late afternoon. She'd stand at the front door of the stairs. "Ed! Yo, Ed!" That was enough; from the third floor he'd answer.

The Kellys lived at 103 North Front Street, close to the corner of Greenway Avenue, which sloped down a short distance to the creek. One of the houses down there - I have no idea which – was home to our parents and us during their short-lived married life together, from October 1915 until March or April of 1918.

Aunt Katie and Uncle Ed Kelly – a plasterer like my father and his father – had five children: Dorothy, Catherine, Eddie, Helen, and Jack. Dorothy was about a year older than I. Uncle Ed had another daughter, Grace, by an earlier marriage. I have no recollection of her; she didn't live in Darby.

103 North Front Street was typically single-family, 2-story, red brick, semi-detached, with a front porch, and on such a slope that the back door to the cellar was above ground. A small grass plot and flower garden in the back. A heavy - laden pear tree in the far left corner. A narrow side yard on the north.

In Grandma's house no one let the cold water run in the sink, because of the nasty odor. So too in Kelly's but only because the delicious "Springfield" water was metered. A bottle was kept in the ice box, alongside the home-made ginger beer or root beer.

Aunt Katie's parlor hid a rare prize, an upright piano that could be played by anyone. A window opened in the middle, above the keyboard, where a roll of paper about a foot wide could be set in and made to unwind downward across a row of tiny air holes in a brass plate and onto another spool. The roll had tiny square holes governing just one key, one note. A lever allowed change in the tempo. Power came from pedals pumped alternately right and left. Song lyrics were printed down the side so that one could sing along.

Like cordwood stacked atop the piano, square-ended cardboard boxes of music rolls. At the right, on a tasseled scarf, a framed studio portrait in sepia of my mother, full faced head and shoulders.

The sisters Lillian and Katie were close in affection as well as age and features. Indeed, Katie had been my mother's maid of honor. They had an older sister, Fanny, who married someone named Joseph Swift, of whom I have no recollection at all. They had no children. Aunt Fanny supervised housekeeping in a Philadelphia hotel. The only contact Lillian and I had with her was on those rare times when she went home to visit while we too were at Grandma's. The poor soul must have borne a heavy cross, one that crowded out patience with small nieces and nephews, in contrast with Uncle Eddie, who was at least pleasant, when not jovial. May she rest in peace.

Mary McLaughlin, first of the five sisters, lived on the same side of Greenway Avenue, a few doors below 70th Street, in a house unusual only for its narrow enclosed back stairs, from hall to kitchen.

Uncle Will McLaughlin was first in the family and the neighborhood to own an automobile, a Studebaker President, four door sedan. The year may have been 1928. Evidently his plumbing business was doing well. I rode in it once when son James drove to New York. After supper we crossed the Brooklyn Bridge, and cruised midtown sightseeing, just James and I.

Houses in that Philadelphia neighborhood were built before the first automobiles. P.R.T. trolley cars served well. Thus no one had a garage, and few had space to build one. Cars were weekend luxuries. After the McLaughlin's moved to Yeadon, to a new house with a built in garage, Uncle Will, as winter approached, jacked up the Studebaker, and covered it with canvas until spring. That was the evolution of the "Sunday driver".

Mary, Lillian, and Katie all resembled their mother and each other in looks as well as mannerisms, the more so as they got older.

The McLaughlin children were John, Catherine, Mary, James, Anna, Margaret, and Billy, the youngest and about my age. Of all these my favorite by far was Anna, vivacious, pretty, cheerful, and best of all, she had time for Lillian and me, an obvious distinction.

Billy McLaughlin was the first relative to have electric trains. That Lionel set had enough tracks to form an enormous loop or a figure 8, and also a semaphore signal tower, station, tunnel, and a headlight on the locomotive. A transformer allowed variations in the speed. Whether the same Christmas or earlier or later, I don't recall, but I also do recall receiving a set of American Flyer trains whose locomotive was powered by a spring wound by a key on the right side. Lots of tracks too.

One afternoon I dropped in while Billy was sitting on the cellar steps shooting with a Daisy BB gun at cans set up against the back wall. I was in time to stand the targets up again. As I was bending over, he shot me in the behind, and laughing, ran upstairs.

Then there was the time we were walking past a church, of which I had taken no notice. In those days devout Catholic men and boys doffed their hats in passing a church, in reverence toward the Blessed Sacrament. Poking my side with his elbow, says Billy "The church; tip your hat!" At once I did so, whereupon Billy laughed and laughed; he knew the church was not Catholic.

My mother once quoted her sister Mary as remarking of someone "Why she'd think nothing of taking a drink, even if only she had a cold". If Aunt Mary held alcohol in a class with say heroin or opium, one must wonder why. It wasn't as though she were reacting to drunkenness at home. Despite Prohibition, bootleggers everywhere were getting rich, and yet only once in my life did I see anything alcoholic in the Foley house. Just once. We had arrived one evening from Brooklyn during a snowfall. I was five or six years old. Grandpa reached into the bottom of the kitchen cupboard, and drew out a bottle with no label but a long tapered cork stopper. God knows how old it was. I recalled the incident years later when my mother said Grandpa kept a bottle that he got filled from a barrel at the Blue Bell, at a time, it must be noted, when it was legal, if not also condoned by such busybody do-gooders as Carrie Nation.

Carrie Nation was a woman who was a member of the temperance movement, she was notable for attacking saloons or taverns with a hatchet.

On the way home from the Baldwin Locomotive works one evening, Grandpa suffered a momentary dizzy spell while walking to the trolley car. As he was hugging a lamp post, he overheard two women passersby commenting on the "drunkard".

In advanced old age my mother used to reminisce with respect and affection about "Pop", her father, sometimes with tears. Several occasions, however, brought out the remark that "My mother didn't want me". "Eddie" on the other hand, "could do no wrong". Never did I judge it wise to press for details, preferring only to lend a sympathetic ear. My suspicion is that Grandma, with no son and four daughters, was disappointed by the fifth, and made too little effort, if any, to hide her despair. Eddie, the last child, was not born until four years later, 1895, when Grandma was 41 years old; Grandpa 45.

John Andrew Foley and Catherine Boyle emigrating from Belfast, and unknown to each other, probably had no formal schooling beyond elementary grades, if indeed they had completed them. He had worked in the shipyards, but both were still young; how young I don't know. Yet they were smart enough to value education, and devout enough to send all six children to St. Clement's parish school and then through high school, probably West Catholic. My mother recalled a sister coming home from school and commenting that Father X ought to go back to the pipe he was giving up for Lent. "He's become such a grouch". Well, Grandma was scandalized and ignoring the validity, if any, of the diagnosis, reprimanded her because one must never speak ill of "God's anointed".

Uncle Eddie often escorted us back to the railroad station on Sunday evenings when he didn't have to work. We'd barely get seated in the trolley car when we'd be grinding past St. Clement's Church, and then, on the other side of Woodland Avenue, St. Vincent's Hospital. where Lillian and I were born, and where my mother nursed me and another baby, whose mother was unable to provide enough milk. A Dr. Boyle – not related to Grandma – had an office nearby. It was he who vaccinated Lillian and me, when we were old enough to go to school, on her thigh and my left arm. It was the same Dr. Boyle who years later was to care for Lillian in her last months. But that's another story.

.

15

Thursday August 13, 1992

Here are some reminiscences about the Foley's.

The census of 1910 lists residents of 7214 Greenway Ave., West Philadelphia, childhood home of John Foley, husband, Katherine, wife, Rose, daughter, Katherine, daughter, Elizabeth G., daughter and Edward B. son.

Because they are recorded as married 35 years, the wedding must have taken place in 1875. John's age is illegible in my copy, as is the year of his birth on his death certificate, where he is said to have died at age 75 in September of 1926. Thus he must have been born on 1851, was 21 when entering the country in 1872, 24 at the wedding and 59 at the census of 1910.

John and his parents are recorded as born in Ireland, with no precise location.

Katherine's age is illegible. Her death certificate, whose data was provided by her son Edward, has her dead at age 85 on February 1, 1939, implying her birth in 1854. May 14, 1854 I believe.

Thus at the wedding she was 21 and at the census 56 years old.

For most of my life, I was sure she had come from Belfast, as had Grandpa Foley, who was reported to have worked there in the shipyards. Her death certificate has Grandma born in Philadelphia, whereas the Census of 1910 says Ireland.

16

On the application for a wedding license in October 1915, my mother gave her mother's maiden name as Catherine Boyle. Now the space on her mother's death certificate for her mother's maiden name is blank, or rather there's a line through it. Could it have been Catherine Boyle?

The Census of 1910 records John and Katherine Foley as parents of twelve children, of whom seven had survived. Of the five who had not survived, three are listed in the records of Holy Cross Cemetery – nearby in Yeadon PA – as Thomas, Francis, and Ellen, all buried on the same day, June 6, 1903 in the Foley plot Section 7 Range 4 Lot 23.

Those records show also that the plot was bought for seventy-five dollars on May 22, 1903, seventeen days before the internment and twenty-eight years after the wedding. Is it not reasonable to infer that the three had died and were buried elsewhere. But where? When? And what of the other two?

Of the seven survivors we've seen three recorded as single and living with their parents : Katherine, Elizabeth and Edward. I can account for the three other daughters: Mary, Frances and Rose, who must have married and left home before the day of the Census, April 19, 1910. Who and where was the seventh survivor? Vaguely I recall overhearing, as a small boy, of a son John who had left in anger. Of course I could have misunderstood.

In June of 1991, while attending a Congress of Secular Carmelites in downtown Philadelphia, I found time that first afternoon to run out on the trolley car to the old neighborhood, of happy memory, and to Holy Cross Cemetery in Yeadon, the first such pilgrimage in decades. The Foley grave (Section 7 Range 4 Lot 23) is a few paces from McDade Blvd. (Route 13) and close to the driveway near the corner with Rundale Avenue.

Mary was the oldest of the Foley children. Frances was the next oldest. Mary Foley married William McLaughlin, a plumbing contractor. They raised Catherine, James, Margaret, John, Mary, Anna and Billy. Billy and I were about the same age. John may have been about ten years older. The Margaret McLaughlin buried in 1906 in the Foley plot must have been another daughter.

The McLaughlin's lived in a two-story row house with an open front porch, typical of West Philadelphia, a short walk up Greenway Avenue from the Foleys. Then in the 1930's they moved to a new house in Yeadon, a bit the other side of Cobb's Creek, the city line.

Uncle Will was the first to own a car, a Studebaker President, four door sedan. First in the neighborhood too.

In the 1920's and 1930's few people had cars, people in places with good public transportation, such as New York or Philadelphia. The first garages were converted carriage barns. In those pioneer days there were no heaters, no air conditioners, no balloon-less tires, no automatic transmissions, no "self-starters". Woolen lap robes were hung behind the front seats. Cars such as Uncle Will's were weekend luxuries, except in winter, when they perched up on blocks shrouded in canvas until the spring thaw.

It may have been in 1930 that I got a ride in the Studebaker. Cousin James had driven on business to New York. He took me joyriding after supper. I fondly recall our racing over the Brooklyn Bridge at 30 M.P.H. and wandering through lower Manhattan, just we two.

John A. McLaughlin married a charming lady, Rose Caserta. She was born on August 27, 1917 in Philadelphia and they were married in 1938 in Philadelphia Index # 688013. Her family had a small grocery store nearby on Greenway Avenue, an oasis in a sea of homes and more homes.

John and Rose raised William, who resembled the McLaughlin's in appearance, and twins Rose Marie and John Michael, more like the Caserta's. One beautiful happy family.

John A. McLaughlin died on January 06, 1956.

William McLaughlin was born in 1938 and died in 2001 and is buried in Holy Cross Cemetery Section N, Range 1.

Rose Marie McLaughlin was born on February 2, 1941 and married William C Downs. "Aunt Lil" and I were honored to sit at the reception with Anna and Billy close to the band. (The rock-n-roll was loud enough for Madison Square Garden. As though we all were hard of hearing.)

John Michael McLaughlin was born on February 2, 1941 and died on August 10, 1997 and is also buried in Holy Cross Cemetery Section N, Range 1.

Rose Caserta McLaughlin Duchat died on August 12, 2007 and she was survived by her second husband Tony Duchat. She is also buried in Holy Cross Cemetery Section N, Range 1.

Catherine McLaughlin married Matthew Gibney (born December 08, 1900 died February 07, 1959). They were married in Philadelphia in 1924. The Gibney's lived close to the St. Clement's Church. They are both buried in Cathedral Cemetery Section X – Range 5.

Anna McLaughlin married William J. Donahue (born August 31, 1897 died June 16, 1963). He too may have been in plumbing. She died a widow on September 22, 1986. They lived at 6826 Paschall Ave. Philadelphia PA. They are also buried in Cathedral Cemetery Section X – Range 5.

Of all the Philadelphia cousins, Anna I loved the most. Pretty. Cheerful. Most of all: Anna always had time for Lillian and me.

James McLaughlin was the victim of a homicide in New York in 1936. He is also buried in Cathedral Cemetery Section X – Range 5.

Frances Foley, "Aunt Fannie", married Joseph Swift. In the late 1920's and early 1930's she used to visit, alone, her mother and brother on Sundays and holidays sometimes when we Brooklyn Dees were doing the same. I believe she was head of housekeeping in a Philadelphia hotel. They are buried in Holy Cross Cemetery Section B, Range 9, Lot 33.

Edward Bernard Foley, only son and youngest child, is recorded as eighteen years old at the census of 1910. Born then in 1892. He's described there as compositor for a newspaper. I knew him to be a Lino-type operator. The name Curtis Publishing Company comes to mind, but in no clear context.

He used to leave for work around suppertime, riding the trolley car on Woodland Ave., two short blocks away, the green one marked "Darby 11". In the small hours of the morning, he'd creep back into the house. My sister

Lillian and I learned to keep very quiet lest we disturb his sleep. His was the rear room on the top (third) floor, where hung a high-school diploma awarded to "Elizabeth G. Foley." Only after many years did it dawn on me who she was. Uncle Eddie's snoring, by the way, could be heard on the second floor. No one closed bedroom doors.

He liked Chesterfield cigarettes, Lifeboy soap, Gillette double-edged blue blades, his hair cut short, vacations in Atlantic City. A member of the Elks, he explained to us that B.P.O.E. meant "Best People on Earth".

Around 1924, Uncle Eddie brought home a handful of unroasted peanuts for us to plant beyond the grape arbor, near the east-side fence. I recall only that they did sprout.

When the country was drawn into the war in Europe, April 1917, Uncle Eddie was working in Louisville. Drafted into the Army, he served in France with a distinguished unit of Kentucky engineers. Afterwards he never spoke of the war, the only reminders being the helmet and gas mask hanging in his closet. Little nephews and nieces crept up there when he was out, fascinated by the trophies.

The Foley house at 7214 Greenway Avenue was semi-detached, the east wall being shared with the neighbors in 7212. In the 1920's and 1930's their name was Walker. The layout of the Walker half was a mirror image of the Foley side. The side windows in the Foley house afforded an unbroken line of sight across broad undeveloped fields and Cobbs Creek Parkway to Darby, hugging the eastern edge of Delaware County.

The Walker-Foley houses were the last on Greenway Avenue, indeed the only ones west of 72nd Street. Moreover, the pavement ended at 72nd Street. But from the side of Quigley's, on the corner, a walk of red brick, set in sand, ran down the slope past Walker's to the maple tree across from the Foley fence. A gas lamp stood close to where the front porches met, a wooden partition between them.

Each of the three floors had two rooms, except for the first which had a one-story extension at the back for the kitchen, as wide as the house. A porch, shaded by unpainted cedar lattice, one step above the ground, extended almost to the fence on the west side. Wooden floor, two steps below the kitchen door. In the inside eastern corner, just beyond the window, a square booth just big enough for a toilet set in concrete. An arbor of grapes shaded the two windows on the side of the kitchen. Another of Concord grapes, on the eastern side of the backyard, formed a shady tunnel from the porch toward the gate, about fifteen feet long.

Between Greenway Avenue and Woodland Avenue to the south lay Yocum Street, narrow and unpaved and without a walk. A path led down to single houses at the far end, occupied by a widow as I recall, Mrs. Flynn, her children and chickens. They were a bit father from 72nd Street than the Foley's.

A large undeveloped lot lay behind the Foley and Walker properties all the way to Yocum Street. Someone in the house on 72nd Street and the corner of Yocum, had fenced in with chicken wires a part of the lot behind his yard for a vegetable garden. It did not, however, bar the Foley's or Walker's from the shortcut to Woodland Avenue. Indeed no one used the front door, except to sit on the porch. Even the letter carrier, Mr. McCann in the 1920's went to the kitchen.

John A. Foley is described in the 1910 census as a boiler maker in a locomotive works. On her application for a wedding license in October 1915, my mother wrote that he was an inspector. Years later she spoke of him as having been a foreman at Baldwin Locomotive.

He invented a steam valve. Baldwin had it patented; for he had devised it in their shop while their employee.

On his way to the trolley car after work, Grandpa became dizzy, enough to prompt him to wrap an arm around a gas lamp. The spell passed quickly but not before a woman passing made a nasty remark about the "drunkard".

My mother revered her father. A song popular in her last years called up happy memories and silent tears: "Oh, My Pa Pa". Then she'd reminisce about a gentle kind man, ever devoted to his family. And he was gone almost half a century.

His hearing as I recall was so poor that we had to shout. Perhaps a price for so many years in a noisy shop. Yet he read without glasses, The Philadelphia Inquirer, The Bulletin, Saturday Evening Post, Country Gentleman and Messenger of the Sacred Heart.

Not only roses, gladiolas, phlox, etc. in the side yard, Grandpa raised also vegetables in a plot against the back fence: string beans, scallions, parsley, carrots, tomatoes and lettuce. Lucky the grandchild who happened to be near when Grandpa washed anything at the garden faucet. I've not forgotten the scent of fresh-picked tomatoes.

Sometimes he liked a cup of tea with milk before going to bed. The huge oaken table in the middle of the kitchen – easily the largest room of all – was covered always with a tablecloth, sometimes checkered in red and white. While the kettle was heating on the coal stove, he'd spread at his place several layers of newspaper. Whenever he found left-over boiled potatoes in the oaken ice box, they became, with a bit of salt dropped from the tip of a knife, a snack to share with the admiring entourage. But we were too young for the tea, though old enough to learn how to cool it in a saucer.

I was about seven years old when he took me along one summer afternoon. I've forgotten where we went and why; I do remember though our stopping on the way at the Blue Bell tavern, on Woodland Avenue, close to Cobbs Creek Parkway and Island Avenue. Grandpa went in, leaving me to mind the wheelbarrow. A couple of minutes later I went in alone. The floor was paved in small white tile, about the size of a quarter. Dark brown woodworking. Ceiling of embossed metal. No customers. A tall man in a white shirt leaned over the bar and handed me a glass of ginger ale. Or was it root beer?

My mother told of how sometimes her father came home from work, grabbed the coal scuttle, and hurried out again. Horse manure was a valued fertilizer, and "road apples" cost nothing.

I still see the old gentleman in his Morris chair in the kitchen, alone in the dark. The only sound: the ticking of the steeple clock atop the oaken sideboard. Baggy woolen trousers. Dark woolen cardigan. Slippers with cloth gussets covering the ankles, and finger loops over the heels like those on riding boots. Dangling from his left hand: black rosary beads.

John Andrew Foley died in his bed on Sunday September 12, 1926. The cause as given on his death certificate is illegible. We know he had suffered from "rheumatism", painful but not mortal.

The ancient custom then prevailing was to wake the dead at home. The undertaker hung black crepe ribbons with a rosette at the front door.

In the Foley house a cozy parlor in Victorian décor separated the front porch from the enclosed stairs. Casket and floral pieces left little room for mourners. Women all in "Sunday best" whispered in the living room. The men sipped spirits in the kitchen. The hall was so narrow that Bart Cavanaugh's pallbearers had to pass the casket through the only window to the porch.

That house held many tokens of devout Catholic faith; each bedroom for example had its crucifix. The one on the second floor rear had also a huge painting or print of St. Anthony of Padua holding the Child Jesus and an open book. Dark reddish brown frame. Next to the armoire in Grandma's front room: a framed Papal blessing occasioned probably by a wedding anniversary. In the upper hall, directly across from the stairs, St. Joseph smiled down from a black oval frame.

That rear bedroom had been divided to make place for a full bathroom on the west side. Uncle Will McLaughlin installed the fixtures. The toilet was flushed by water from a wooden tank near the ceiling, released by pulling a chain on a side. My mother told of having as a child to walk a line of boards to an outhouse.

In front of Grandma's favorite chair, which was in easy reach of the Philco radio, there stood in the living room a foot-stool with Queen Anne legs and upholstered in colorful tapestry. The hinged top concealed a compartment about the size of a shoebox that often held a cache of Whitman's chocolates or salt-water taffy from Fralingers in Atlantic City.

At the right of the hall door – closed only in the winter – a "Victrola", a popular phonograph in a handsome wooden cabinet having a partitioned and or closed space to store records under the speaker. "Victor Red Seal" fragile records in individual paper envelopes. Easily scratched. The 78 r.p.m. turntable was powered by a spring wound and rewound often by a crank on the right side. Enrico Caruso. Fritz Kreisler. John McCormick. The vaudeville comedy team of Gallagher and Sheen etc.

A massive round table of dark brown wood stood in the center of the room, draped with lace that overlapped about a foot. A vase of fresh-cut flowers. When I had grown tall enough to reach, Grandma had me polish the top with lemon oil, buffing until she was satisfied.

Other chores for Lillian and me included sweeping the concrete walk from back porch to front gate, dusting the furniture, fetching Mason jars of preserves stored in a cellar cupboard, (the cellar floor was not paved.) and fetching groceries from the Acme store on Woodland Avenue, across from St. Clement's church.

Grocers in Philadelphia did not provide paper bags. Customers brought wicker baskets. They didn't have to be large, especially in summer, because primitive refrigeration made frequent shopping necessary. And so Lillian and I would set out through the backyard with a written note and cash that Grandma had excavated from a small leather purse buried under layers of white cotton shirts that fell to her high black shoes. Seldom was that basket needed.

Breakfast after Sunday Mass was special: crisp fried scrapple and fried eggs. Occasionally ham or sausages with the eggs. Grownups sometimes preferred the eggs soft boiled. These they spooned from the shell held upright in a footed cup. One at a time. Bread. Butter. Jelly. Marmalade. Red and black pepper shakers. A cut –glass jar full of table spoons. Salt in tiny shallow dishes. Milk for children. At every meal youngsters were required to eat at least one slice of bread. Anyone who did not clean his plate did not get desert. This policy imposed no burden on me.

I don't recall ever seeing bread toasted at Grandma's. But I do remember seeing Aunt Rose Leggett toasting over the gas stove when we lived on Glenmore Avenue, Brooklyn. The toaster of thin steel looked like a stunted tapering obelisk. A shallow ledge at the bottom edges held the slices that leaned against perforated sides. The toasting demanded full attention to avoid burning and to turn the slices with a fork.

While Lillian and I were still very young, Grandma used to wash us at the kitchen sink. She'd draw a chair close to a basin of warm water. With a towel on her lap and a washcloth in hand, she soon had us shining, ready for supper. Not hands and face only, but knees, arms, ears and necks too.

One hot summer day Billy McLaughlin and I walked about a half-mile east to an indoor public swimming pool. We were about ten years old. Just before I left to pick up Billy on the way, Grandma gave me a quarter, a lot of money when a loaf of bread sold for a dime. And she was by no means well off.

But then it wasn't unusual after supper for a grownup to buy peach ice cream, a favorite flavor, from a dealer on Woodland Avenue. It was not pre-packaged. Customers brought a suitable bowl. The dealer covered it with a sheet of wax paper.

At Grandma's funeral February 1939, Bart's pallbearers weren't needed. Six grandsons felt honored to serve. Bart did provide the grey gloves.

Katherine Foley, "Aunt Katie" was twenty-five years old at the census of 1910 and working in a "soap works". That had to be the nearby Fels factory. "Fels Naptha", bars of yellow laundry soap competed with Kirkman's and Octagon.

In June of 1991, it was only an abandoned red-brick shell at the junction of Cobb's Creek and Darby's Main Street; a short walk from what in happier days was the Foley house, but now literally falling apart, although still lived in. Tom Wolfe was right: you can't go home again.

When the Foleys were young, Fels began the day at 8 A.M., at which time the gates for employees were locked until the noon lunch hour. Then again at one o'clock. And so to arrive late was to miss a half day's pay. Incidentally Grandma Foley used to wake up her children for school or work only once each morning. She was not given to coaxing

On February 12, 1916, Aunt Katie married Edward J. Kelly. My mother served as matron of honor. They were married at St. Clement's Church on Woodland Avenue. Ed Kelly was a plasterer and union member.

Aunt Katie and Uncle Ed raised five children in their house at 103 North Front Street Darby. By the way, it is still well preserved. They were Dorothy, Kathryn, Helen, Edward and Jack. Dorothy and my sister Lillian were close in age and close friends.

Dorothy M. Kelly married John Ballas in Philadelphia in 1947. They lived at 103 North Front St. in Darby. They had a daughter Sheila Ballas who lived just six days. She is buried in Holy Cross Cemetery Section 7, Range 4, Lot 23.

Dorothy Kelly's older daughter Susan Ballas (born in 1951) married Edward W. Zinkan.

Helen M Kelly Schaeffer was born on March 3, 1921 and on died January 5, 1994.

Edward (Eddie) volunteered for the Army in 1942 or 1943 assured of an assignment to artillery or armor. I don't know which. From basic training he was shipped to Europe in the Infantry. After the war he sold cars.

Jack Kelly was rumored to have left home after a dispute of some kind in the early 1940's.

Wednesday, February 21, 1990

My father, Leonard Jerome Dee, aged 26, and my mother, Lillian Gertrude Foley, age 24, were married Wednesday October 20, 1915 at their parish church, St. Clement's, on Woodland Avenue near 72nd Street, West Philadelphia.

He had lived with his parents, brothers and sisters in Darby at 27 East Main Street. She with her family nearby at 7214 Greenway Avenue, West Philadelphia.

They set up home in a rented single-family house in Darby, on Greenway Avenue, somewhere between North Front Street and Cobbs Creek, the city – county line below the hill.

The small house on Greenway Avenue, Darby, was on the eastern end, where it slopes down from North Front Street toward Cobbs Creek. The back yard may have abutted that of his parents' house at 27 Main Street. Either way, the houses were close.

The Kellys were just around the corner at 103 North Front Street in Darby. The grade down to the creek, by the way, was so steep that the rear cellar door in the Kelly house opened at ground level.

Like his father and his father, Leonard was a plasterer, a union plasterer. Lillian had been a secretary to a physician in downtown Philadelphia.

Her father, John Andrew Foley, was born in 1851 in Ireland, perhaps Belfast, from which he had emigrated. Her mother, Catherine Boyle Foley, was born, Sunday May 14, 1854, in Ireland, perhaps Belfast, from which she too had emigrated. John was a foreman of steamfitters at Baldwin Locomotive, Philadelphia.

Leonard – baptized Dennis – was born Saturday April 27, 1889, in Philadelphia. His father, John Francis Dee, was born Monday April 2, 1866, in Philadelphia. Leonard's grandfather, Dennis Dee, was born somewhere in Ireland, where the family name was O'Dea, not Dee. In Philadelphia, as elsewhere in America in those days, anti-Irish and anti-Catholic bigotry was so widespread, that Irish Catholics had great difficulty finding work, just as they still do in Belfast today and the rest of Northern Ireland. Consequently Dennis Anglicized the name – a change some of us descendants regret – while rigorously adhering to the faith, for which we are indeed grateful. Leonard's mother, Mary Ellen Leonard Dee was born Sunday May 1, 1870 in Castleisland, County Kerry, Ireland.

My sister Lillian was born nearby at St. Vincent's Hospital on Columbus Day Thursday October 12, 1916, shortly after which she came down with a mysterious ailment that even doctors at the University of Pennsylvania could not diagnose. Finally they discharged her, providing scant hope in a special diet.

While my mother was eating cereal one morning, oatmeal perhaps, with Lillian watching intently, she was tempted to give her a taste. To her surprise, Lillian gulped it. Then a spoonful. "Well, if she's going to die, let it be on a full stomach". Down went the cereal. Out went the diet. By the grace of God, Lillian recovered, although never was she robust. Indeed, illnesses caused her to lose time in school so that I graduated from elementary school a year before she, while we pretended she was a year younger than I. She was about 14 years old when she suffered a ruptured appendix. The surgeon commented that she had come close to death, very close. Evidently God had other plans.

I was born at St. Vincent's on Thursday, October 4, 1917, feast of St. Francis of Assisi. At St. Clement's I was baptized Leonard Jerome on Sunday, October 21st.

In less than six months, in March or April 1918, my mother took Lillian and me to live with her sister Rose, Mrs. Henry Stanley Leggett

Sr., in the City Line section of Brooklyn. Then in April 1918 my mother began working in the Credit Department of National City Bank of New York, 55 Wall Street, head office. Then, and ever after, she represented herself to everyone as a widow.

Leonard enlisted in the Navy at Philadelphia Navy Yard, he and his brother Thomas, whether before or after our departure from Darby I don't know. More likely it was very shortly after.

Veteran's military records indicate Leonard Dee enrolled in the U.S. Navy in Philadelphia on April 13, 1918. He completed a course in the Navy Signal School on September 1, 1918 and was a Seaman Signalman 3rd class. He served on the U.S.S. Ohio in September and October of 1918. He was relieved from active duty on February 16, 1919 and was then in the U.S. Naval Reserve. He was issued the Victory of Atlantic Fleet Clasp on August 8, 1921. On September 30, 1921 he was honorably discharged from the U.S. Naval Reserve force.

His brother, Thomas Leonard Dee also served in the U.S. Navy during World War 1.

Thomas Leonard Dee enlisted in the Navy on May 6, 1918 in Philadelphia and was honorably discharged on September 30, 1921 in Philadelphia. His address at the time of entry into the service was 27 Main St. Darby Delaware County PA. His rank was Apprentice Seaman and his service number was 134-83-70.

He served at the Section Base Training Camp -Wissahickon Barracks Cape May New Jersey from 05-31-1918 to 07-05-1918, the US Coast Guard Station No. 135 Cape May NJ from 07-06-1918 to 11-16-1918 and the US Coast Guard Base Gloucester City NJ from 11-16-1918 to 02-21-1919.

In March of 1933, he was at the Sawtelle Soldiers Home, a care home for disabled veterans located in the west side of the city of Los Angeles.

He died on December 7, 1973 and is buried in San Jacinto Valley Cemetery in Hemet CA Plot Number GLA-48.

Never were Leonard and Lillian reconciled, nor canonically separated, nor divorced. The underlying causes of the rift, who did what to whom, who was at fault, who – if either – was blameless, I don't know. Oh, I haven't forgotten all the mean things that my mother attributed to her husband, nor the rancor that she carried to the grave almost sixty years later.

Even though she had told us our father had died, and for years we believed it, while Lillian and I were very young, she poisoned our minds against him, largely by the power of her own hostility rather than any evidence of wrongdoing, so that there was no room for anything but a sympathetic contempt. Later, in middle age, my contempt had evolved into cold indifference. A more mature perspective eventually opened my eyes to the sorry truth. I had condemned the man on only the flimsy testimony of a bitter plaintiff. It was like reaching a verdict without hearing the defense, or evaluating a mosaic after viewing a few scattered tesserae.

Leonard lost his job once, my mother said, but she didn't learn of it for about a week, because he went off every morning and returned at night just as usual.

Leonard enjoyed music on his phonograph, such as "The Whistler and His Dog". When he left for work, he took with him a critical part, so she said, insuring that no record could be played in his absence.

Few homes had telephones then. A messenger from Western Union delivered a telegram to my mother, purporting to come from her sister Rose and begging her to come help in some emergency. The wording was cryptic but ominous, and so off my mother went to Brooklyn, probably leaving the babies with her parents. Rose was glad to see her, but puzzled, for she had not sent a telegram. By the time she got back to Darby, Leonard, said she, had sold all or most of the furniture.

Assuming that this latter allegation be substantially true, does it not cry out for so much more than its bare bones? Assuming that, on the other hand, it not be substantially true, does it not raise even more troublesome questions? Surely it testifies to my credulity, yes my stupidity, that in opportune times I failed to ask such questions.

Leonard served during the war on warships escorting troops and supplies across the North Atlantic. Once when he got leave at the Brooklyn Navy Yard, (at least once that I know of,) he rode out on the Fulton Street El to City Line. My mother and Aunt Rose wouldn't even open up the door.

On several occasions Leonard tried to see his babies in Brooklyn but was rebuffed every time. Not once was he even allowed in. If it wasn't my mother, then it was Aunt Rose who turned him away.

His letters, unopened, they mailed to his parents' home in Darby.

Leonard waited at the employee's entrance to the bank on Exchange Place. My mother again rebuffed him. No, he could not see the children; they were "boarding" in New Jersey, says she.

Long after his death in 1967, and in fact after her death in 1975, I discovered that Leonard had in 1920 emigrated to Los Angeles. Not long afterward he was joined by his parents, brothers, and sisters: Thomas, William, Christopher, Maurice, Anna, Mary, and the youngest Frances. Leonard, the oldest, was thirty-one years old when he left for California. Frances Julia, the youngest – the only survivor as I write this – was then ten years old.

Lillian and I grew up in what was in effect, if not in fact, a conspiracy of silence among the Foleys, Kellys, McLaughlins, and Leggetts. It was as though Leonard and his family had never been born. To be fair, I must add that not only was I prejudiced against a mere phantom, fashioned by my mother, but also during the early years, despite suspicions, I lacked the wit to ask probing questions until it was too late, for all those with answers were gone.

Uncle Eddie Foley and Grandma were talking in the kitchen when I overheard a vague reference to "my relatives in California". "Who? What's their name?" says I. "Armstrong". I let it go at that.

On another occasion, as I sat in Grandma's easy chair reading the Sunday funnies, Uncle Eddie and Grandma in the kitchen were talking about Leonard. I was not so absorbed with the Katzenjammer Kids that I failed to catch the name, and to see that they spoke as though he were still living. This confirmed my secret suspicion at last. I went on reading in silence. I must have been about nine or ten years old.

Sunday, March 25, 1990

Although I was baptized Leonard, my mother's enmity toward her estranged husband, father of her two children, was such that while I was still in diapers, she began calling me Harry, in tribute to her brother-in-law whose home we were sharing. The change was not legal, let me add. The Commonwealth of Pennsylvania was not petitioned, nor informed.

A baptismal certificate survives, dated "05/11/31" from St. Clement's giving my name as "Leonard (Harry) Dee". There must have been another submitted for admission to St. Joseph's seven years earlier. School records listed me as Harry only. I thought of myself as Harry, even after learning the truth at an early age, for my mother had so poisoned my mind against her estranged husband. With respect and affection for Uncle Harry Leggett, (who in fact was Henry) had the choice been mine, I'd have preferred Leonard.

A year or so before she died in December of 1975, when I was fifty-eight years old, my mother surprised me with a birth certificate, recently issued by Pennsylvania, listing my name as Harry. Why she applied for it, and how she managed the change, I don't know. In 1985, it was not returned when I sent it with an application for a passport, as Mary, Libbie and I planned to visit Ireland.

It was probably in the autumn of 1972 that my mother came out to spend a few days with us, and to celebrate Thanksgiving. Afterwards I drove her back to her apartment in Brooklyn, one that she had first rented in the summer of 1932, among neighbors of mixed national ancestry, all very pleasant, although somewhat aloof.

Some person or persons unknown, aware probably of her absence, had broken in from the fire escape. It looked as though it had been ransacked by a tribe of barbarians. Missing was everything that could have been pawned. What was left was severely damaged.

Two uniformed patrolmen responded to our call. Neither showed any interest in possible clues to the identity of the criminals, or the retrieval of her property. Their concern was only for filling out a form, one presumably to be filed at the station-house. It was as though such incidents were of daily routine, and utterly bothersome.

My mother lived the last fourteen months or so of her life here with Mary, me, and her three grandchildren. On a day in December 1975 while I was setting up a walnut grandfather clock I had made from an Emperor kit, she stepped into the hall from her room, and seeing me in the living room, paused at the bathroom door long enough to say "I'd like to talk to you some time about when we first came to Brooklyn".

What was it she wanted to tell me about "when we first came to Brooklyn"?

A few days later she grew so ill that we called an ambulance to take her to Huntington Hospital. She had suffered a stroke and lingered a few days in Huntington Hospital. She never spoke another word. Her eyes were open. I presumed she recognized me, that she'd have said something if she could. She could not have fed herself, nor, I suspect, had anyone spoon fed her. One day I brought in chocolate ice cream from Friendly's, hoping she'd like it. She did.

We were awakened one night by a telephone call from a doctor on duty on her floor. She had gone to meet her Maker. It was very early on Sunday morning, December 28, 1975. She would have been 85 on January 24th 1976.

Three Franciscan Friars from 31st Street offered to come out - I had not had presence of mind to ask them - to offer the funeral Mass and to pray at the grave. My mother, you see, had been an active member of the Third Order at St. Francis Church. Moreover, beginning in my early years at Callicoon, she had often raised money for the seminary and for Franciscan Missionary Union. The Friars do not forget their benefactors.

The three old friends were Fr. Dominick A. Dean, O.F.M.; Fr. John Sullivan, O.F.M.; Fr. Arnold F. Brown, O.F.M. Dominick and I were classmates, John was in the following class, and Arnold was a year ahead of us.

I never did learn what she would have said about "when we first came to Brooklyn".

35

Tuesday, February 27, 1990

When my mother brought my sister Lillian and me to the City Line section of Brooklyn from Darby, Pennsylvania, it must have been on or around 1918 or 1919. (Leonard, my father, was serving in the Navy.) My mother's sister, Rose Leggett, and her husband, "Uncle Harry" lived in a "cold-water flat" on Glenmore Avenue, above the shop-store room of a tobacco merchant, near Autumn Avenue. The parish was Blessed Sacrament, until it was divided to form St. Sylvester's, (where, in due course, Stanley Leggett was to serve as altar boy.)

Aunt Rose and Uncle Harry had John, Bill, Chloe, and Stanley. Eddie was to be born in 1920.

My mother found a job at National City Bank of New York, 55 Wall St., Commercial Credit Department, where she stayed, at modest salary, until retirement at age sixty-five. Being a woman, promotions were out of reach to her, even though she used to train young men, some of whom became vice presidents. Yes, it was a man's world.

When I grew old enough to go to school – it must have been in September 1924, - my mother learned somehow of St. Joseph's parish, in Brooklyn, that had a school and a day nursery, where pupils, whose parents were working, could go for lunch.

The front of the church, a magnificent treasure, faced Pacific Street, with twin towers that may have been bells. Across the street stood the day nursery, in what originally must have been a small wooden house. A spacious play yard lay at the rear and the left side.

36

At the time the school was housed in an ancient redbrick building that was soon to be torn down. Two red-brick buildings served as toilets for the boys, one at each end of the property. (Accommodations for the girls I can't recall.) The plumbing was primitive: a long trough over which a row of wooden seats that made no provision for privacy. Flushing, such as there was, was achieved by a sporadic flow of water flowing slowly by gravity down the trough. The stench was enough to preclude loitering. Draining one's bladder therefore, was a torment.

When the old school was torn down, after my sister Lillian and I had completed first grade, and while the new building was being erected, classes were held in the lower church, a spacious area with a high ceiling and wide side aisles. Classes must have been small, for there was no sense of crowding. Every class was taught by a Sister of St. Joseph. Whether we pupils, a mix of boys and girls, were well-mannered or whether the Sisters were domineering, or both, I recall no disciplinary problems. They never laughed nor smiled. They were there to teach, and we were there to learn, a very serious matter.

By the time the new school was ready, I was promoted to third grade, which I completed before my mother found an apartment in nearby St. Teresa's parish: top floor third left at 832 Washington Avenue. The parish school had separate buildings for boys and girls. Miss McCormick taught fourth-grade boys. She maintained discipline, and yet she earned our respect and affection. In June 1932 I graduated, "with honors".

The City Line section of Brooklyn lies at its eastern edge, next to Woodhaven, Queens. The name, as you may have surmised, dates back to the former City of Brooklyn, before it became one of the five boroughs of the City of New York. Residents are, or were in the early century, a mix of many ethnic groups, Irish, English, Scottish, German, Italian, Polish, etc. I don't recall seeing any Blacks, however.

Originally the neighborhood was part of Blessed Sacrament parish, before St. Sylvester's was created. Sunday Mass was said for a while in what had been a movie house on the north side of Liberty Avenue, the Sheridan. When, in her mid-thirties, Aunt Rose Leggett died on Wednesday, Christmas Eve, 1924, she was the first to be buried from St. Sylvester's Church.

We three Dees lived with Aunt Rose, Uncle Harry, their sons and daughter from the spring of 1918 until the fall of 1924, when I had grown old enough to enter first grade.

During those six years we all shared three successive cold weather flats, each a short walk from the others. The last I remember well. The house occupied the south west corner of Glenmore Avenue and probably Autumn Avenue. Behind the house stretched a vast undeveloped tract that was destined, as it turned out, to become the right of way for Conduit Blvd. from Atlantic Avenue southeast to Cross Bay Blvd., Ozone Park.

It had three stories, two flats over a shop used to store tobacco products. Our rooms were on the second floor. Because the house stood on the corner, we were blessed with outside windows in all rooms but the bathroom. It opened onto an airshaft.

The kitchen came equipped with a gas stove and a tall water tank heated by a gas burner. Wooden matches hung in a metal holder. Coffee grinder behind the kitchen door. A steel bread toaster, shaped like a tall pyramid with its top half missing. Holes in the sides allowed heat to toast four slices, on one side at a time, an operation calling for complete attention. Wooden-handled hair curlers, warmed in the flame, my mother used to touch up the ends of her black tresses before leaving for work. John and Bill were responsible in turn for emptying the pan under the icebox. Near the sink, hung on a roller. A long wide hand towel, formed into a loop by sewing the ends together.

The tables in the kitchen and dining room were draped in a fabric of light felt coated on one side with a soft waterproof material, and decorated with flowers or geometric designs. We called it oil cloth.

Linoleum covered the floors in kitchen and hall. When the bare base showed through, outlining the floor boards, it was time to shop for a new roll.

In summer, at the open kitchen window, the scent of mint wafted up from the back yard, competing for attention with the chatter of the parrot upstairs.

In winter, the other rooms were warmed by round black kerosene heaters with pans of water on top. Scatter rugs alongside the beds, a comfort on cold mornings. Some days we'd wake up to find beautiful patterns of ice crystals on the windows, painted while we slept by "Jack Frost".

Balconies and stairs of black steel ribbons and rods, called a "fire escape", were bolted to the back wall at the kitchen windows. A slender wooden pole, as tall as the house, and fitted with spikes for climbing, stood at the back fence holding pulleys and laundry lines.

Most of the family clothes were collected each week by a "wet wash". A couple of days later they were returned in a cloth bag, damp. A line the length of the kitchen served in freezing weather.

The outer door on the ground floor, kept unlocked, opened into a vestibule with a locked inner door. Thus the mailman had access twice a day to the boxes set in the left wall. To summon a tenant for a parcel or special delivery, he'd press a button that rang a bell in the kitchen. The tenant then pressed a button that unlocked the inner door while sending a buzzer, and so allowing the letter carrier to step inside, where he blew his whistle. Incidentally, we had a family code: three short dashes. Of course, grownups had keys.

In the ground-floor hall, behind the stairs: a beige wicker stroller, extra-wide so that Lillian and I could ride side-by-side.

Uncle Harry was a telegraph operator for stock brokers, Harris, Upham & Co., 11 Wall St. My mother said he was first, or among the first, to learn, via Morse code, of the war's breaking out in Europe in August of 1914. Born in North Carolina, he was probably baptized a Baptist. Whatever his religious convictions, however, he gave no hint of church affiliation. My mother recalled that on a Saturday afternoon he walked from the office in downtown Manhattan all the way home to City Line.

For his entire seventy five years, Harry Leggett was ever the well-groomed gentleman: immaculate shirt and tie, three piece suit, well pressed, shined shoes, hair just right. An alert ear could detect faint echoes of a Southern childhood.

John Andrew, named after his mother's father, was first born. Then Bill, Chloe, Stanley, and Edward Bernard, named after his mother's only brother. Stanley was in fact Henry Stanley Leggett, Jr. Eddie, the youngest and only survivor as I write this, was born on Monday March 29, 1920.

Uncle Harry saw a sharp division between the roles of husband and wife. A Southern legacy perhaps. At any rate, his was to go out and work and return with cash wages. Hers was to care for the children, shop, cook, bake, wash, dust, sew, etc. He expected to sit down to meals on schedule. Of Aunt Rose I must say she played her part heroically. Her family was as well provided for as her means allowed. Eddie, alas, was too young to remember. The youngsters were taught – including, of course, Lillian and me – to be polite, to say "Yes, sir", "No, sir" "Yes, ma'am," "No, ma'am", proper table manners, good posture, responsibility for chores. When naughty we were swatted on the seat with a hairbrush, but not in anger; Aunt Rose radiated love.

Our Leggett cousins used to play a game with their father on Sundays. He'd sit reading the paper and smoking a cigar. They'd take turns climbing into his lap and begging for money, a dime each, for the movies. "Ah, come on, Pop". "Sorry, I'm broke". After the ritual we'd all scamper around to the City Line, on Liberty Avenue. (A generation later the name was changed to the Earl.)

Those were the days, as you know, of silent films and cartoons, long before the "talkies" and the greater artistry of Walt Disney. Nevertheless, the children's matinees I found delightful, especially the cartoonist who began the fun with a bottle of India ink. As he pulled up the stopper, clowns and other characters popped out, like the genie from Aladdin's lamp. The films had terse dialogue printed in panels interspersed among the pictures. However, for the small fry who hadn't learned to read, it made little difference. The fast actions, the spectacle, were enough.

While the screen was silent, the movie house was not. An upright piano stood between the screen and the first row of seats. A pianist, with no sheet music but a vast repertoire of memorized compositions, kept watch on the screen. As the emotional tone and the action changed, he switched to something appropriate. I wasn't aware of it at the time, of course, but we tots were being imbued subtly not only in popular Broadway-show tunes, but also in the best of the classical European treasury.

On Sundays the only shops open were drug stores and what were called variously candy, stationery, or cigar stores. They sold all of these and newspapers too. Few homes had telephones. But these shops had public phone booths in the back, dark varnished boxes, side-by-side, with embossed sheet – metal inner walls. A ledge in the left corner served as a seat. A fan and the ceiling light went on when the two-panel folding door with narrow glass windows was closed. Local calls cost a nickel. Outside, at the shop's front door: a round white enamel plaque bearing the phone company's blue logo, in the shape of a bell.

The drug store on Liberty Avenue, below the Grant Avenue El station, had in the front windows flanking the door two large fancy glass bottles of a bright blue liquid, reminiscent of ancient amphoras. Maybe they were sentimental relics – like the barber's pole, and the pawnbroker's three balls – of days long gone, when few customers could read.

One addressed the pharmacist as "Doc". If you walked in with a speck in your eye, he'd have it out in a jiffy, and at no charge. Physicians were called on only in serious illness or injury. Mothers depended on local pharmacists for free advice.

Bergin Street trolley cars ran along Liberty Avenue, under the El, as far as Grant Avenue. Trucks and automobiles were few, indeed rare, and so there was little risk from traffic in sending children on errands or to the movies.

On weekdays, however, there were the ice man, milk man, and coal dealer, all of whom used horse-drawn wagons. The ice man delivered at regular intervals, the same size block. Customers who wanted more or less put in a front window a square cardboard sign with the number of pounds on each side. His cue was the number on top.

His stock came in one hundred pound blocks, which he kept covered in canvas. Leather apron and leather sleeveless jacket. Neighborhood urchins waited until he trudged through a doorway, whereupon they hopped onto the rear bumper and salvaged the ice chips.

Those flats having coal stoves were supplied by burly dealers laboring under canvas bags. To homes heated by coal furnaces, trucks delivered larger chunks that fell by gravity into a wooden barrel that was then trundled over to a cellar window, and dumped into a steel chute.

At Thanksgiving in those days in City Line, boys used to beg, especially from shop keepers. "Got anything for Thanksgiving?" The harvest included small coins, candy, cookies, fruit, and chewing gum, whatever.

Except at Christmas and Easter, we saw little candy. Bill Leggett shared with me once a piece of what seemed to be white paper tape, attached to which were colored hard round candies arrayed in ranks like infantrymen.

Well I do remember a special treat on Washington's Birthday, cardboard hatchets with bright red blades and black hollow handles filled with chocolates.

Then too there was the surprise. We lived a short walk from the Crescent Street station of the Fulton Street El on Liberty Avenue, access to Manhattan. Also the Long Island Railroad used to run above ground along Atlantic Avenue, between the terminal at Flatbush Avenue, Brooklyn and Jamaica, a faster means to Manhattan's financial district. I recall walking down the stairs with my mother as she left for work each morning. Out on the sidewalk she stooped down and kissed me, then pressed into my hand a chunk of Kerr's butterscotch.

John Leggett and his father put together the first radio I ever saw or heard. They called it a "crystal set". Were they delighted when it picked up a station from another city! Fantastic!

After we three Dees moved to 398 Park Place, we would often return to visit on Friday evenings, sometimes via the Fulton Street el. Either way, we'd pass street vendors on Liberty Avenue. Men with portable charcoal braziers roasting chestnuts, none of which my mother bought. Another with a small table like a high stool, with small bottles and a grinder. Fresh horseradish.

Those Friday visits to Aunt Rose's were the highlight of the week. It always seemed that everyone was as glad to see us again as we were to see them. Then when it came time to leave, Lillian and I used to cry, the first few nights, for we really had two mothers. Down at the foot of the stairs we were coached to call up to Aunt Rose: "Thank you for your hospitality!" Hospitality indeed. Surely far more than either of us could then have had in mind.

Friday, March 2, 1990

After we had lived six years with the Leggetts in City Line, my mother, by the grace of God, learned of St. Joseph's parish, in the center of Brooklyn, a blessing because it had a parochial school and, what was critical for working mothers, a place that, for a modest fee, provided hot lunches, St. Joseph's Day Nursery.

The facade of our house, on the south side of Park Place, between Washington and Underhill Avenues, was not easily distinguished from the others in the row of so-called "brownstone" townhouses, which were in fact of granite. One had to be alert for the 398 in gold leaf on the outer door at the top of the stoop.

Typical basement, parlor floor, and two floors of two bedrooms each. Flat roof. Lush carpeting up the stairs and along the halls. White woodwork. Plaster ceilings embossed with rosettes and wreaths. Bathroom on the third floor. Double-hung windows with solid wooden blinds recessed into the massive walls. Central steam heat. Parquet floors.

The top floor was ours, what had been originally two large bedrooms, each with a marble sink and a large mirror off a narrow connecting passage. Between these rooms, off the outer hall, a small kitchenette, in what may have begun as a walk-in closet. Table, icebox, cupboard, two-burner gas range, sound-proof walls and floors.

A small galvanized garbage pail with a sturdy bail it was my task to leave alongside the stoop as we set off for school. One day Lillian and I had just reached Underhill Avenue, the northeast corner, where now stands

44

Mount Prospect Laboratory, when I discovered hanging on my arm the garbage pail.

In those days that corner was landscaped with shrubs and trees and guarded by an iron picket fence, jewels of an old mansion. Best of all: in the center a magnificent magnolia. Down Underhill Avenue, at the left of the mansion's door, and in the shelter of the porch, a mounted head with antlers, deer perhaps or elk.

Just as in City Line, here too were few automobiles and trucks. Walking the half mile or so to school posed little threat from traffic. The Bergin Street trolley cars were noisy and not very fast. Slow-moving were the chain-driven Mack trucks that collected garbage.

A man stood on top in the pan and emptied the cans lifted up to him. A folded tarpaulin attached behind the cab he unfurled over the load as he packed it from front to back. The truck's doors bore the monogram "D S C" (Department of Street Cleaning).

North Star Hand Laundry, on Underhill Avenue near Prospect Place, a modest operation serving the neighborhood, washed and ironed a few things.

My mother had a colleague and friend at the bank, Lillian Martin, from Glendale, whose brother took a fancy to the "widow" Dee. He was a civil engineer, handsome, soft – spoken, pleasant. My sister and I were glad to see Paul come to take our mother out; he always brought us Loft's candy. By the time they got back, we'd be asleep.

Our not having a fireplace didn't frustrate Santa Claus. He managed somehow to get in, to leave presents, and to refresh himself with the cookies and coffee. The oldest of the toys I still remember was a set of brightly enameled wooden circus figures: clown, elephant, horse, and a solid half-barrel. Their heads and limbs were articulated and strung like beads on flexible cords so that they could be moved to various poses. The ears of the elephant were leather.

Boys of elementary-school age wore knickers, baggy short pants buckled just below the knees, over the tops of high stockings. Men wearing knickers were obviously golfers, like Bobby Jones. The fly was closed by four concealed buttons. Shoes came up over the ankles. They were held snug by a row of tiny globular buttons. You passed a special hook through the button hole, looped under the button, and pulled it through.

The only fun was a bit of furtive deviltry. One cupped his right hand, as though to scratch, and in a swift left-to-right sweep, tried to unbutton a classmate's fly. A gap of four buttons was a home run.

Here in the desk lies a green shoe horn that may be sixty-five years old. The engraving reads "Thom McAn $4 Shoes For Men – Boys $3 Shoes – Shoes For Women $4". Attached at a hole in the top: a rod of two inches with a round button hook 3/8 inches across. The flattened loop at the top reads: "Thom McAn $4 Shoes".

Wednesday, March 7, 1990

St. Joseph's School stood – let's hope it still does – on the North side of Dean Street, and just a bit east of Vanderbilt Avenue. The faculty were Sisters of St. Joseph, whose mother house is in Brentwood, Long Island.

The sequence consisted of sixteen half year grades from 1A to 8B. Depending on one's date of birth, he entered 1A in September or January, was promoted (or left back) a half-year, and finally graduated in either June or January, having had possibly sixteen teachers. The course of studies for all sixteen grades covered academic basics, reading, grammar, penmanship, writing, arithmetic, geography, history and singing. Religion too, of course. Very bright pupils sometimes skipped a grade. On the other hand, no one was promoted who had failed to meet minimum standards, no one.

The school day began at nine A.M. with prayer and the pledge of allegiance, broke for lunch with the Angelus at noon, and resumed for two hours at one o'clock. Classes were all co-ed. Pupils raised their hands when wanting to ask or answer a question, kept silent until called upon, stood up to speak, answered "Yes, Sister'" "No, Sister", remained seated unless called to the blackboard, and spoke to the sister only. When asked to spell, one said the word, spelled it, said it again. If, as rarely happened, a priest walked in, the whole class stood up. Pupils were addressed by last names only. This called for an exception the year we had both Thomas A. O'Brien and Thomas E. O'Brien; not related.

Sisters of St. Joseph were most conscientious. No on laughed or smiled, as though fearing that to do either would be to lose control. Indeed, one,

47

years later in St. Teresa's Boys School, had a permanent frown that earned her the nickname "Stoneface". And so there was at all times a certain tension; only the insensitive could feel at ease. I recall being scolded in grade 7A by "Stoneface" for chuckling at the mention of "Flathead Indians". Little wonder, then, that having graduated one did not feel comfortable enough to visit these dedicated teachers to whom we owed so much.

Forbidden were chewing gum, eating anything, whispering, passing notes, lingering in the toilet, daydreaming, and running. Infractions brought at once a sharp blow to the palm from a wooden ruler. Then too there was the grave threat of being sent to the principal's office, there to suffer whatever horrors Lillian and I, by the grace of God were never to learn.

Ah yes, Sister G., the only one whose name after sixty-five years I still remember. Sister G. had us tots trembling, literally trembling, maybe others as well, whenever she strode about, ruler held high like a mace, screaming "red hot bloody murder!" That's verbatim.

I've a hazy recollection of a puddle under or near my seat, perhaps on the first day of the year. Toilets were in separate red-brick outhouses serving the original school. The urinal in the boys' room near the west end, toward Vanderbilt Avenue, was a long iron trough anchored to the wall about a foot off the floor, whose wetness testified to the contest to see who could stand farthest away. The other boys' room, close to the east end, had a row of toilet booths, all drained by a single trough. Our eagerness to get in and out quickly gave dramatic testimony to the inefficiency of the drainage system, an urgent consideration, no doubt, in deciding to tear down the school and rebuild the following year.

Lillian, a year older than I, though I had grown bigger than she, had entered first grade with our Leggett cousins the year before in City Line. Thus we were in different classes.

The classrooms were furnished with a crucifix, American flag, pictures of Washington, Lincoln, and Governor Alfred E. Smith, he was to run against Herbert Hoover for president in 1928. For the lower grades at least there were also black placards of white Arabic numerals and of capital and lower case cursive letters of the Roman alphabet.

Texts used in teaching reading were graded story books. Damon and Pythias. Androcles and the lion. The fox and the grapes. David and Goliath. Noah's ark. Cornelia and her jewels. The name peony I had learned before I saw or sniffed the first one.

Similarly I could recite the Ten Commandments before I learned what adultery meant, a sequence by no means to be disparaged. It was a grave sin of "impurity", still another term to be pondered. To listen in the schoolyard, however, was slowly to gain muddled, puzzling insights, while building one's informal vocabulary.

The basic text in religion was the Baltimore Catechism. Well do I remember:

"If God is everywhere, why don't we see him? We don't see God because He is pure spirit that cannot be seen with bodily eyes".

"Why did God make me? God made me to know Him, to love Him, and to serve Him in this life, and to be happy with Him forever in the next".

"What is a sacrament? A sacrament is an outward sign instituted by Christ to give grace".

St. Joseph's, a magnificent Romanesque church with twin towers, well suited to be a cathedral, stood east of the school and rear playground, its high front steps off Pacific Street, sacristy close to Dean Street. Spacious interior of lavish marble. Sanctuary lamp of intricate bronze filigree. Baldachino inscribed "ITE AD JOSEPH" (Go to Joseph, the instruction to the Egyptians during the seven years of famine.) Stairs right and left of the main lobby, and of the sanctuary. Confessionals in the lower church, with its high blank white walls and pillars.

There in the lower church, classes were held, at least for the lower grades, from September 1925 to June 1926, while the old school building was being replaced on the same site.

And it was down there I learned to loathe drills in multiplication. We were to have memorized the products of 2 X 2 through 12 X 12. Sister held a device of cardboard having two covered discs, each with one hole in the cover. Each hand could rotate a disc so that any number from 2 to 12 could be shown through the hole. She could, of course, turn one or both discs. Thus the pupil, looking at the holes, didn't know what combination to expect. Now, memorizing was no great challenge to me, whether the alphabet, verses, spelling, whatever. Yet in this drill I usually stumbled, often blurting the wrong product. The fast pace so unnerved me that I could barely concentrate. In other words, I wilted under pressure.

In our third year at St. Joseph's, then in the new building, with inside toilets, among other improvements, one night I confided to my mother distress at not being allowed to go to the boys' room. Sister seemed blind to my raised hand, so that I almost wet my pants. "Well, if it happens again, get up quietly and leave". Next day it did happen again. I did leave. Sister said nothing then or later, but thereafter demonstrated improved vision.

All pupils were obliged to attend Sunday Mass in a body, class by class, at nine A.M. Boys on "the Gospel side". The higher the grade, the closer to the sanctuary. Taking up the collection was the privilege of boys in 8 B. There we sang beautiful old Catholic hymns that were, alas, to lose fashion in the liturgical revolution following the Second Vatican Council, hymns of devotion to the Blessed Virgin Mary or to patron saints, hymns foreign to heretics.

One such, especially dear to me, I can still hear in the secret chapel of my soul:

Mother dear, oh pray for me

While far from Heaven and thee

I wander in a fragile bark

O'er life's tempestuous sea

Oh, Virgin Mother, from thy throne

So bright in bliss above,

Protect thy child and shield my path

With thy sweet smile of love.

We learned early to hold priests in reverence, those few chosen we endowed with such awesome authority, power and dignity, delegates of Christ Himself, whose lives were dedicated entirely to serving the Church. They were easily recognized by the black biretta, white Roman collar, and black cassock with its score of tiny buttons from throat to ankles. Away from church, on a sick call, for instance, they wore a black fedora, suit, shoes and a coat, all black and of course the white Roman collar.

A few years later, in the confessional, when I had said the Act of Contrition, and the priest had granted absolution, just before he closed the window he sometimes said: "Please pray for me." I probably did, but I was baffled. How could a priest, of all people, need others to pray for him? Who prays for the saints?

Sisters of St. Joseph in those days wore a traditional, age-old habit, so full of black layers and folds as to conceal whatever feminine pulchritude they had brought to the convent. Starched white linen boxed in the face, covering forehead, shoulders and back. Sleeves down to the wrists. A large, stiff white linen bib with rounded bottom edge lay over the bosom. Suspended below the bib: a crucifix inlaid with ebony. Black rosaries hung at the right hip. Shoes of black leather. Eyebrows were the only visible hair.

Such a costume, you may surmise, made difficult estimating one's teacher's age.

Charles A. Lindbergh was a young airman pilot in 1927, when he flew the Spirit of St. Louis from Long Island to Paris nonstop in thirty-three and one-half hours. It was a feat that electrified the world and galvanized public acceptance of the airplane and commercial aviation.

I have a vague recollection of walking two-by-two with my class, standing along a curb, and waving to Charles A. Lindbergh as he rode by in a touring car in the Brooklyn parade following his historic flight from Roosevelt Field, Long Island to Paris. It had to be the spring of 1927. I was 9 years old.

Saturday, March 10, 1990

In the 1920's school buses were unknown, excepting as we heard of them from time to time in exotic rural areas. Elementary – school pupils walked to schools in their neighborhoods. High–school students either walked or, at parents' expense, rode trolley cars or subways. In St. Joseph's, at noon the sisters retired to the convent; pupils hurried home to lunch. There were, however, about a dozen of us from several grades, whose mothers worked full time. We scampered over to St. Joseph's Day Nursery, across Pacific Street, opposite the church and school yard.

The building had been evidently a one-family house, two story, flat roof, wooden frame, with an extra fenced lot on the west side that served as an additional play yard. Behind the high board fence at the rear were the back yards of houses on Atlantic Avenue. The front door, at the left, and above three wooden steps, opened into a hall and stairs to the rooms where babies slept, except, of course, when we were too noisy. The front room, furnished with long tables and benches, was where we enjoyed a hot meal at mid-day, and at three o'clock, milk with bread and jelly.

The staff of three or four kindly matrons, led by a Mrs. Leddy, served a varied menu. For example, green pea soup, milk, bread, butter and a banana. Or beef stew, milk, bread, butter and a juicy Red Delicious apple as big as a man's fist.

One of the ladies reprimanded me, promising in the future to wash out my mouth with soap. She had overheard me saying "P-P", in whatever context I've since forgotten.

The welcome aromas from Mrs. Leddy's kitchen often came to meet us at noon, competing with the heavenly fragrance of fresh bread wafting east from Ward Baking Co., just beyond Vanderbilt Avenue.

Incidentally, Ward had a "Day-old" store on Dean Street, where in later years I bought turkey-stuffing bread. My mother believed it served better. Ah yes, the time a friend and I paid a dime for a pound cake. Charlie McNally and I then sat near the door devouring it.

After lunch at the nursery we'd spend the remaining time in the yard, the girls chatting or skipping rope, the boys lounging, horse playing, or teasing, and all of us being warned not to wake the babies. Once or twice I had to trudge around after school to a house on Atlantic Avenue, and ask permission to retrieve my hat from the back yard.

During the first fall, 1924, Bill or John Leggett several times fetched Lillian and me on Friday afternoon, and shepherded us back to City Line for supper. We'd march down Vanderbilt Avenue, across Atlantic Avenue with its cobblestones – becoming mementos even then of horse and wagon days – past the massive Schraeder Valve Co. plant on the left, to the El station above Fulton Street.

The fare was five cents. The wooden coaches had on each end open porches with iron gates on each side. The operator straddled the two coach ends and swung open the gates, swung them closed, and then pulled a cord signaling the motorman. There may have been four such coaches, able to be driven from either end. We got off at Crescent Street.

By the way, there used to be in a corner of the Franklin Avenue B.M.T. station, at the shuttle to Prospect Park, a sign: "Commit No Nuisance." I used to wonder why we needed a sign forbidding our making pests of ourselves. If there were no sign, we'd still have to behave. Then someone pointed out that during the late hours the toilets were locked.

While making a visit to the Blessed Sacrament, I found on the church floor a coin, a nickel or a dime. With later finds I had come to concede a duty to drop such coins into the poor box, but on that first happy occasion I skipped around the corner to the multi-purpose "candy" store on Vanderbilt Avenue. Due to subsequent depredations of inflation, the beloved institution of "penny candy" has faded, alas, into history. Today even a nickel buys nothing. Then a grand alluring assortment lay spread out. "Green Leaves" of sugar-coated, mint flavored gum. Licorice "shoe laces". Wax whistles. "Mary Janes", taffy-coated peanut butter. Caramels. Chewing gum. Sour balls. Peppermint sticks. Gum drops. Lollypops. Blocks of black licorice-flavored taffy. Chocolate-coated peppermints. The critical question always: "How many for a cent?"

A popular boys' hat in the 1920's was a soft, close-knit, gray wool, without a brim or visor, but with a flap that could be lowered to cover the ears, and buttoned at the throat. They were warm, light-weight, and easily stuffed into a coat pocket. I hope they were not expensive because I had twice to report to my mother the loss of my Timm's hat, nor did I know where or how I had lost it, nor indeed whether it had been stolen.

The people who lived in the area did not have automobiles, nor horses; yet there was a small stable on Pacific Street, a few doors east of the rectory, probably serving merchants having horse-drawn wagons, such as hucksters and ice men. A common sight: a man in white pants, white tunic, and boots, pushing a cart with two large and two small steel wheels. Standing erect in the cart: a long – handled shovel with a blunt edge, a long - handled broom with long, coarse bristles, on either side of tall steel can. An employee of the Department of Street Cleaning, the "White Wing" faded into history with the horse and wagon.

The first birthday party ever was at the home of a classmate on Pacific Street, just a few houses down from the nursery and opposite the convent. His family was Italian, as indeed were so many others in the neighborhood. Richie and his guests were all dressed up in our "Sunday best", and it was only Saturday afternoon.

Then there were the annual Christmas parties at the nursery, from which we toted home armfuls of hard candies and games. It may well have been there that I was introduced to dominoes and checkers. A half-century later, finding somewhere an appeal from St. Joseph Center, Venice, California, a small group helping the local poor, I recognized a way to balance the scales. "Go to Joseph".

Thursday, March 15, 1990

By the time I had passed through grade 3B at St. Joseph's, we had moved from Park Place to Washington Avenue near Lincoln Place, in St. Teresa of Avila parish.

Number 832 is a four story walk-up with two apartments on each floor. High stone stairs rose to a vestibule and halls paved in tiny white hexagonal tiles. Go there today and you'll find that the stairs are gone, and two shops doing business at ground level. So too with the other houses in the row.

Our apartment was on the top floor, left. Near the top of the stairs a door opened into an inner hall. Turn left into the bedroom shared by my mother and sister, or go straight past the bathroom and my room into the dining room. The kitchen lay at the rear. The fire escape hung at the dining room window. An airshaft gave light as well as ventilation to the bathroom and bedrooms. Pass through the front bedroom into a kind of back parlor before a living room half the width of the house. That spacious front room had bay windows, a door to the outer hall, and a fireplace with a cast-iron gas heater shaped like three wooden logs, a convenience rarely used; the steam-heated radiators were enough.

The doors to the outer hall, as well as that to the bathroom, gave light to the halls through a single large pane of cloudy glass in the upper half. A double-hung window with the same kind of glass allowed light and ventilation between the dining room and my bedroom.

The kitchen was equipped with the usual gas stove, double sink, cabinets, broom closet, ice box, a door that swung both in and out, a backyard laundry line at the window, whose stove sill my mother used to sharpen knives.

Ah, then there was the dumbwaiter, based on the original of Thomas Jefferson at Monticello: a square shaft from the basement to a booth on the roof, housing a wooden box with two compartments, raised or lowered, like a double-hung window, by a stout hempen rope hung over a pulley at the top of the shaft, and counter-balanced by flat iron weights riding in grooved channels along a side wall. The pulley shared its axle with another pulley over which was draped an endless loop of hempen rope that hung along both sides of the shaft to the basement. The balance was such that the box stayed at any level, excepting when it was overloaded. The pulleys turned or stopped together. Pulling down on the left strand raised the box. To collect garbage, the janitor pressed a button that sounded a buzzer in the kitchen.

Transoms over the doors to the outer hall permitted ventilation as well as a blending of aromas from the eight kitchens. Originally there must have been a door and transom between the dining room and inner hall. In our day, however, only the lintel survived, a perch on which our cat, Lindy – named after Charles Lindbergh – liked to nap, leaping all the way from the floor.

A couple with three daughters lived in the other apartment on the top floor. Alas, the husband took sick and died, leaving the widow broken hearted. For days we heard her through the wall wailing "Oh, Mike! Oh, Mike! Oooooh!" Of course no one had the heart to complain of the disturbance when we were trying to sleep. A month or so later she remarried.

The landlady, a widow named Buttafuoca, lived with a large family in the house, daughters, granddaughters, and a brother, "Uncle Angelo", who livened gatherings with his guitar and kazoo.

We Dees were guests several times for Sunday dinner, a leisurely and lavish affair of classical Italian cuisine: anti-pasta, soup, pasta, wine, celery tonic, veal, meatballs, chicken, fruit and spumoni. When we thought dinner was over, out came another course. Incidentally, our hosts were not overweight.

Nick Lorenzo, son-in-law, had a three chair barber shop on the east side of Washington Avenue, a few doors north of St. John's Place. Mrs. Lorenzo was a seamstress. A sign in a window on the first floor left said simply "Hemstitching. Dressmaking". I recall once - though he may indeed have done so more often – Nick's coming to our apartment and there cutting Lillian's and my hair. We were as one big happy family. He spoke of their summer home in Patchogue, perhaps my first inkling of Long Island. Christine Lorenzo, about our age, went to public school. One day she went off in a beautiful gown, made, no doubt, by her mother. She was to play Beauty in a skit, <u>Beauty and the Beast</u>.

The janitor, Colonel Jones, occupied rooms in the front right side of the basement. He served in either an Army Reserve unit or the National Guard. I used to see him leaving in uniform. Spurs, saber, campaign hat. My mother had occasion on day to talk to him about something or other. She came away impressed by his speech. One fragment stuck with her: "I'll get in communication with him.......".

In addition to the basement room where coal was stored, there were eight bins, each about seven or eight feet square, for tenants to keep unneeded furniture, baby carriages, luggage. whatever. They were made of 2 X 4's and horizontal boards a few inches apart. The bin was a convenience common to most if not all apartment houses. Padlocked, of course.

The landlady's men folk used to make wine in the basement, with wine press, barrels and crates of white grapes. Legally to be sure, even under Prohibition, the Eighteenth Amendment.

The first radio my mother bought was either an Atwater – Kent or a Crosley. Electrical power came from a storage battery, cylindrical, about 2 ½ inches in diameter and 6 inches tall. Its electrodes were threaded to accommodate knurled nuts. The single speaker stood apart on a round base, like a table lamp. The antenna consisted of a single strand of bare wire stretched across the roof between two glass or ceramic insulators held aloft by two poles. From there the radio signals were borne along an insulated wire, over the parapet, and down to a convenient window.

The Dempsey – Tunney championship fight was one of the earliest broadcasts in our experience.

On weekday mornings we tuned in to WOR, 710 kc, "Rambling with Gambling". John B. Gambling kept up a stream of pleasant chatter, gave frequent time checks, and thus allowed listeners to pace themselves as they made ready for school or work. Programmed exercises, sponsored by Metropolitan Life Insurance Co., were a regular feature. One of these was the "bike ride" to musical accompaniment setting the pace, while Gambling spelled out the Manhattan itinerary.

At first the telephone was tall, dull black, of either hard rubber or Bakelite, an early plastic, had a base of about five inches in diameter and a cylindrical column about seven inches tall. A blunt megaphone-type microphone swiveled slightly at the top. The earphone, a short tapered cylinder, rested on the arms of a y shaped cradle jutting from the column. The dial was fastened to the base. To make or answer a call, one lifted the earphone off the cradle, which then rose a bit, thus sounding the dial tone or completing the call. The weight of the earphone depressing the cradle again ended the call.

Telephone numbers of four digits were preceded by two letters and one digit that identified the local telephone exchange. For instance, NE 8 indicated our neighborhood, "Nevins". My mother's office, National City Bank, Wall Street, had the number BO 9-1000, "Bowling Green". The Leggetts out in City Line had an "Applegate" number.

An encyclopedia, The Book of Knowledge, published in twenty volumes plus index by the Grolier Society, and designed especially for school children, was easily the best investment my mother could have made in the late 1920's. Lillian and I found it not only helpful with school work, but also the source of many hours of fascinated browsing. The wooden box it came in served for years to hold my toys and treasures. The set found its way in 1940 to the Franciscan Sisters at Holy Cross School Callicoon, New York, shipped in the original box.

Saturday, March 17, 1990

My mother made and kept friends easily. A cheerful persona she affected at all times outside home, keeping ups and downs to herself. Had she been a man, she could have done well in Brooklyn politics. Indeed, for years she was active in the local George Washington Democratic Club, serving for instance as Secretary of the County Committee, whatever that was. Yet she had no political ambition. The club meant to her friends, campaigning for friends, meetings, parties, annual balls, a counter balance to the routine world of commercial credit. Thus she knew on a first name basis senators, congressmen, councilman, judges, influential law clerks and lawyers.

Marcellus Evans, our congressman, had a season pass to Ebbets Field, home of the Brooklyn Dodgers. I saw a game once in his place while he was in Washington. There could have been others too, had I been eager.

On Saturday evenings my mother occasionally played hostess to non-political friends who enjoyed playing cards: sisters Julia and Jane Boden, and brothers Walter and George Carroll. Sometimes also a man whose first name was Austin.

Around the dining room table they'd play pinochle, bridge, whatever, while smoking cigarettes, sipping high balls made with bootleg whiskey, and munching saltine crackers with Roquefort cheese. Pretzels too. Sometimes Perrier water, in its distinctive green oval bottles, was preferred to ginger ale.

One such night I was sent across the street for ice cream. Wohl's drug store, on the northeast corner of Washington Avenue and Lincoln Place, had a soda fountain serving Breyer's, of which "burnt almond" was then a popular favorite. Bulk ice cream was packed into tapered cardboard boxes, held in a metal form, the same kind of box used elsewhere for chop suey or fresh oysters. With ice cream the custom was to load it so high that the four top flaps could not be closed completely, perhaps to compensate for trapped air. Our house was close to the middle of the block. As I stood behind a parked car, looking to the left and waiting for a car to pass, the parked car at my right backed up, the driver evidently not seeing me, gently knocked me down, and then slowly pulled away. Only my composure was hurt. The ice cream did not touch the asphalt.

Julia and Jane Boden, both single, shared an apartment in the nearby Crown Heights section. Ours, by the way, was Prospect Heights. Julia worked for a stock brokerage house at 40 Wall Street, E. A. Pierce and Co.. Jane close to home, on Flatbush Avenue, for a dress shop. Well, dresses and under-garments for matrons with bulges in places unflattering.

Jane was standing in the street one afternoon, chatting with the driver of a parked car. A passing car knocked her down, breaking bones, as it turned out. At once her friends lifted her into the car and sped off to a hospital, thus causing additional injury, for they didn't know that she ought not to have been moved before an ambulance arrived. For the rest of her life Jane walked with a decided limp.

Wohl's drug store was memorable for two more reasons. First, because from time to time it held "one-cent sales". Buy an item at the regular price and another for one cent. Second, because the manager-owner was so disagreeable toward children, as though they were not customers but pests. Naturally Lillian and I stayed away when we had a choice, even when we were no longer children.

Across from our house was the Lincoln Rotisserie, where the aroma of chickens, broiling in clear view, tormented passersby.

Prospect Heights Hospital stood at the southeast corner of Washington Avenue and St. John's Place. A fenced lawn and tennis courts separated it from houses and shops on the Washington Avenue side. Small boys played marbles between the fence and sidewalk.

Behind the hospital, on St. John's Place stood a two-story single-family house. Beyond that house, and across from the twin firehouses, was a large vacant lot where urchins used to build fires and roast potatoes, "mickeys", until they looked like coal. Only sissies would not devour the whole thing.

That lot has since become the site of an apartment house, 500 St. John's Place. But the single-family house still stands, overshadowed on both sides. Rumor had it that the homeowner held out for his price, confident of selling to either the developer or the hospital, which later expanded southward, onto the lawn and tennis courts.

Alongside the hospital there were usually a few parked cars. Strongest was one powered by batteries, with a tiller rather than a steering wheel, and a high black cubic body that looked almost the same from front or back. A man could run faster. As you have no doubt surmised, electric automobiles did not survive the competition from many with gasoline engines. So too with battery-driven trucks, such as those of the Burton Dixie Mattress factory that plodded along Washington Avenue to and from their place near Ebbets Field.

The automobile that precipitated Jane Boden's downfall could have been an Essex, Nash, Studebaker, Willys Knight, Cord, Whippet, Pierce Arrow, or Packard, among others. These early competitors shared many features, even though styling made them easily recognized. Each was black all over. Each had to be started by a hand crank under the radiator. Each had a running board on both sides from fender to fender. Each had a manual transmission. Each had bumpers, back and front, of sturdy chrome-plated steel straps held several inches away from the body. The motor could be exposed on either side by swinging up a hinged vented hood between the radiator and dashboard. Most wheels had stout wooden spokes. Others had wire spokes, the Cord, for example. Some had thermometers built into the radiator caps, in easy view of the driver. The Pierce Arrow had its headlights built into the fenders as one unit, while the others had separate lamps on either side of the radiator. Radiator-cap ornaments came to be distinguishing features. Willys Knight, for example, had a standing chrome-plated knight in armor.

Traffic lights stood at each of the four corners at all intersections along Washington Avenue, regulating two-way traffic everywhere. Along nearby Eastern Parkway the traffic lights stood on tall stanchions above massive concrete bases on the line separating opposing lanes. They were eventually removed as traffic hazards.

At intersections with heavy traffic, policemen wearing white gloves and blowing whistles superseded the lights, thus preventing conflicts and collisions in turning left. Those early-model cars had no lights to signal turns. The left arm out the window informed other drivers. The forearm up straight, perpendicular to the pavement, meant "I'll turn right". The arm parallel out to the pavement meant "I'll turn left". The arm down, pointing to the pavement meant "I'll stop".

In the Police Department the rank below sergeant was then patrolman, not police officer, a name well suited to one who in fact patrolled alone on foot the same neighborhood every day. As there were at some corners red boxes at which to summon fire engines by pulling down a lever, so too there were telephone call boxes for patrolmen to check in with the station house, or to call for help.

The police tunic had a military-style collar held closed at the throat by two hooks and eyes. High slits on the sides of the tunic allowed fast access to the 38 caliber revolver, blackjack, handcuffs, extra ammunition, and a device that could have been called a vademecum for it helped in holding an arrested suspect. A short chain between two short steel rods, one of which nestled against the other, was wrapped around the right wrist. Black brogans. A hard-wood club about eighteen inches long and one and one quarter inches in diameter, secured to the wrist by a leather thong, the "night stick", was standard equipment for patrolmen.

Wednesday, March 21, 1990

The "candy store" at the southwest corner of Washington Avenue and St. John's Place, Kristol's, stocked the usual packaged candies and chewing gum, but also a chocolate – coated ice cream bar wrapped in foil and kept with dry ice in an air-tight cylinder, "Eskimo Pie". Five cents each. When a man asked for cigarettes, the clerk laid them on the counter with matches. When he asked for cigars, the clerk held out the open box. A cigar lighter on the counter had a lever that, pushed down, tilted the cylinder forward while igniting a jet on top.

As was common with such shops, Kristol's had a wooden stand outside, next to the door, in view of the clerk. Newspapers were arrayed side by side. A rope, attached to one side of the stand and weighted on the other, lay across, a precaution against gusts whipping around the corner. Customers dropped coins on top, unless they were going inside for something else. The reading public enjoyed choosing among both morning and afternoon newspapers. The Times, Herald Tribune, Daily News, Mirror, Graphic, Telegram, Post, Journal American, World, and Brooklyn Eagle.

Bulky Sunday editions were stacked inside on a low bench. Some had rotogravure sections, short on text but long on photographs in sepia. The funnies, of course, were my favorites. Hairbreadth Harry managing finally to rescue Belinda Blinks from the nefarious Rudolph Rasendal. The Katzenjammer Kids, Hans and Fritz, scheming up some deviltry to the annoyance of the Captain, the Professor in his stovepipe hat, and the poor Mama, wielding her wooden spoon. Officer Pup at wit's end to some Krazy Kat from the brick - hurling Ignatz Mouse. Barney Google and his racehorse, Spark Plug. Moon Mullens, Mamie, and Lord Plush-bottom trying to coexist. Texas Slim. Happy Hooligan, who wore a tin can on his head. Boob McNut.

Prospect Heights Pharmacy, diagonally across from the hospital, had a soda fountain to which my mother sent Lillian and me on occasion for a dose of castor oil mixed into a chocolate ice cream soda. At other times it would be for a glass of citrate magnesia which, kept cold in their refrigerator, tasted like carbonated lemon soda. One Sunday after dinner we said we had no room for desert, a rare occurrence indeed. "Run down to the drugstore and see what time they close". By the time Lillian and I got back, we found, oddly enough, that we did have room.

Fondly do I recall three Christmas presents. A gyroscope that stayed erect no matter how much it was moved, as long as it kept spinning. "Erector Set No. 4" : perforated and slotted steel ribbons in several lengths, shallow perforated trays, wheels, pulleys, axles, angle irons, nuts, machine screws, screw driver, a battery – run motor. With a little imagination a boy could construct a variety of small toys. Best of all presents was a set of carpenter's tools. Not even Lionel electric trains would have delighted me so much. One of my mother's friends confided a concern that I could damage the furniture. The apprehension proved unwarranted.

Airplanes and boats of my own crude design were favorite projects. "Lumber" came from boxes begged from storekeepers. Mascoli's Produce gave me apple and pear boxes from Washington State. Grape crates too from California. Orange crates from Florida proved to be flimsy and hard to dismantle without splitting. Loaves of Kraft's American cheese came in boxes greatly appreciated : yellow pine, straight grain, no knots. Breakstone's boxes, however, were usually junk.

Other tools were accumulated gradually, a coping saw, for instance, and a block plane from a kind neighbor on Sterling Place. At first, as a substitute for a drill, I made do with an ice pick heated on the gas stove. My mother was gracious about the mess of chips and sawdust on the kitchen table and floor. She knew I always cleaned up.

The coping saw I misused once, gashing near the tip of my left index finger. The bleeding upset my mother more than me. She bandaged the finger and wrapped the hand in a towel. Off went Lillian and I to the hospital where we climbed the steps into the lobby, for there was no emergency room. Most patients were new mothers. A doctor led us into a small office where he stopped the bleeding without stitches. A day or so later, after changing the dressing, he refused payment.

On Washington Avenue, along the three blocks from Lincoln Place north to Park Place, we were blessed with a rich variety of retail shops. Three drugstores, one with a Post Office sub-station. Three delicatessens, one of which was Kosher. A shoemaker who also cleaned and blocked men's felt hats. Cushman's bakery. "Al's Sanitary Dairy". Ruder's department store. Boston Fish Market, especially busy on Fridays. Three "French Dry Cleaners and Tailors". A pool hall over a luncheonette where on occasion "The Masked Marvel" challenged all comers. Two ice cream parlors. Ray's market, where sometimes rabbits were hung near the side door on Sterling Place. Nick's barber shop. Scharf's hardware, with boxes of merchandise stacked up like file cabinets, row on row, and each with a sample wired to the front. Then there was Roy's radio shop selling replacement tubes, batteries, wire, insulators, whatever.

Butchers wore white aprons and shirts, boater-type straw hats, and wide black leather cuffs like snug gauntlets. Sawdust covered the floor. Hot dogs and sausages came in strings, like beads. Meat was cut to order. So too was hamburger ground. Chickens, their heads swathed in paper, were carried from the walk-in refrigerator whole, excepting the feathers. Bones for soup were added for no charge. A slice of bologna was usually given to children in tow.

Self-service shops had not been conceived of in the 1920's, no clusters of retailers sharing parking spaces. We walked to stores close to home for day-to-day needs. Yet we did not have chain grocery stores, small affairs serving the immediate neighborhood. Largest was The Great Atlantic and Pacific Tea Company, popularly known as the A & P, with three departments: produce, groceries, and meat. The three competitors in groceries had Irish names: James Butler, Thomas Ralston, Daniel Reeves. Some of their managers and clerks spoke with a brogue.

Bread was not sliced. Some loaves were not wrapped. Coffee beans were ground at home as needed, but the A & P would grind the whole pound if asked. Tea came in bulk, to be brewed in pots. Butter came in large wooden tubs. The clerk hacked out a chunk onto waxed paper to be weighed. Similarly with several kinds of cheese. Milk, in heavy galvanized cans, was drawn up in a long-handled ladle that held about a pint. The customer provided a pail and a lid. Ours, of aluminum, held a quart. Also in bulk were cookies and crackers such as ginger snaps, lady fingers, shortening bread, social teas, fig newtons, etc. They were displayed in cubical cardboard boxes having hinged glass lids.

When business was slow, part-time delivery boys weighed potatoes into five pound paper bags from one-hundred pound burlap bags. Likewise with sugar from wooden barrels. The paper bags were then held closed by a couple of turns of string.

The customers stepped directly to the wooden counter, where he either handed his list to the clerk, or read from it, one item at a time. Big orders, to be delivered at no extra cost, were assembled in a corrugated carton or cartons. With others, the clerk tore off a length of brown paper from a roll, spread it out on the counter, and proceeded to gather the order. After placing each item, he wrote the price in pencil on the edge. Finally, everything was bundled up and tied with string dangling from a globular basket overhead. Heavy bundles were given handles of cardboard tubes pierced with wire hooked at each end.

Chain stores printed weekly circulars listing sale items. These were stacked on the counter or near the door. Collecting them on Saturdays was my chore. Then my mother drew up shopping lists for Lillian and me. Thus we often had to make the circuit. Shopping to me was a bore and a distraction that had to be borne, but I hated to fetch the circulars. Now I can't recall why.

Radio in its infancy did not compete with newspapers in informing the public of important national or world events. (Incidentally, Governor Alfred E. Smith used to pronounce radio to rhyme with sad, at least until radio became the universal fashion.) Well, as we've noted, the papers were competitive, so much so they tried to scoop each other with special

editions, "extras", that they hawked through the streets shouting "Extra !
Extra !" adding enough to whet curiosity but not enough to satisfy it.

Pflaumer was the name of friends George and Anthony, next door,
number 830. Their father was building superintendent. When the boys and
friends set up a "club house" in an unused bin, Mrs. Pflaumer flushed us out
to the sun and fresh air. At Christmas they used to assemble on the living
room floor a vast miniature landscape of electric trains winding through
villages, farms, and woods. Fabulous.

De Forest Billyou, another friend, on the south side, at number 834,
was about my age. The first of three older sisters taught in Danbury,
Connecticut, and drove a handsome convertible. Helen and Lydia were
a little older than we. Ferris Jr. was a toddler. I especially admired their
parents, Mary and Ferris Sr., soft-spoken, affable, relaxed. The Billyou
family radiated serenity. De Forest served as a navigator in Europe with
the Army Air Corps during World War Two. Afterward he practiced law
in Manhattan. When I saw him last, in 1949, he was planning a move to
Texas.

Neither of us cared much for sports. Whether because – to speak for
myself only – I was poorly coordinated, I'll never know, at least not in this
vale of tears. It could have been the other way around, perhaps, that I was
poorly coordinated because I took so little interest in sports. I suspect it's a
question of genetic endowment, talent. Well, leaving that moot question,
after a snowfall De Forest and I used to hike over to nearby Prospect Park,
dragging our sleds up to the Sugar Bowl, just west of the Sheep Meadow.
In those early days there really was a flock of sheep in Prospect Park,
sheltered in winter near the site of the present zoo. On Saturday afternoons
Brooklynites would gather from all directions on adjacent hills.

The challenge in sledding was to see how far you could coast, farther,
one hoped, than anyone else. Hoping to build momentum, one stood back
from the crest of the hill, holding the sled out in front, and then ran as
fast as he could. At the crest he threw himself down prone on the sled
and grabbed the steering bar. Two boys could ride together, the second
pouncing on top at the critical moment of contact with the snow. But this
wasn't much fun; they usually tumbled off or stopped short.

Friday, March 23, 1990

When we moved from Park Place to Washington Avenue, the neighborhood had several vacant lots that were soon developed. Most notable was that opposite Brooklyn Museum, at 135 Eastern Parkway, the site now of the biggest and tallest apartment house in all of Brooklyn. Except for a small stretch in the northeast corner of Brooklyn Botanic Garden, behind the museum, and possibly part of Highland Park, farther east, that lot may lie at the highest part of Brooklyn. The view from the roof in all directions must be spectacular.

I recall wandering over that lot when excavation was just beginning, depriving local boys of a playground. It stretched back from Eastern Parkway to Lincoln Place. I was ten or eleven years old. Construction fascinated me so much that when classmates and neighbors were playing ball after school, I was standing as close as I could get, studying the steam shovels, concrete workers, iron workers, masons,...... The teams that riveted girders earned my special respect. One man hurled red-hot rivets up to another who caught them in a kind of cone. Rivets never went wild, nor were they ever fumbled. Neither did the riveter wear a safety belt.

As the framework rose higher, the contractor built an elevator close to where the front wall would be. A gasoline engine, operated on the ground, lifted supplies as needed. White code marks on the steel cable told the operator what level the car had reached. Bell signals told him when to lower the car. In the meanwhile a team of laborers was mixing concrete in an enormous wooden trough in the street, and shoveling it into wheelbarrows. A wooden canopy ran the length of the sidewalk. Along the curb a string of shacks provided office and storage space for the architect, contractor, plumbers, etc.

That house of luxury apartments was named Turner Towers. (Who was this Turner?) Its neighbors also had liveried doormen in white gloves, "service entrances", southern exposures in front, and high rents: Copley Plaza, Peter Stuyvesant, George Washington, etc.

Directly behind Turner Towers, facing Lincoln Place, a smaller house was built. In its early stages of construction I wandered through on a Sunday afternoon, perhaps in search of discarded scraps of lumber, perhaps out of curiosity only. Whatever the motive, I stepped on a nail that pierced my left sole. By the grace of God, a dab of iodine was enough. I've forgotten whether I salvaged any of the scraps.

George Mc Caffrey, only son of the first superintendent, became a classmate at St. Teresa's as well as a friend. A cheerful family, with an older sister, Kay, the Mc Caffrey's lived in an apartment off the rear courtyard, a convenient place for George and me to toss a ball forth and back.

The apartment house lobby had a lush oriental carpet, several antique chairs, carved, high-backed, and upholstered in velvet. Also a handsome table was in the middle holding a dark bronze sculpture on an oval base of marble. Best of all was the affable middle-aged doorman, Gene, who loved to reminisce when he wasn't jumping up to let some tenant in or out.

He told of hoping, with no experience, to become a waiter at the best known restaurant in Coney Island, Feltman's. In preparation he spent several days observing the staff, studying their movements until he felt confident. With self-assurance and luck he landed the coveted job.

Wages were low; waiters depended on tips, as they still do. Feltman's was always busy at night; tips were good, but there were thorns in the rose garden. A clerk at the kitchen door kept a detailed record of everything carried out. At the end of the shift, each waiter paid his total. After the last course, a diner might order brandy or a cigar perhaps. Sometimes Gene returned to find the party had sneaked out.

When we were about fourteen or fifteen, George invited me to a party. Whatever the occasion I don't recall, but I remember well enough being enthralled by the most charming young lady in the entire world. Poised, smiling, self-assured, affable, fashionably dressed, blonde, an angel on a secret mission. Friends called her Lee, short for her name, Lillian E. E....... A Christian Scientist, she lived up in Mount Vernon, New York. For days, maybe weeks, I stumbled around in a trance, unable and unwilling to focus on anything but the celestial Lee. I worked up the nerve to telephone once. A servant answered. She did not return the call.

It was either the August of 1927 or of 1928 that Lillian and I spent a week or so at a Catholic camp in Glen Cove, Long Island, at Garvies Point, the site of the present day Nassau County museum devoted to local pre-historic American Indians, or in the current fashion, "Native Americans", as though the rest of us were immigrants. In those days the camp site was a spacious fairly level meadow on the east edge of Hempstead Harbor. In several spots below the cliff, close to the high water line, were pockets of soft clay. The gray decaying hull of what may have been a small wooden schooner lay aground at high tide. We campers were warned away, of course. My mother visited Camp Aquinas. It happened to be the Feast of the Assumption, August 15th, and so she went with us for a swim, encouraged by her belief in "a cure in the water" that one day. Not, incidentally, that she had been afflicted by any malady.

The staff and fellow campers were pleasant enough, and the food good. Lillian and I saw each other every day. Chances are we sat at the same table. Even so we knew homesickness, especially on chilly nights as we shivered on our cots and heard the wind whipping the tent flaps. One morning after a storm, counselors took us for a walk where we saw smashed boats, some upside down on the beach.

Tuesday, March 27, 1990

St. Teresa's had two schools. The Boy's stood on the north side of St. John's Place, just east of Classon Avenue. Four stories. A classroom in each corner. Higher grades on the higher floors. The broad paved area in the back served only for assembling in the morning and after lunch.

Had games been allowed, it could have been called the boys' playground. The only sport was a bit of deviltry. One cupped his right hand, as he would to scratch, and with a quick left-to-right sweep, hoped to unbutton a classmate's fly. A gap of four buttons was a "home run". Then there was the feint. One boy made a sudden motion as though to strike another. If the "victim" reacted so as to ward off a blow, the prankster chortled "Gotcha !".

Any lad so imprudent as to bounce a ball off the auditorium, risked a clout from a black-robed enforcer of propriety, also the loss of the ball. The auditorium, next to the school and on the corner of Classon Avenue, was completed while Lillian and I were new transferees. Indeed, I recall how fascinated I was with the grinding and polishing of terrazzo in the lobby.

A handsome spacious hall, it had banked theater-type seats in the balcony as well as in the back of the orchestra. A vast level area in front of the stage had wooden folding double chairs that were stored under the stage when not needed. The building proved a most valuable asset to the parish over the years, socially and liturgically. Graduations. Sunday afternoon dances with professional bands. Annual bazaars. Communion breakfasts. Basketball games. Boxing matches sponsored by the Holy Name Society.

Midnight Masses. Amateur dramas by Father Mooney's Avila Players, e.g. My New Curate, in which Lillian and I had a small part.

Except for two laywomen in the lower grades, the classes were taught by the Sisters of St. Joseph. My introduction was to 4A, with Miss Mc Cormick, who, we were to learn, had been a neighbor on Park Place. Like everyone else, she was strict and demanding, but fair, a fine teacher. The no-nonsense unsmiling persona that characterized the faculty must have been a studied affectation for most, if not all.

Sister Francis, teacher of 7A or 7B, had a gruff air outside the classroom. A relief was it, therefore, when we reached her grade to discern a gentle soul behind the mask.

An entertainment of some sort being held in the auditorium, all pupils, boys and girls, were told to attend on the following Sunday. Price of admission was to be comparable to that of a local movie. With our mother's consent, Lillian and I went to the National on Washington Avenue, near Prospect Place. The next morning Sister Francis called me to her desk. I didn't know what to expect, but it had to be bad.

"Where were you yesterday afternoon?

At the National, Sister.

Oh, and what did you see?

Janet Gaynor and Buddy Rogers in

Follow Through.

Did you enjoy it?

Yes, Sister.

You may sit down."

School policy obliged all pupils to attend nine o'clock Mass on Sundays. Boys on the Gospel side (left). The higher the grade the closer to the sanctuary. Like a mother hen, each sister kept a watch over her restless brood. A cricket signaled all moves: when to sit, when to kneel, when to stand, when to march out. Boys in 8B had the privilege of taking the collection, only the boys. The whole school sang hymns in unison to organ accompaniment. Of course we were dressed up in our "Sunday best". Shoes shined. Hair slicked down. Impatient to get home to change to play clothes, or at least take off the neckties.

A few sisters on Monday used to ask why, of those who had not gone to receive Holy Communion, even though they always got the same answer: "I broke my fast, Sister". In those days Catholics were obliged to fast from food and drink, even water, from midnight, before receiving. What boy would have revealed, or was obliged to reveal, to the sister a troubled conscience?

St. Teresa's had an excellent boys' choir that sang at High and Solemn Masses. A classmate, Thomas A. O'Brien – not to be confused with Thomas E. O'Brien – sang beautiful soprano solos. He and the others must have been recruited while I was at St. Joseph's. Calls went out for altar boys. Bob Giles and I were happy to serve, yet at no time was my class invited to try out for the choir.

Bishop Thomas E. Molloy confirmed us. The good sister drilled us well, in preparation for answering whatever questions he might put to us at random. Moreover, we were told to expect a blow to the face, a symbol of what we must expect to endure as devout Catholics for the rest of our lives. In the sacrament, however, the Holy Ghost would presently pour upon us the graces to fight the good fight. Thus we were about to become soldiers of Christ.

At an early age St. Paul in his epistles had made a deep impression on me, as indeed he still does, and so at Confirmation I chose the name Paul.

At last the great day dawned, the day of our marvelous metamorphosis. I glided down the main aisle in happy expectation, like a small child getting out of bed on Christmas morning. Ah, but what a letdown! Bishop Molloy barely grazed my cheek, and what was even worse, as I crawled back to the pew, I was no different at all, but the same timid bunny. What went wrong? Are the sisters to be trusted again?

Friday, March 30, 1990

We moved to nearby Sterling Place probably in the spring of 1930. Number 431 was similar: four floors, each with two apartments of the familiar plan. Ours was the third floor left.

In clear weather the panoramic view from the roof was fabulous. The tallest building in Brooklyn, maybe of all Long Island, Williamsburg Savings Bank, with its four enormous lighted clock dials, stood out like the Washington Monument. East River bridges. Manhattan skyscrapers. And none of us had a telescope.

At the top floor right lived a retired fireman, Hugh Gallagher, Mrs. Gallagher, their daughter, Mrs. Hill, and infant grandson Jackie. Captain Hill, master of a merchant ship of Mallory Transport, and a Navy war veteran, was usually at sea. When his S.S. Malltran was docked at Mariner's Snug Harbor, Staten Island, he invited me and a friend and classmate, Charlie Mc Nally, to visit on a Sunday afternoon. Of course we were delighted to board a ship that had sailed all over the world. The rain did not keep us home. Everyone was on leave excepting one officer, who treated us as family.

I noisily bounded down the stairs on an errand one evening. Almost to the vestibule, I caught sight of a man, a stranger, hurrying out the door. Mr. Gallagher lay near the foot of the stairs, dazed from a blow to the back of his head. Luckily he had not been robbed.

Between our house and the corner to the east stood another with ground-floor shops facing Washington Avenue. Where its backyard had been, there were two small one-story shops. Mr. Fishkin did tailoring in the one next to us.

One of the signs in his window read "Buttons Sewed on Free". With a pair of knickers and a loose button, I marched in. Mr. Fishkin laughed, but stopped what he was doing to accommodate me. My mother laughed too when she got home from work.

Mr. Fishkin proved an interesting character. As a Doughboy rifleman in France with a New York division, he had come under heavy fire in what came to be called The Last Battalion, because it had been cut off a long time from the rest of the regiment.

In those days shopkeepers used to provide free delivery. Grocers had sturdy bicycles with wire baskets on the front wheel. Department stores had fleets of trucks: John Wanamaker's, Frederick Loeser's, Abraham & Straus, Macy's Namm's, etc. At five cents per house call, Mr. Fishkin hired me to deliver garments, whether one or several. Most were suits and gowns that had been dry cleaned and steam pressed. Tips were either five cents or ten cents. Dr. Bowie always gave a quarter. Some weeks I'd make close to a dollar.

We were going away for a weekend to Philadelphia. Miss Foster had agreed to mind Lindy, our cat, the huge one with an extra claw on each paw. She had an apartment on the first floor of the house we had shared, a short walk. After supper I managed to get Lindy into a corrugated cardboard box. With a five dollar bill in my pocket, Lillian and I set out. Because he evidently had other plans, we had to stop several times to stuff Lindy's head back into the box. We arrived at Miss Foster's, finally, with Lindy but without the money. Of course I had no idea when or how it fell out of my pocket. My mother was furious; it was a lot of money.

Bicycles were almost as rare as tennis racquets and golf clubs. There was, however, a shop on Grand Avenue, near the 80th Precinct station house, where bikes were rented by the hour. As security a boy had to leave his coat.

Every boy and girl had roller skates. Steel wheels an inch wide. With a leather strap and a metal clamp near the toe, they were worn with regular shoes, not like ice skates. Replacement wheels cost about a quarter. Small fry carried the skate key on a ribbon around the neck. Union Hardware was the common brand.

Skates were useful in running errands, until one had to cross cobblestones. I used to pay the bills, for example, at Brooklyn Union Gas Company on Fulton Street, less than two miles away. Once I got a quarter for returning a small pail for chop suey to a Chinese restaurant on Atlantic Avenue, near the railroad terminal.

Among regular chores were washing and drying dishes. We both preferred washing because drying took longer, and so Lillian and I agreed on a scheme. Whoever called out "washer!" first became washer at the next meal. Cleaning the cat's box was my monopoly. A huge roasting pan with newspapers, some shredded. Also emptying the pan under the ice box. Shopping. Making beds. Sweeping. Dusting. Putting potatoes on to boil at five o'clock so they'd be done by the time my mother got home. Setting the table. Redding the table. Emptying the mailbox.

Saturday was a mixed blessing. We didn't have to go to school. We could stay up on Friday until eleven o'clock. We could sleep late. There was the special children's matinee on Saturday at the National. On the other hand, there were tedious chores, especially shopping.

Banks were open Saturday mornings. When my mother got back early in the afternoon, if we had not done the work to her satisfaction, she sometimes became angry and punished us in various ways. My mother evidently hated housework. Mopping the kitchen floor or scouring a wash basin made her grouchy. Lillian and I developed a secret code, an early warning signal. When either was returning from an errand, the other, after opening the door, silently wagged his or her tongue. "She's in an ugly mood."

Whenever Lillian was not allowed out to play, she sat and sulked, whereas I'd get out my tools and make something.

Monday, April 2, 1990

We in Prospect Heights were blessed in living so close to the Brooklyn Museum. The original plans called for further construction in the back, which intention is evident even today in the stark facade back there. The area serving now as a parking lot for the museum and Brooklyn Botanic Garden, was in the 1920's partly excavated, leaving a high mound, a natural berm, running parallel to and set back from Washington Avenue, hiding a makeshift playground for neighborhood boys.

The original front had high granite stairs, like those at the Metropolitan Museum, a little wider than the present main lobby. Huge front doors were opened on rare occasions, such as visits from foreign dignitaries. The public entered through an inconspicuous door at the right, where a guard took count on a round, hand-held device no bigger than a hockey puck. No fee was paid at any time. At five o'clock visitors were encouraged to leave. The door at the far right, on the same level, that today opens into the art school, was used then only to accommodate a local election board. Voting machines and tables were surrounded by cases of mounted butterflies and moths. My mother served there for years as a clerk for the Democratic Party.

Today's main lobby occupies space originally the site of a spacious auditorium with banked seats, stage and projection room. Programs for children were presented on Saturday mornings. Those for adults on Sunday, but parents could bring children. Lectures. Movies. Drawing lessons. Travelogues with slides of exotic peoples and places, perfect geography lessons. I learned to look on Sundays for a family heading toward the door, and then to walk close behind until we had passed the guard.

In the 1930's there was an interesting character who called himself "The Tune Detective", adept at recognizing classical roots of fragments of popular songs, Sigmund Spaeth. He wrote a book and lectured on How to Listen to Music, a program I had to sneak in to hear.

The magnificent Sculpture Court was the ideal setting on Saturday afternoons for superb symphonic concerts. Orchestra and soloists were employed by the federal Works Progress Administration (W.P.A.), first-rate artists suffering from the Depression that followed the stock market crash of October 1929. Organ recitals also were given there on Sundays. Over the years I accumulated a large stack of programs, one with the autograph of American composer Henry Hadley.

The W.P.A. sponsored a concert one evening in the auditorium of the Y.W.C.A. near Borough Hall. The major work was to be the Cesar Franck symphony. A fierce snowstorm did not deter the orchestra, nor force a late start, for they performed the program as scheduled, even though the entire audience consisted of two teen-age boys, strangers to each other.

Wednesday, April 4, 1990

We were about ten or eleven years old when my mother brought Lillian and me on a Sunday afternoon to visit a little old lady in the wooded hamlet of Wortendyke, New Jersey, between Wyckoff and Midland Park. Mrs. Smith, a widow, was mother of Lillian, who lived at home, and Arthur, was a colleague of my mother at National City Bank on Wall Street. He and his family met us at the railroad station in Ridgewood, where, incidentally, Lillian used to commute by bus to a real estate office.

The house, on the North side of Park Avenue, about a quarter mile up from Godwin Avenue, was set back thirty or forty feet, one of the few spaces in the area cleared of trees. The few neighbors were separated from each other by so much foliage that in the summer everyone seemed isolated. A world so different from any other we had known. The wooden house was a bit deeper than wide, with two stories, gabled roof, front porch, hardwood floors, and varnished woodwork. Near the back door was a well with a hand pump, though the house had running water. A swing hung from such a high branch that with a little effort a lad could soar with the birds.

We became such good friends that Lillian and I spent a few days at Christmas and Easter, and even longer in summer. My mother would escort us to the train, probably in Hoboken, and we'd hike up from the Wortendyke station, past Babcock's charming white country house with its white picket fence, shrubs, flowers, and covered well out front that looked like a tiny white gazebo.

79

Grandma Smith, as we came to call her, was a loveable soul who was full of tales of her younger days in Indiana. She used to scold, for example, a group of men for cruelty in holding cock fights. She had a huge brown dog, Daisy, part Golden Retriever, whom she spoiled. Grandma had a small flock of chickens too, Leghorns, Rhode Island Reds, and a gray variety with white lines, that may have been called Barred Rocks. Like pets, each had a name.

The hens held back when she strewed feed on the ground, until the rooster began to eat. Similarly at dusk he perched on the roost first. Then the hens snuggled together, each in her regular place, like cows that find their own stalls. Of course a hen with a brood slept on the nest, the chicks crowded under her wings. During the day they followed her everywhere until, in due course, she shooed them away to fend for themselves.

The Smiths drank Postum, not coffee, and on occasion home-brewed sassafras tea. Thus I learned to recognize the tree from its three different leaves. Far better would it have been, had I learned to recognize poison ivy. Wearing short pants, I shimmied up a tree shrouded in it. Commenting only that sugar of lead brought no relief, I'll pass over the indelicate clinical details.

Whatever their religious convictions, Grandma and Lillian Smith gave no evidence of church membership. This is not to say, of course, they were atheists. Indeed Grandma appeared in her daily life to be a devout Protestant. When others would sing popular songs at home, she would sing hymns, so much so, in fact, that with no effort at all, I memorized many. Every Sunday she dressed up as though to go out, even donning gloves and hat, then she'd excuse herself, turn on the radio, and sit in the living room, listening to and singing along with a church service.

Two Catholic ladies, from a farm house further up the oiled road, shepherded Lillian and me. A bus marked "Oakland" took us a couple of miles north on Godwin Avenue to Wyckoff, where Franciscans from the Paterson monastery had a mission chapel, St. Elizabeth's.

The Wortendyke railroad station housed the small post office, where residents had boxes. There may not have been home delivery in the 1920's. A grocer nearby stocked fruits and vegetables which he regularly loaded onto a small truck with awnings over the open sides. In so small a community, where everyone new everyone else, his making the rounds was a social event as well.

Grandson Buddy Smith, about my age, a Boy Scout in Englewood, spent part of the summer at a Scout camp with a name easy to remember: "NO-BE-BO-SCO" (North Bergin Boy Scouts).

Monday, April 9, 1990

My mother had a friend at the bank, a young woman with no family, who often went to the movies several times a week. In my eyes she ranked up there with those who could buy licorice drops whenever they wished. Lillian and I knew we were lucky to get to the National on Saturday. Today there's a supermarket where it used to be, on the west side of Washington Avenue near Prospect Place.

It opened at ten or eleven in the morning and ran continuously until about midnight, repeating without intermissions. An avid fan, therefore, could sit through the program again, or until closing. A couple of times Lillian and I stayed longer than our mother approved of, and so she marched down to fetch us, the ticket-taker being sympathetic.

Whenever we couldn't go together, the late arriver knew a seat would be held, preferably near the center of the orchestra. Lillian said she had no trouble locating me; my laugh was a beacon.

The program usually included a "Double Feature", two full length films. There were also "Selected Short Subjects": a comedy, Movietone News, and "Coming Attractions", samples of films soon to follow. The National's program changed perhaps three times a week. Evening rates were charged beginning at five o'clock.

Children were catered to on Saturday mornings, with a serial of about fifteen installments. These were typically long on action, stereotypes, and pageantry, but short on all else. Settings may have been the Western frontier, American Revolution, a jungle in Africa, a mythical planet of

82

Buck Rogers, wherever. Every episode ended abruptly with hero or heroine in grave danger, followed by the promise "To Be Continued". For example, the hero would catch an arrow or spear in his chest, or be carried into an abyss in a car hurtling over a cliff. The next episode always took up the story before the arrow or spear hit, and before the car flew over the curve, and lo, the arrow or spear missed, and the car managed to round the curve safely. Hooray! By the way, after Gene Tunney beat Jack Dempsey, he was made the hero of a Saturday serial.

Short comedies featured such loonies as Charlie Chase and Thelma Todd, Stan Laurel and Oliver Hardy, Buster Keaton, Charlie Chaplin, Harold Lloyd, or the implausible gang in Our Gang Comedies.

The double bill often included a prototype Western starring such cowboy heroes as Tom Mix, Tim McCoy, George O'Brien, Ken Maynard, and Hoot Gibson, all slight variations on the basic persona. Like the vast majority of movie stars, their predictability was both a strength and a weakness.

Downtown theaters, such as the Fox and the Paramount, that showed first-run films, added on weekends a "stage show" with an orchestra – called a dance band then – singers and dancers, and an occasional movie star "live". An impresario well known in the early 1930's, Nils T. Grantland, (N.T.G.), used to specialize in such entertainment.

One Sunday afternoon a friend and I attended the Metropolitan, on Fulton Street, close to the department stores. Among the entertainers was the glamorous platinum-blonde movie star Jean Harlow, enchantress in, for one, Hells Angels with Ben Lyon and Beebe Daniels.

On the way to the St. John's Place trolley car, George Mc Candles and I left through the back door, on Livingston Street. Standing there at the curb, a big black limousine awaited N.T.G. and his troupe. We waited, but not long. Out they filed, all smiles, and close enough to rub elbows with the handful of admirers. In that fleeting moment I was impressed by two features of the great Jean Harlow: she was more petite than I had expected, and her stage makeup was not attractive close up.

Years later I was reminded of the incident in passing the stage door of the original Metropolitan Opera House. Two ballerinas, in tutus and make up, were getting a breath of fresh air. Distance lends enchantment.

Still more years later, as a young man I wandered into the ballroom of the Hotel Astor on Times Square. Some car manufacturer was introducing his new models. Live entertainment had been promised. The place was packed like the rush-hour subways. A hand touched my right shoulder while a gruff voice behind me said: "Pardon me, Buddy". It was Jimmy Durante.

Tuesday, April 10, 1990

During Prohibition laws outlawing the manufacture and distribution of alcoholic beverages were enacted. In 1919, the Eighteenth Amendment to the U.S. Constitution established Prohibition, but enforcement, through the Volstead Act, failed to abolish bootlegging and the widespread lawbreaking associated with it. In 1933, the Twenty-First Amendment repealed Prohibition.

Under the Eighteenth Amendment, Prohibition, beer as well as wine could be made legally at home for home consumption. Shops sprang up in most neighborhoods selling wine presses, kegs, malt, hops, yeast, and all the equipment necessary to make and bottle wine and "home brew".

Several gallons of beer could be made by first boiling the black thick malt and hops held in a cheesecloth bag. After the hops were discarded, the liquor was transferred to an earthenware crock with yeast. Fermentation took about a day, in the course of which thick foam that rose to the top had to be spooned off several times. When the frothing stopped, the "green" beer was siphoned into bottles, which were at once capped and laid on their sides for a week or so.

"Bathtub gin" was made quickly by mixing grain alcohol and flavorings, a process favored for its simplicity and speed, although more costly than homebrew; bootleg alcohol was expensive.

Some restaurants and private clubs that served bootleg booze operated openly, as though legitimate and law-abiding, yet they served liquor to known patrons in tea or coffee cups.

Others functioned in secret places behind various fronts, with a hidden entrance from the rear of a cigar store, perhaps, or other retail shop. Despite the elaborate pretense, however, even neighborhood boys came to see where the some "speakeasies" were. The giveaway was exuberant patrons coming and going. Sometimes the odor too.

A common sight after sunset was large trucks, completely shrouded, excepting the cabs, in tarpaulins, bearing no markings, and rumbling up Washington Avenue.

My mother and her friends used to take the Brighton Line, B.M.T. to Sheepshead Bay for "shore dinners" and an evening's revelry at The Boat, which was in fact a barge aground on the north shore of the bay, across from what was then called Oriental Beach. The Boat disappeared long ago, as indeed that entire row of picturesque wooden piers, bait shacks, and clam bars that had endowed Emmons Avenue with its unique charm.

Gone too is Glory, a sleek handsome yacht of varnished mahogany and brass that stood out among the party fishing boats like a swan among mallards. She was reputed to have served as a cutter with the Coast Guard during the Great War, and more recently as a rumrunner. If that were true, then she was forced into retirement in 1933 with the repeal of the Eighteenth Amendment.

In Roosevelt's campaign against Hoover the year before, he promised to work for repeal, and so when he won, the disgruntled heirs of the Woman's Christian Temperance Union (W.C.T.U.) and of Carrie Nation, those saintly souls who so zealously had striven to save the nation from itself, those champions of compulsory virtue, clamored for "light wines and beer" only. In the end they could at least console one another with the boast that the term saloon was still a dirty word. The new era bars and taverns all enshrined President Roosevelt in framed photographs, hung appropriately over the cash registers.

Wednesday, April 11, 1990

The building that stands where Prospect Park West and Union Street meet at Grand Army Plaza, now Madonna House, was originally the clubhouse of Columbus Council 126 of the Knights of Columbus. As such it was ideally suited to its purpose, with various meeting rooms, living quarters, restaurant, gymnasium, steam room, swimming pool, ballroom, billiard room, members' grill, and a roof fitted for summer dances and parties.

In the 1920's and early 1930's the pool and gym were open to Catholic boys twice a week for several hours, three times in summer. Annual dues in the Boys' Club was nominal, maybe five dollars.

Few of us spent time in the gym; the heated pool was the big attraction. Ten by twenty yards. Low and high boards. Bathing suits were left home. Members took showers before climbing the stairs to the pool. Mr. Reilly, the lifeguard, inspected each boy to see that he was wet and clean. Then, with an unlit cigar, he leaned against the stair railing, ready to sound the whistle at the first sign of horseplay, and if necessary to dive in. Fortunately, I never knew him to get wet. The tattoo on his right forearm he explained as a souvenir he regretted of his war service in the Navy.

My friend Charlie Mc Nally and I were members for two or three years, before we lost interest at about the time we entered high school.

Uncle Harry Leggett had moved his family in the late 1920's to a big Victorian house in Sheepshead Bay, a few doors up north from the venerable Tappen's Restaurant on Emmons Avenue. The best place for swimming in that area was Roeder's Beach, on a nearby inlet, where I learned to swim while a frequent guest.

How proud I was the day I boasted to my mother of having swum across the bay to Oriental Beach. Of course, I didn't mention fear of shark bite, or how often I had stopped to rest, or how narrow the bay.

On a hot summer day when I was twelve or thirteen years old, I was invited by a neighbor to go along for a swim at the Central Y.M.C.A., on Hansen Place, near the Long Island Railroad terminal. While we were hiking down Carlton Avenue, Earl Woods explained to me that at the door, we'd be asked what church we belonged to. He'd answer "Duryea Presbyterian". With little if any reflection, I agreed to say the same. I don't know even now whether my saying "St. Teresa's" would have made a difference, nor did I think to question Earl, and so to the question I parroted: "Duryea Presbyterian".

That evening when my mother got home from the bank, I related all that had happened. She was aghast and ordered me to march back down at once and tell the truth. By that hour I had become ashamed of myself, and so I was eager to recant.

The side door we had filed into was locked by early evening. Thus there seemed to be no way for me to confront the afternoon sentinel. Up the front steps, through the main door and into the lobby. There were only three men in sight, playing pool off to the left, none of them the one I had hoped to find. Well, I had come to confess the truth; one of them would have to do. The man about to strike the cue ball drew back, leaned on the stick, and asked what he could do for me. Patiently he listened as I told my tale in full details. For a moment in silence he looked me in the eye. The other men said nothing. Finally he said in effect "All right, son. I'll tell him. You can forget it. You can forget it." I glided back to the door relieved.

Thursday, April 12, 1990

During Lent boys and girls customarily gave up some indulgence: candy or ice cream or desert perhaps. On Holy Thursday after supper, families visited neighboring churches praying before the special altars of repose lavishly banked with spring flowers. With school closed, we kept silent, or tried to keep silent, during the hours on Good Friday when Jesus hung in agony on his cross, from noon until three o'clock. Lillian and I found the nearby Brooklyn Botanic Garden an ideal setting for this devotion. From the gate we'd wander our separate ways, pretending not to recognize friends and classmates doing the same.

On Easter Sunday parents decked out their children in new outfits from hats to shoes. My mother said that back home in Philadelphia, a lady without a new bonnet on Easter was a fair target for birds, and of course she wouldn't dare go to church bareheaded.

I can't talk for girls, to be sure, but the typical boy got all dressed up only when he had no choice, as in going to Mass or visiting Grandma. This disposition faded away, however, shortly after the first young lady made his heart skip a beat.

Tuesday, April 17, 1990

While dairies sold milk in bulk, poured into customer's pails, delicatessens sold milk and cream in glass bottles, and, like those for home delivery, plugged with cardboard discs and further protected by bonnets of heavy paper. Cream rose to the top from where it could be poured off or shaken.

Some few customers didn't bother to return the bottles for the two cents deposit, nor even soft-drink bottles for five cents. Finding these in the cellar was almost as good as finding the money. We got to know what store sold the various brands, Rinken or Borden for instance.

Borden had a fleet of horse-drawn milk wagons fanning out from a plant on Sterling Place in Park Slope, near St. Augustine's Church. After their runs, several teamsters used to have breakfast at a luncheonette at the corner of Washington Avenue and Sterling Place, the one with the pool hall upstairs. Their horses and wagons school children would pass, lined up on Sterling Place. On our way over to Classon Avenue, Lillian and I often brought sugar cubes, which, by the way, were in fact oblong. A beautiful and alert chestnut, Tommy, we'd find with his forelegs up on the sidewalk, charming passersby. Do you know that draft horses such as Tommy get to know the routes so well that they don't have to be told where to stop?

Newspapers were another source of money. A junk dealer on Bergin Street near Grand Avenue paid twenty cents per one-hundred pounds. Once when Charlie Mc Nally and I were almost there, a housewife called us to her door. A trap had caught a rat, both of which she had swept into the back yard. We were relieved to find the beast already dead. It was a small matter then to pry up the bar, drop the corpse into a garbage pail, return the trap, and collect a quarter.

Neither of us owned a shiny red express wagon to carry the papers. Oh, there had been times when I hoped for one at Christmas, as indeed later for a bicycle, but in the Depression these were luxuries beyond reach. Let me add that eventually, when I could have paid for a bike out of my wages, the appeal, like knickers, had vanished.

City boys in those days made their own wagons. Wheels and axles from a discarded baby carriage. Scrap lumber from packing cases or foraged from construction sites. A handful of common nails. A spike or bolt to serve as a pivot. A few feet of rope, usually clothes line.

Home-made scooters were more common, for they were easier to build, and more fun to use. All one needed: one roller skate, an orange crate – apple boxes were too low – about three feet of 2" X 4" board, and a few nails. The front and back parts of the skate were nailed to the ends of the 2" X 4". Narrow sticks on top of the crate, one on each side, served as handles. Some boys added tin cans in front, simulated headlights. Those noble chariots were typically garaged in apartment-house cellars. Oddly enough, I never heard of one being stolen.

The public library, where Flatbush Avenue meets Eastern Parkway at Grand Army Plaza, is the second building on the site. A concrete and steel shell, surrounded by a high wooden fence, stood there all during my childhood, a sad eyesore a white elephant.

Small boys used to climb through a break in the fence along the Parkway, near the back. Pigeons made the top floor their rookery. Water filled the cellar. Floating abandoned lumber we used to push around with sticks, like lumberjacks maneuvering logs.

It was torn down around 1940. As the present library was going up, with its massive pillars framing the main door, an ad' appeared in The Brooklyn Eagle for a left- handed stone carver.

When my pals and I were thirteen or fourteen years old, we began hitching rides on the back of trucks, not that we had someplace to go, but just for the adventure. Trucks in the early 1930's were only rarely sealed boxes, but most often rolling platforms with wooden slatted sides and canvas covers. They moved slowly in traffic, stopping often at red lights. Thus it was tempting to hitch a ride standing on the bumper while climbing to the tailgate.

Where space permitted, we'd climb aboard. Sometimes we'd have ridden a mile or so before the driver, discovering us in the mirror, persuaded us to get off, too often with an earthy stream alleging our addiction to unspeakable erotic perversions. Yet there were, of course, some knights of the road who either didn't see us or didn't care, and so we learned more of Brooklyn geography, and had lots of fun on summer afternoons.

The design of trolley cars made hitching rides risky or impossible, due to the lack of footholds and handholds. In the early days, moreover, each had a motorman and also a conductor who would have scared off a freeloader. Incidentally, I recall on the St. John's Place line in the 1920's special summer cars, somewhat like the San Francisco trams. All passengers sat facing forward, on benches stretching from side to side, with hand rails at each end from floor to ceiling. Wide running boards extended along the sides from front to back. There being no aisle, the conductor collected fares as he shuffled from bench to bench along the right side. Cars in winter opened in the middle, at the conductor's station.

This calls to mind an incident on the same line when I was about twenty years old. I boarded one night at the northeast corner of Sterling Place and Washington Avenue, heading downtown. The entrance was at the front where riders dropped the fare into a hopper at the right elbow of the motorman who stood in the dark with his back to a movable canvas curtain. Where I was going and what I was thinking I don't recall, but I climbed in and sat down without paying. Just then the light turned green and the car swung right into the avenue, stopping before the red light at the next corner, Park Place. Brushing aside the curtain, and pumping his index finger over the hopper, the motorman called out for all to hear "Hey, Buddy ! Donaaate ! Donaaate

Thursday, April 19, 1990

It was in 1930 or '31 that I joined the Boy Scouts. Sam Hall, a neighbor around the corner on Washington Avenue, was a patrol leader in a troop that met in Central Methodist Church that snuggles against the eastern side of Williamsburg Savings Bank on Hanson Place, across from the Long Island Railroad terminal. He was kind enough to introduce me to the scoutmaster, Mr. Theodore H. Kenworth, parishioner, World War 1 Army veteran, and attorney, with an office on Montague Street near Borough Hall.

The church sponsored the troop in graciously allowing use of its basement gym on Friday nights, but it did not proselytize. Indeed few scouts were parishioners, far fewer than Catholics. Moreover, no one lived near the church. Mr. Kenworth came from Park Slope.

Troop S 32 had five or six patrols, with names such as Eagle, Beaver, Fox, Wildcat, etc. A patrol had about five or six members, in rank from Tenderfoot to Eagle.

Meetings featured competitions among the patrols in skills, e.g. knot tying, semaphore signaling, fire starting with flint and steel or with wool and friction. Incidentally, the "S" stood for Standard, a proud distinction that acknowledged the meeting of certain criteria set by the National Council.

The uniform shirt was as it still is today. Merit badges, however, were clustered on the right sleeve at the cuff. Only after many had been won were they transferred to the sash. The black neckerchief was secured by a ring of golden cord woven like a Turk's Head knot. Rings of other materials and design were optional. The color of the neckerchief varied from troop to troop. Pants were like riding breeches, but not baggy. Ribbed cotton stockings came up to the knees. Brown oxfords. The official hat was styled like the campaign hat still worn by state troopers and park rangers, among others. Mr. Kenworth wore one, as did a couple of senior scouts. To the rest of us they would have been an extravagance.

Several times a year the troop went hiking in Staten Island on Saturday. The nearby I.R.T. subway sped us over to Bowling Green, Manhattan, a short walk from the ferry to St. George. Fare on each: 5 cents. The bus labored up Victory Boulevard. to an undeveloped wooded region called, for no obvious reason Four Corners. At lunch we shared fires, but each one cooked his own meal, most often frankfurters and Campbell's "Pork and Beans", the pork being a lump of suet the size of a postage stamp. Beef stew was another favorite, canned, of course.

Among the requirements for a Tenderfoot to advance to Second Class was a hike of fourteen miles, followed by a written account. We were allowed to fulfill this if we made the trip on our own and eliminated the bus in both directions. My friend Charlie was not a scout, but he joined me on the outing, hiking up from the ferry. On the way back down, he took the bus to save time.

Palisades Park was also a good place for the troop, but we didn't go often; we spent so much time just getting there and back.

One summer most of the troop spent two weeks in a camp of the Brooklyn Council at Ten Mile River, up near Narrowsburg. The Erie Railroad dropped us off at a trail through the woods. The only sign of civilization was the tracks. How did the engineer know where to stop?

The vast Ten Mile River reservation had more acreage than some towns up there. Also an enormous lake surrounded by wooded hills. Headquarters, infirmary, p-x, chapel, cabins for arts and crafts, all huddled close to the shore. A central commissary provided all meals in insulated cases and jugs to satellite camps sprinkled over the hills. There was one exception: the camp serving Kosher.

Our camp was named Ste-ha-he, whose translation I don't know. Tents on raised wooden platforms. A huge square wooden screened mess hall, also 2 feet off the ground. A tent with telephone for scoutmaster and staff. Flagpole. Totem pole. Flush toilets. Cold showers. Clearing with a shallow pit for a bonfire.

Each camp had its own bugler, who added to every call distinguishing grace notes.

Before a camper was allowed to swim in deep water, he had to demonstrate his skill in the "crib". I recall having later to jump from the raft fully clothed and then swimming a short distance. I've forgotten why.

Lifeguards enforced a "buddy" system. No one was permitted to swim alone. Whenever the whistle sounded, and the guard called out "Buddies", you had better hold up your buddy's hand, even on the raft or dock.

Fortunately, rain was brief and infrequent, and so almost all of the time there was a good variety of things to do. Canoeing, boating, swimming, arts and crafts, picking berries, watching salamanders and sunfish, working for merit badges, writing home for money, etc. The tacit postulate was that we were there for vacation. No one was pressured to work toward advancement in rank. There was no regimentation; everyone could do as much or as little as he wished.

Mr. Kenworth – we addressed him simply as "T-H" - was the perfect scoutmaster. For example, though a devout Methodist, on Sunday mornings he made the rounds to tents waking all the Catholics in time for Mass. A Franciscan friar drove down from the seminary in Callicoon. Afterwards T-H made sure a hot breakfast was waiting.

While I was foraging for blackberries one sunny afternoon, a misguided bee stung my instep, a gratuitous affront, surely, but a dab of mud proved effective therapy.

Some experienced campers find enjoyment at the expense of the credulous, in sending them, for example, in search of keys to the oarlocks, a can of striped paint, twenty feet of shoreline, a left handed monkey wrench. a bucket of steam, etc. These fools' errands, I suspect, are usually recognized by would-be victims.

Speaking of the variety of things to do, I almost forgot the snipe hunt. The snipe is a small game bird that, like the chicken doesn't fly. It sleeps in the day and feeds at night, preferring thick brush and woods. Coordinated team work is required to capture it.

About seven of us set off after taps one night. As quietly as we could, we crept through the woods to a small clearing where tactics were spelled out. Now because snipe run ahead of approaching danger, they can be herded to a given point. The trick is to have hunters, spread out in a great arc, beating the underbrush with sticks while they all head for the center, the place of ambush. In the meanwhile, at the critical point, one or two of the team are hiding in silence, ready to scoop up the snipe into burlap sacks.

After this had been explained and understood, two were chosen to stay there in ambush while the rest set off to circle around.

It took about a half hour for those two to awaken to the fact that they had been left holding the bag. The rest of the troop were asleep when we crawled back to camp.

Tuesday, May 8, 1990

In the boy's school, St. Teresa of Avila parish, each class was commended to a special patron saint, whose virtues were acclaimed for our edification. As a member of this or that sodality in the upper grades, we were required to pay "dues" of five cents each month. One day I didn't have the nickel; when the rest of the class left at 3 o'clock; I had to stay and to write a zillion times: "I must not forget my sodality dues. I must not forget my sodality dues I must not forget........."

Desks were fastened to the oaken floors in six rows of five. As class average changed with each report card, the seating plan changed. Whoever had the highest was awarded the first seat in the first row, at the teacher's left, nearest the door. In our class it was always James Cuneen, always.

On the first Friday of the month, the Blessed Sacrament was exposed all day on the main altar, and so the classes were escorted for short visits. We boys were lead two-by-two down the back stairs, through the yard to the passage east of the convent, and across Sterling Place to the church. Every day at noon, however, sister led us two-by-two down the front stairs to St. John's Place. We, who lived on Sterling Place, or beyond, were marched down Classon Avenue, where we were dismissed at the corner. Once I leapfrogged over the fire hydrant, a breach of decorum that earned a clout to the back of the head.

I've forgotten the occasion; maybe we were returning from church. Sister allowed the class to go to the boy's room, in the basement, a few at a time. She stood at the door playing traffic cop. Because the first group was taking too long, she pushed the door open a bit and yelled in: "Come out, or I'm coming in!" Out they stampeded. Would she really have gone in?

In the Tridentine liturgy there were degrees of ritual and ceremony. In the most simple, the Low Mass, there was no music. In the High Mass, Missa Cantata, the celebrant and choir sang certain parts, with or without organ accompaniment, in either Gregorian Chant, (Plain Song,) or four-part harmony, (polyphony). In Solemn High Mass, Missa Solemnus, the celebrant was joined by a deacon, who chanted the gospel, and sub-deacon, who chanted the epistle all three ministers in matching sleeveless chasubles. Six candles were lit. The organ accompanied the choir. The missal, altar and congregation were incensed. Most often the festive occasion called for a sermon or homily; sometimes too a procession.

The girl's school, fronting on Sterling Place, across from the church, stood back-to-back with the auditorium. Only once in the five years did I have occasion to go there, when, in 8A, Joe Wertman and I were sent to draw maps on the blackboards in 8A, Geography text in one hand, and chalk in the other. Most classrooms, if not all, in the upper grades were equipped with assorted cloth maps on rollers, like window shades. What we drew and why we were chosen I've since forgotten.

A classmate, delivering The Brooklyn Eagle, was standing at the basement door of a brownstone town house on Sterling Place as I strolled by. We were friends; yet I whipped out my home-made slingshot and fired a tiny pebble. He ducked, a window shattered, and I ran home, a few doors east. While we were at supper that evening, our apartment bell rang, third floor left. The aggrieved homeowner said she had followed me home that afternoon. That's what she said. My mother paid.

There was no school uniform, but boys were required to wear neckties. Incidentally, in 4A we had a classmate who several time came late, explaining that he had to shine his shoes. Indeed they glowed. A certain sister had the habit of grabbing the tie as though it were a halter, when a pupil aroused her displeasure by gazing out the window, or not moving fast enough, or whatever. Until one day she yanked the tie of a lad who had it knotted to a rubber band under his collar.

The pastor, Monsignor Peter Donahue, had the sisters make an announcement; it may have been 1930. Boys belonging to Boy Scout troops sponsored by Protestant churches were to resign at once. No rationale at all. Just that bold decree. Well, I was stunned. On the one hand, pastors are Christ's surrogates. On the other hand, I respected and loved our Troop S-32. My mother mulled over the dilemma during supper that evening, deciding finally that we'd wait for further word from the pastor. A wise choice, for no word ever came.

The parish sponsored a new organization, The Catholic Boys Brigade. We met in the school basement. Khaki uniform with burgundy trim. Bugle and drum corps. I had previously taught myself to play the bugle, to the annoyance, I must add, of at least one grumpy neighbor. In the Brigade I learned the snare drum. We gave a performance on night in the ballroom of the Elks club down on Livingston Street, in the building that today houses the New York City Board of Education.

The Brigade, alas, did not survive, largely, I suspect, because it had so little to offer the many boys who flocked to it at first. Moreover, close-order drilling and military discipline had short-lived charm. The vacuum could have been filled easily by a Boy Scout troop, but in those days all or most Catholic pastors, for whatever reason, misjudged the Scouting movement as vaguely anti-Catholic, an error that even today persists here and there despite the truth.

In the Tridentine Mass we had two altar boys, vested in black cassocks and white surplices. The altar stood on a platform against the back wall of the sanctuary, three steps above the floor. Side altars were raised one step. After the regular memorized penitential prayers, in Latin, said before the bottom step, the priest, with his back to the congregation, arose and read, in a low voice from a large missal on a portable lectern at the right side of the altar, prayers and the epistle appropriate to the liturgical calendar. The server who knelt on the bottom step, on the left, watched for the priest to touch the altar with his left hand, his cue that the epistle had been read. Having genuflected in the middle, before the tabernacle, the server walked around to the right and up the steps, while the priest moved to the middle, bending in silent prayer. That moment was for me the beginning of nervous torment. The Latin responses and the rubrics I had memorized:

they were no problem, but carrying the missal and lectern was. They had to be carried down the steps to the floor, and after genuflection, up to the left side, where the priest stood waiting to read the gospel. You see, they weighed a ton. If I had dropped them, I'd have died of shame. Only God's grace saved me, every time.

All academic subjects were taught, with cumulative intensity, of course, through the upper grades. Formal instruction in geography, however, ended in seventh year. Not, certainly that we had learned it all; probably to allow more time for matters of greater urgency, maybe preparing for the Preliminary Examinations. They were written tests from the Board of Regents in Albany, designed to measure competence in all academic subjects before we moved up to high school, all but religion. Everyone about to graduate was tested, everyone, in both private and public schools.

It was in the late spring of 1932 that my voice changed abruptly. I recall being sent around the corner to Butler's, where I chatted with the delivery boy, Mixie McDonald. He remarked how strange it was that I had a cold in warm weather. Only then did I notice that my voice had dropped about an octave, an event destined to distinguish me from my classmates. In preparing for graduation, on the stage of the auditorium, we were rehearsing the awarding of diplomas, having been admonished to be silent until we said "Thank you, Monsignor". During the practice, however, most of us whispered as we waited our turn to file up. The sister, playing the role of the pastor, interrupted long enough to scold us and to call me up for a clout to the back of the head, dramatic evidence that indeed I stood out in my class.

Pupils whose parents could afford the tuition – very few – applied to Bishop Loughlin High School or St. Augustine's. Shortly before graduation, a handful was sent on Saturday mornings to compete for scholarships to St. Augustine's and Regis, a Jesuit high school in Manhattan. I never learned my scores, but then no news was bad news.

Academic subjects were taught through the eight years, excepting Geography, which ended with the seventh. Not, of course, that we knew it all, but perhaps to afford more time to prepare for the critical Preliminary Examinations before graduation. They were from the Board of Regents in

Albany, written tests measuring achievement in the full range of subjects, whether in private or public elementary schools.

In June 1932 our class of boys was rehearsing for graduation on the stage of the auditorium. Standing in the middle, Sister was playing the role of the pastor while we sat in rows behind her, most of us whispering despite the order to be silent. Now it happened that a week or so earlier my voice had changed from tenor to baritone. A sister pretended to hand out the rolled-up diplomas, we filed up one at a time as our names were read aloud, coached to say "Thank you, Monsignor". Well it wasn't long before our buzzing became too much for "Little Annie", for she interrupted the ceremony long enough to reprimand the offenders and to summon me for a clout to the back of my head, dramatic proof that I stood out in my class.

Prescribed for graduation was a certain costume for boys, two of whose items I'll never forget. Whereas knickers were the customary school-boy fashion, on that great occasion we were to wear "long pants", custom-tailored trousers of cream-colored heavy woolen flannel, having conventional bulky cuffs. That shade was suited surely to the summer just begun. But the fabric would have been appropriate in Anchorage. The shoes had to be oxfords whose toes and heels were brown, separated by white insteps. It chanced that I had a new pair similar, whose insteps were tan.

While we were assembling in the school yard for the last time, I was embarrassed to see that I alone was out of uniform, even though it seemed to me my shoes went better with the flannels. Afterwards, on the way to Lewne's for a soda, my mother remarked that due to the lighting and the height of the stage, she couldn't see anyone's shoes.

Tuesday, May 22, 1990

A girl who had just graduated, a friend and neighbor on Sterling Place, invited me to a bon voyage party. Kathleen's father was to take the family Farrell on vacation to England and Ireland, sailing on the maiden voyage of the ocean liner <u>M.V. Georgic</u>. Having had a secret crush on the smiling colleen, I was of course delighted.

Two Checker cabs sped us in style to the Cunard Line pier. From the start I was impressed; it was probably my first ride in a cab, certainly the longest. The <u>Georgic</u> turned out to be much more enormous and luxurious than I had imagined. Staffed with ministering stewards eager to please. The kind of ship that seamen such as Capt. Hill dreamed of commanding. The contrast with the primitive square-riggers that had ferried our forefathers across the same Atlantic Ocean must surely arouse our gratitude. Do we not reap where they sowed?

Later in the summer of 1932 we Dees moved from 431 Sterling Place. What prompted the change I don't recall; the rent maybe, or the absentee landlady. Roaches were no problem; she had an exterminator service the whole house regularly. Mice were rarely seen; our cat had little excitement. During the previous summer, however, we were plagued with bedbugs. We guess the tiny devils migrated from the apartment below, immediately after it was vacated.

Spraying with Black Flag or Flit was not enough, alas, and so every few days I pulled the mattresses off, and held burning rolled-up newspapers under all the coiled springs. (Candles had not been hot enough.) With God's help we eventually won that war.

The new house at 427 St. John's Place had four handsome apartments on each of four floors. At the right and left of the double front door, shielded by iron fences, garden plots, about twenty feet square, harbored low shrubs, for example, forsythia, blessed relief among the stones, bricks, concrete and asphalt.

The landlord, Mr. Louis Miller, and his family lived on the second floor. Re-painting was assigned to professionals, but routine maintenance he himself took care of promptly. The janitor swept and mopped the tiled halls and marble stair treads.

We moved into the four rooms and bath, steam-heated, apartment 16, top floor, northeast corner. Lillian and our mother shared the larger bedroom, at the back, where two north-facing windows gave a partial view of the house on Sterling Place. Linoleum on the kitchen floor, but excepting the narrow bathroom with its small hexagonal tiles, the other floors had oaken parquet, all in excellent condition. Woodwork was of solid oak, so hard that nails or screws for curtain brackets required pre-drilled pilot holes. The living room was blessed with a large double-hung window between two smaller ones, through which the morning sunlight flooded in, while it cheered also the kitchen and my room. So well insulated were the walls and floors that we heard little from neighbors when the windows were shut.

In September of 1932, no news of a scholarship having come, I hiked out to Alexander Hamilton High School, where I enrolled in the liberal arts program, a.k.a. academic program. Freshman classes were held in an annex, on the top floor of an elementary school at the southwest corner of Dean Street and Schenectady Avenue, eleven blocks east and six blocks north of our new home. The main building, at 150 Albany Avenue at the northwest corner of Albany Avenue and Bergin Street, was a short walk, two blocks west and one south of the Dean Street annex, even shorter when we cut through the Bergin Street trolley barn and yard.

Originally Hamilton had been named Boys Commercial High School, but the confusion with Boys High School and Girls Commercial High School prompted a change. Yet it remained for boys only.

After eight years of tutelage under the strict Sisters of St. Joseph, I entered the secular public school expecting laxity and even a subtle, corrosive moral assault. Why I don't know. But Hamilton was in fact a no-nonsense school with high standards and high morale, operating on the tacit premise that the faculty was there to teach; we to learn.

Corridors had stripes down the middle, never to be crossed. If the next class were directly across the hall, the student or teacher had to make a U turn at the end or intersection. Infrequent disciplinary measures were recorded on color-coded cards, pink perhaps. Among the laurels listed in the yearbook, the vast majority of graduates were said to have had no pink cards in the four years.

All programs through the four year sequence were organized in eight terms, not in four years. And so, as in the elementary schools, students were promoted, or required to repeat, after each term. The state Regents exams were taken in academic subjects after every two terms. With English, however, only after the eighth term. Moreover, with foreign languages the first Regents exams were taken after the fourth term.

Each term was divided into three marking periods. Although Regents exams were mandatory, excellent grades in the thirds earned exemption from school exams.

Most courses covered at least two terms. Exceptions were, for example, Civics and Economics, which, by the way, were required of all students. Commercial Art was nominally optional; yet in my first term I was registered to take it as filler, because, except for lunch, everybody had to be in some class every period of the day. It turned out to be instruction and exercises in block lettering, no more. At the time it seemed to be mere busy work; I did not foresee enduring value to be exploited some day in intaglio woodcarving. The teacher was all business, colorless. Never once did she smile, in contrast with most of the faculty, who were not only competent but also relaxed and humane.

Mr. Bedwin opened up a vast new fascinating world of Biology. Families of beautiful white mice competed for attention as they huddled among other exhibits on the window sill. He had a clever way to demonstrate germination. We each took home a piece of white blotting paper pressed between two small rectangles of clear glass, a tiny seed embedded in the damp paper. Amazing!

Mr. Rayback introduced us to the treasures of Shakespeare with <u>The Merchant of Venice</u> and <u>A Midsummer Night's Dream</u>. Their Elizabethan English was at first a baffling foreign language, as were algebraic and chemical equations. Yet, with all of them, perseverance did exorcise the demons. In a lesson on spelling, Mr. Rayback commented that some people are better at remembering what they see written; others what they hear. This trait prompted me to conclude that in memorizing we ought to write and recite at the same time.

Two or three periods a week were spent in what was called Physical Training, (P.T.) or gymnasium, (gym), even though at the annex there was no gymnasium, nor in fact training. When not playing softball out on Dean Street, we were in the basement broad-jumping (standing broad jump) or chinning the bar. This activity was a pleasant respite for most students; we were required only to bring sneakers. Yet for us few uncoordinated, unathletic fumblers, it was embarrassing and dull. Whether coordination could have been achieved through training I'll probably never know.

A vivacious attractive young lady, a recent graduate of an upstate college, taught Civics. I've forgotten which college; I recall though her amusement with "the milk train." Miss Molinari sat on the front of her desk, legs crossed, the focus of pubescent fantasy.

A gracious motherly sort, Mrs. Bernadette Carey taught music and led the Glee Club. She tested everyone, enlisting those with promising voices. In a few weeks she had us entertaining at the regular Friday assemblies, in four part harmony, with or without piano accompaniment. "We gather together to ask the Lord's blessing........." "Stars of the summer, night deep in yon azure sky........." "Drink to me only with thine eyes, and I'll not ask for wine........" "We're poor little lambs who have lost our way. Baa, Baa, Baa,....."

In September 1933 I became a sophomore in the main building, easily awed by the husky varsity athletes in their gray and scarlet cardigans, the envied elite, many of whom were black, and all good students too. Failing grades brought team suspension.

On arrival in the morning we went first to "homeroom", where hats and coats were locked in one large closet. It stayed locked until the end of the day. Thus we carried from room to room books, sneakers, lunch, etc. Individual student lockers, as indeed study halls and chairs in the lunch room, had not yet been invented, and so we had no occasion to feel aggrieved.

Mr. Zeiner, the principal, was the one official that prudent students hoped to avoid, at least until graduation.

Mr. Hansen, Music Department head, conducted both the symphony orchestra and the Glee Club. A gifted musician. Natty dresser in double-breasted vest with lapels. Dignified, soft-spoken, self-confident. He had us all in the palm of his hand.

Fridays were best, because of the assemblies in the spacious auditorium, always featuring enchanting music. An evening concert before Christmas that year was especially memorable. The strings played <u>Andante</u> <u>Cantabile</u>. It haunted me for days.

Just as in the Dean Street annex, the lunchroom offered sandwiches, drinks, candy, etc. In those rough days of The Depression, however, almost everyone brought lunch from home, sandwiches in waxed paper. My favorite was peanut butter and Concord grape jelly. Usually the jelly had had time to soak through, not a pretty sight, but boyish appetite added its peculiar condiment. For those with nickels to squander: candy, as for example, a bar of peanuts drowned in chocolate, "Mr. Goodbar" or "Baby Ruth". Then there was Borden's "Mel-O-Rol", a paper covered cylinder of ice cream, about two inches across and three and one half inches long, served in a spongy cup, a giant edible thimble.

As we poured out onto Bergin Street at dismissal, we were teased by the aroma of hot potato knishes waiting near the door, an allurement I managed to resist. Whenever I had the nickel, I preferred to save it or to spend it for "a nickel's worth "of hard round licorice drops bearing the diamond trade mark of Henry Heide. Ice cream parlors had them in huge glass jars.

The hike home, ten long blocks west and five shorter blocks south, afforded many zig zag routes, a variety not wasted on me, nor was it a hardship at all, for I enjoyed walking. At a good pace too; the books made little difference. Oddly enough I got home refreshed, not tired, and breathing normally. Maybe I ought to have inquired about the track team. My mother once quoted her father: "If foresight were as good as hindsight, we'd all be better off by a damsight." Amen.

Saturday, June 2, 1990

While Sunday excursions by train to Philadelphia were a bargain, on other days it was cheaper though slower to go by bus. I must point out that it was long before multi-lane, high-speed, toll roads, and before buses had toilets. From midtown Manhattan we preferred the Quaker City Bus Line, which made one "rest-stop" on U.S. Route One below New Brunswick, in view of the Raritan River. Then it cruised down through beautiful farmlands and villages – Cranbury and Heightstown, - for instance – quaint, charming places away from rail lines, God's country. Because those gasoline motors were designed to run efficiently at thirty-five m.p.h., and also because traffic through villages and towns was even slower, alert riders could enjoy a rich variety of sights, much more than possible from a speeding train. Even so, having to return home the same day made the faster train a wiser choice.

We schoolboys in Brooklyn had been hitching rides on the backs of trucks, as I mentioned earlier. One summer morning three of us happened to be carried down Flatbush Avenue, across the Manhattan Bridge, along Canal Street, between Chinatown and Little Italy, and close to the Holland Tunnel, where cars and trucks were lining up. Well, we just had to meet the challenge. Soon we were flying along the Pulaski Skyway toward Newark Airport.

Before we got home that evening, starving, we had seen a lot of rural New Jersey. A lake in a wooded area looked so good that we decided to go for a swim. But while we were stripping, a rowboat glided into view. A man and a woman. Spotting us, he dropped the oars and began to yell and wave his arms. We didn't wait to refute his objections.

That escapade was the first of many similar adventures for me, and one of the last with others, for it became obvious that there were many more trucks on the road with room enough for just one gypsy. Later it occurred to me that if I were dressed neatly, wearing a necktie, hands and face clean, hair combed, shoes shined, I could do better at hitchhiking, "thumbing" rides from motorists as well as truck drivers. Thus came an end to the days of hitching rides on the backs of trucks, dressed like a ragamuffin.

My cousin Billy Leggett once spun a tale about his trip to Philadelphia in a boxcar. It got me wondering if I could get that for hitchhiking. (Hopping freight trains had no appeal for me, though I admired Billy for his daring.) It turned out to be easy for one who liked walking, even easier with experience. The most profitable insight was that the best prospect was a man driving alone, when asked face-to-face at a red light, gas station or toll plaza.

Even in sparsely populated rural counties, New Jersey had excellent roads, with intersections well provided at the four corners with arrows pointing in all four directions, each bearing a place name and mileage. With these and road maps that were available at gas stations, there was little risk of getting lost, at least in daylight.

I would set out on a clear night to visit Grandma or the Foley's in Vineland New Jersey, my mother's cousins, all of whom I loved, and those who were most hospitable, but I confess that the adventure was more than half the attraction. Then too I knew I'd meet memorable characters, like the melon farmer from Delaware.

Although it had been dark a couple of hours, I had gotten only a few miles above Camden on the way home. Traffic was sparse. An open truck with Delaware plates, heading north, and loaded with watermelons, pulled into a gas station. Yes, I could have a ride as far as Newark, if I would help unload the melons. Along the way the driver asked what I had in the small black valise. I told him the truth: pajamas and toilet articles, though it was none of his business. Not that I pointed that out. Strange that he should care.

When we got to the area of the Newark wholesale markets, he slowed down and waved to black men loitering at the corners, some four or five of whom followed the truck. With it backed against the loading platform, and the new recruits alongside, I was told to climb up and toss the melons to be carried inside and stacked. If any should be found broken, and so of no market value, we would be permitted to stop and eat them. While the work progressed, the driver was in the office, too far to see a couple of his helpers fumble, the load having proven to be in excellent condition.

Upon climbing into the cab for the return to Route One, I noticed that my valise was not quite where I had left it, and the contents were a bit messed. Maybe with the cash from my sale, my host feared that I might have been hiding a gun.

It was after midnight when I stood at an intersection near Newark Airport, waiting for the next lift. Light traffic still. But Providence provided. In just a few minutes along came a touring car, a salesman, presumably, with cartons stacked on the rear seat. He was in no hurry to get to New York, evidently, for he drove slowly, a fact which proved good for us both. As we rolled along, he held the wheel in his left hand and while from time to time he stretched his right behind the seat for a bottle of whiskey. He could have driven to the time-saving Holland Tunnel, whose toll, incidentally, was fifty cents, or to any of several ferries, whose toll was half that. A drinker, yes; a fool, no; he chose the Erie ferry to Chambers Street.

Charlie McNally, a long time-friend, went along once on a trip to Philadelphia. We arrived so late at Grandma's – ten or eleven o'clock – that the lights were out; she had gone to bed, a white-haired matron near eighty. It wouldn't do to wake her, certainly, and so we lounged on the front porch until Uncle Eddie got home from work several hours later, in his usual cheerful mood.

That night sticks in my memory because of two changes. Uncle Eddie, seeing me in bed without a pillow, persuaded me to use one for my neck's sake. Then observing my hair in disarray – it wouldn't lie flat – he suggested I comb it straight back, with no part. Thereafter I followed his advice. Problem solved. Oh, incidentally, Grandma told us that we should have knocked; she had been awake for hours.

Then there was the sunny afternoon on the way to Vineland, in the middle of vast farmland, cornfields and pastures, where a young man and woman, not much older than I, let me climb into the back of their Ford Model T, in those days – about 1933 – not quite a rare antique in country places.

One chilly fall night on another trip to Vineland, I was given a ride by a farmer down near Hammonton. The open truck was empty except for a tarpaulin sprawling close to the cab. Well, almost empty; a man sat huddled beneath the canvas, his back to the cab, under the rear-view window. He uncovered his head to let me share the windbreak. As we bounced along, shoulder-to shoulder, he regaled me with pleasantries, or what I presume were intended as pleasantries, for he spoke in such broken English that I couldn't understand most of it. Yet of course I lent a respectful ear, speculating the while on his native tongue. Surely not Nordic, German, French, Spanish, nor Italian. Judging from his breath, if not his speech, he had had a few drinks, a fact so evident in those close quarters. Only later did it dawn on me that he had said he was a deep sea diver, a "dye-were."

Between New York City subways and Philadelphia trolley cars, these expeditions involved long series of rides, mostly short, and of course lots of hiking in between. Ah, but once I was really lucky. At the toll plaza of the Holland Tunnel, a man heading for Washington picked me up, a salesman happy to have someone to talk to. We chatted all the way to Lansdowne, PA, about three miles from Darby, a pleasant stroll after sitting so long.

Monday, June 4, 1990

My mother had a cousin who lived in Vineland, New Jersey, Edward Foley. We called him "Cousin Ed." Because her maiden name was Foley, one would presume that their fathers were brothers. Yet I believe that her father had neither brother nor sister. None was ever spoken of by members of the family, as though he had emigrated from Ireland alone. Moreover, she remarked cryptically on one occasion, regarding this cousin, that a "Foley married a Foley." At the time I wasn't curious enough to ask questions, or smart enough.

Being her first cousin, Edward Foley had to be, if not her father's nephew, then her mother's, which is to say son of her brother or sister. Now if he were son of her brother, his name would have been Boyle. But if he were son of her sister, then that sister, also a Boyle, would have had to be married to a Foley, one not related to her brother-in-law, my mother's father.

If it were true that Grandma Foley had no brother nor sister, neither did Grandma have a brother nor sister, as far as I ever knew, with only one possible exception. I recall as a boy of five or so that Grandma and several other adult family members to a house on Paschall Avenue, behind St. Clement's Church. An old lady was being waked in the parlor, probably a relative. Other grandchildren were there too. The name Aunt Katie comes to mind. Her last name was Irish; it sounded like Micanamie, Aunt Katie Micanamie. It wasn't Foley. The mystery remains.

The Foley's lived is a spacious Victorian house on the grounds of the Garden State Dairy, of which Cousin Ed was the manager. Just beyond the side yard lay the railroad right-of-way that linked Camden and Millville. Landis Avenue comes to mind, maybe their address or the main street, with the Chevrolet dealer and J.J. Newberry's and the bowling alley and the diner and the bakery and Sacred Heart Church. A charming country small town, where everyone knew everyone else, slow-paced, relaxed, and where an ordinance forbade fences among the houses.

Cousin Ed Foley and my mother were about the same age. Edward Foley married Mary Davis in Philadelphia. They had two daughters and three sons. 1 Joseph, 2 Mary, 3 John, 4 Isabella and 5 Edward Jr. Isabella and John were about my age. When they were teenagers, Edward Jr. was an infant.

Their father – I addressed him as Cousin Ed – was tall, husky, soft-spoken, placid devoted to his family. Cousin Mary was much the same though petite. If she resented my dropping in, she never showed it. On the contrary she was always gracious. Indeed the whole family treated me with affection. Cousin Ed was seldom without his pipe and Prince Albert tobacco. No one else smoked.

During vacations and on weekends I often hitchhiked from Brooklyn. It never occurred to me that I ought to wait to be invited, so gracious and hospitable was the whole family. Nor did they show any annoyance if I trumped in close to midnight. The large wooden house stood close to the dairy.

Cousin Ed, when John and I were freshman in high school, was manager or superintendent – whatever his proper title – of a dairy farm in Vineland New Jersey, "Garden State Dairy," which collected raw milk from farmers for miles around, pasteurized it, bottled it, and delivered it to homes in Vineland, Millville, and other nearby towns.

Joseph, John and I enjoyed two special treats. Early in the morning, we were allowed to ride on the back of the truck on its route collecting the cans of raw milk at the dairy farms. Then there were the times when we were permitted to accompany the home-delivery route men on their rounds. Theirs was another world. We'd go to bed early. Cousin Ed or Mary would wake us up in the middle of the night. I recall the route through Bridgeton, a charming quiet little town. I helped to retrieve the empty bottles waiting near the doors. We may have heard a dog bark, but through several houses we saw not one person. Of course we never, we cousins, rode together as we did in collecting the raw milk. The route men were all very pleasant and glad to get the help, mostly in silence, lest we disturb anyone's sleep.

Dairy farmers for miles around would set out their raw milk in wide-mouthed galvanized cans about three feet high, to be picked up by the dairy's truck. One of the pleasures as a Foley guest was making the rounds with Joseph and John, preferably on the back of the truck while there was room. My cousins knew many of the farmers' children, and so, while the cans were being loaded, and empties returned, we'd jump down for a chat. I loved every minute of it, the sights, sounds and smells. An enchanted world.

Another delight was making the rounds with the milkmen on their early morning routes. Cousin Mary would wake us up in the middle of the night, while the trucks were being loaded. It was my good luck to help on a route through a neighboring town, Bridgeton. I collected empties and crept up back stairs. During the whole tour we saw few lights, heard no sounds, not even a dog barking. In all of Bridgeton, the driver and I seemed to be the only ones awake.

The name Carew comes to mind, disassociated after sixty or so years. It may have been that of the dairy's owner, or one of the owners. Incidentally, the milk pasteurized and bottled in the small plant next to the Foley's house, had a high percentage of rich cream. Delicious!

On hot summer afternoons Joseph and John took me along to their favorite secluded swimming hole, where we romped around undraped. Mark Twain would have approved.

I recall the interest at the time, the early thirties, during the Depression, in a new fad, "Marathon Dancing," wherein couples vied for cash prizes, to see who could dance the longest, dancing being defined loosely when exhaustion set in. People paid money to watch. As bizarre as it was, it made no less sense than "flagpole sitting" in resorts like Atlantic City where Shipwreck Kelly set an endurance record perched atop a pole at one of the piers, a latter-day parody of St. Simon Stylite.

In Vineland's Sacred Heart parish, whose school my cousins attended, the family were friends with the pastor. After he was transferred to Runnemede, close to Camden, we all piled into the car – all the boys, that is – one afternoon for a visit. To know a priest socially, as a friend, to sit with him informally and make small talk, had been for me undreamt of. Then for the first time I saw a priest just like other men, and inside the rectory too.

When it came time for me to leave Vineland, Cousin Ed used to drive me out east after breakfast to the road that runs from Millville north to Camden. One day I carried home a bugle that I had begged from my cousins, a souvenir of happy days, very happy days.

Wednesday, June 6, 1990

The rich milk at Cousin Ed Foley's in Vineland was a treat I've not forgotten, nor another from a local bakery: "sticky buns" or "honey buns", swirls of raisins and cinnamon baked to perfection and then covered with honey. Said to be "Philadelphia-style." Sticky indeed; we had to wash our fingers afterward.

At home, in Brooklyn sometimes on payday we indulged in mixed buns from Jahn's. In the early 1930's they cost twenty five cents per dozen, actually thirteen. Incidentally, kaiser rolls cost two cents each.

There were other bakeries on the avenue, some even closer, but we had a special affection for Jahn's. They had a few tables and chairs and a waitress who served their goodies with coffee or tea. When Lillian and I were kids at St. Joseph's, we'd stop often on the way home, at the north west corner of Washington Avenue and Prospect Place. We didn't buy anything, yet whenever we asked for a glass of water – it was ice cold- they were always kind, always.

Cakes and pies my mother baked on occasion. Molasses cookies too, around Christmas, big, thick and crispy.

No one made more tasty deviled eggs; she knew just the right combination of spices, including Coleman's English mustard.

Especially talented was she at making soups. She'd send me down to Flax's, on the other side of Jahn's, for "five cents worth of soup greens," a few stalks of celery, two or three leeks, and a handful of parsley. With these and a chicken – she called it a fowl – or a ham hock or a "soup bone," plus barley or rice, she'd concoct the best in the world. Oh, yes, and great bean soup too.

She boiled a pork tenderloin, and when it was done, she'd take it out, and then boil cabbage in the same water.

Boiled potatoes were a regular part of most evening meals and Sunday dinners. By the time my mother got home from the bank, Lillian or I would have had cooked several, with or without the skins. We shared that chore. They'd be served with hamburgers or chops or steak (fried) or liver and onions or dried beef fried in cream sauce, the beef bought packaged like bacon and cut paper thin. In summer sliced tomatoes were fried in cream sauce.

Meat being forbidden on all Fridays, we'd have fish cakes or Manhattan clam chowder from a delicatessen, or home-made oyster stew or pancakes or waffles or spaghetti or Campbell's tomato soup.

Two other dishes my mother prepared to perfection, both of which, for whatever reason, have, alas, fallen from fashion: kidney stew and beef tongue. I recall when beef tongue, sliced thin was a regular feature for sandwiches in delicatessens, along with pastrami. As familiar as pickled herring, dill pickles, pigs knuckles and Jewish rye bread.

As a late-night snack, my mother often served guests welsh rarebit, principally cheddar cheese spiced with Worcestershire sauce, pored over toast and washed down with beer.

The only home-made candy was chocolate fudge. I can still see Lillian hovering over the pan at the gas stove, stirring and stirring and stirring the molten bubbly mass. She knew it was ready to be poured out finally when a drop hardened in cold water. Then came the long wait for it to cool. Patience! Patience!

Wednesday, June 20, 1990

During what came to be called "The Great Depression", families struggled to make ends meet. In 1933 at the depth of the Depression, 16 million people – one third of the labor force – were unemployed. In January 1934 while sixteen years old, I was a sophomore, a Liberal Arts major, at Alexander Hamilton High School at Albany Avenue and the corner of Bergin Street. My mother worked in Commercial Credit at National City Bank, 55 Wall Street, Manhattan. I walked both going to school as well as returning, regardless of the weather; ten cents would have been the round-trip Bergin Street trolley car fare. I'd rather have spent the nickels for licorice drops.

One of my mother's colleagues at City Bank had a friend with ties to a nearby stock-brokerage house. He (or she) suggested that I look for a job as a runner, a bonded messenger to deliver stock and bond certificates. Timing was critical in that business, and so the messenger did in fact often race through the streets, dodging among pedestrians everywhere.

Our company had a half-dozen or so runners, each of whom was assigned his own area. Thus we learned short-cuts, doors back and front, and where public men's rooms were, those never locked.

In those days the State law demanded school attendance until high school graduation or one's eighteenth year of age. The drop-out could attend part-time "Continuation School", an option I ignored, for I was too stupid to recognize the value of a high-school diploma. A real jackass first class. Nevertheless, in time I enrolled at Brooklyn Evening High

School, sharing facilities with Boys' High School, Marcy and Putnam Avenues. Even so, I skipped many sessions, for I was tired, had no goals, no ambition, nothing to make the effort reasonable. And so, after a few months, I dropped out.

I dropped out of Hamilton in the third of the eight terms, in February 1934, the fourth month of my seventeenth year, when I took a job as a runner for a firm of stock brokers. My mother had a colleague at National City Bank who had learned of the vacancy. Had I not lied about my age in saying I was 17, I probably would have been turned down, if only for the lack of "working papers". The prospect, moreover, of Continuation School would have been a scheduling nuisance to employers free to choose among the many adults canvassing the local employment agencies. Previously I had applied for part time work delivering Western Union telegrams, but their messengers – as with waiters everywhere – were paid low wages, even after buying the uniforms.

Walter P. Mc Caffray & Co., 25 Broad St. across from the New York Stock Exchange, was a small brokerage house with few partners, members of both "The Big Board" and the Curb Exchange. Clientele were mostly out-of-town brokers and investment bankers, Chandler Hovey of Boston, for example, for whom they traded in stocks and bonds. There being little or no face-to-face contact with customers, office furniture and equipment were utilitarian, sparse, and in fact drab compared to the wealthy houses that catered to individual investors and speculators. Assets then were largely the seats on the exchanges and modest bank balances. Office clerks, trading-floor clerks, and runners totaled about twenty-five.

Investors could have their securities registered in their names, or they could have the firm register in its name, holding them for safekeeping and further instructions. Those who bought with less than the full price, the firm providing the balance, had no choice but to let the firm register in its name, holding the certificates as collateral. This was buying "on margin", a convenience favored by speculators who hoped to sell quickly. "Selling short", by the way, was selling what one didn't have, in the expectation of falling prices. The conventional Buy low – Sell high in a "bull" market, becomes Sell high - Buy low in a "bear" market. A gamble either way.

The big brokerage houses, E. A. Pierce, for example, stored securities during late afternoon in safe-deposit boxes in bank vaults. Mc Caffray, however, took out a trifling overnight loan at National City Bank, putting up as collateral all its stocks and bonds.

Brokerage transactions were conducted over the telephone: customer to broker, broker to broker, broker to trading floor. Every such vocal purchase or sale had to be confirmed in writing, if possible on the same day. Thus brokers needed runners, messengers who in fact ran to meet deadlines or to get there before closing time. Especially during the mid-day lunch breaks, when the narrow canyons were packed with pedestrians, and Nassau Street closed to vehicular traffic, we runners were hard pressed to get there on time, and without bowling anyone over.

Because the securities we carried were worth fortunes, some negotiable, we were bonded. These bundles were tucked into a black leather pouch, nestled under the left arm, and secured with a leather-sheathed chain around the wrist. Once as I hurried out of Stock Clearing Corporation, I happened to see a bundle of certificates fall from under the arm of a runner trotting across Broad Street ahead of me. He would probably have been fired, had I not caught up to him.

Runners usually were assigned a regular territory, going from office to office to office. Their experience developed time-saving knowledge of every building's design, short cuts, elevators, customers' floors, unlocked men's rooms, etc. But not all deliveries were made that way; both exchanges provided "clearing houses", rooms where member firms had boxes, similar to post-office boxes, where papers that did not require a receipt could be dropped into the boxes of several members in a small fraction of the time otherwise.

At Mc Caffray's employees worked nominally from nine to five, Monday to Friday, with a thirty minute break for lunch. On Saturdays, the exchanges being closed, from nine to twelve. Brokerage houses, however, in contrast with the neighboring sedate banks, oscillated between frenzy and a climate merely hectic. Noise and paper-littered floors were normal. We runners often were told "Go to lunch; be back in twenty minutes".

For clerks who could not get away, we fetched lunches from Lessing's, off the main lobby (where countermen moved with remarkable speed and grace). Then too there were the Automat, Schrafft's and the Green Line. By the way, the district had also cafeterias, most notably a chain, Exchange Buffet, where patrons ate lunch standing – the tacit premise being that no one had time to sit – after which they told cashiers at the doors what they owed. The monogram E B was said by some wag to mean "Eat 'em and Beat 'em". Farther down on New Street, close to Beaver Street: Max's Busy Bee, less elegant in decor, more homey, more relaxed, and what was appreciated by runners especially, it had chairs.

A company named Horn & Hardart operated cafeterias in New York City (Manhattan) called "The Automat". I recall one on Park Row, close to City Hall, but there were others in busy areas around Manhattan. I can't recall any in Brooklyn or elsewhere. There used to be a Horn & Hardart retail shop in the mall on Route 110, Melville, near the A & S store.

What distinguished the Automat from competitors was the ease and time-saving of self service. The various dishes were available in banks of cubbyholes behind glass windows that were opened when the appropriate number of nickels was fed into the slots. Rows of beverage dispensers, equipped with ceramic mugs, dispensed beverages, hot and cold. There were tables high enough for those in a hurry, and, of course, the conventional tables and chairs, enough that one did not have to wait for one to be vacated.

The prices were reasonable. Excellent coffee cost five cents per cup. All the dishes were fresh. It must have been inflation that put the Automat out of business, because more and more nickels were needed.

There used to be a cafeteria on New Street, behind the Stock Exchange, where a clerk at a cash register knew at sight the price of every item. He scanned the trays and said the total cost, there being no need for price tags. Down the street, close to Beaver Street, was a similar place: "Max's Busy Bee", where the atmosphere was more relaxed, and less noisy.

At least one of us worked past five o'clock every day or past noon on Saturdays. Someone had to wait at Fitch's until the market reports had been printed. The extra time earned no extra pay.

Sixteen dollars in cash was paid to me every Friday. Presumably to the other runners too. Salaries were secret, though I learned somehow that the cashier earned seventy five dollars. Of course there was no way for the staff to know how much the partners were taking home; one of them, William Hosford, was office manager. The senior partner Walter Peck Mc Caffray, kept aloof; when not on the trading floor of the Big Board, or lunching at the club, he kept to his hermitage, his private rooms off the lobby.

To my mother I gave ten or eleven of the sixteen dollars. Lunch I usually brought from home, two sandwiches and fruit, which I ate in the storeroom, a library of dusty ledgers. A haircut at Nick Lorenzo's cost fifty cents. At several shops downtown twenty-five cents. Every morning a fresh white shirt which had been done at the Chinese laundry for about twelve cents. Shirts with detached collars were more economical; only the collar need be changed so often. Neatly-pressed three piece suit, double breasted. Shoes shined. Subway fare was five cents. The run between the Brooklyn Museum station and Wall Street took about twenty minutes, usually standing at least part of the way.

On a beautiful Saturday in the Spring I left for home at about one o'clock. Down on the street I found I had no money, not even a nickel. How that could be on the day after being paid, I've forgotten. Ah, well. The weather was ideal, and so I strode up Nassau Street to the Brooklyn Bridge. No great feat for a professional walker, one who hiked from home to Coney Island on a Sunday afternoon. Then too Uncle Harry Leggett had made it all the way out to City Line. Speaking of the weather: we in the financial district could tell when the wind was from the east; the aroma of coffee roasting on Water Street.

The newest buildings in the area had high-speed elevators, completely enclosed and operated by professionals. Dials on the lobby walls (columns of lights, one for each floor for each car) allowed the uniformed starter to judge when to signal with his clicker so as to keep the cars well distributed. Cars in older buildings were slower iron baskets, with walls and grates like wrought iron fences. Such were those at 25 Broad Street.

The most memorable elevators were those in that venerable red brick 2 Broadway, The Produce Exchange, across from the Custom House.

There my cousin John Leggett ran a one-man office. At least he was alone whenever I dropped in. Those elevators were engineered like grill-work dumbwaiters, with two steel cables piercing ceiling and floor. Either of these the operator, wearing leather gloves with thick palms, pulled down the choice depending on the direction desired.

My regular route was lower Broadway, which included such prominent brokerage houses and investment bankers as Laidlaw, Hornblower & Weeks, E.F. Hutton, Charles D. Barney, Kidder Peabody, and Harris Upham, where Uncle Harry Leggett worked as a telegrapher in the wire room.

Typical runners delivered their documents and got receipts through a small wall opening protected by a metal grille or milky glass door, a design efficient but hardly conducive to humane rapport. In some offices eye contact was impossible. Nevertheless there were a few cheerful men who managed some pleasantry, if only a smile and a thank you. Such, for example, was our cashier, Edward Michael Curran. Also there were two customers' men at Barney's who took a moment to chat, after three o'clock when the markets were closed. One day they recommended the Rolls Razor, an English import that had a single permanent blade, homed like a straight razor, but with the safety of a Gillette or Gem. The price, alas, kept it out of my reach.

One of the elevator operators asked me to buy a bottle of whiskey at a nearby shop. Evidently an immigrant, he spoke with such an accent that I couldn't remember the brand name, even after hearing it several times: "Krabooch". Fortunately, however, the clerk must have served that customer more than once; when he heard "Krabooch", "Oh yes. Crab Orchard".

Senior staff members used to reminisce during slow moments about the good old days before October 1929, before the market crash, when at Christmas they brought home fabulous bonuses, in some years equal to a full year's salary. More recently we were grateful for a turkey. Business was especially poor in 1935, so much so that all runners and many of the clerks worked for a month or so "Scotch weeks", during which crisis we worked only every other week.

As I was about to pass the rear entrance to 42 Broadway, on the way to Max's Busy Bee, three city cops trudged out, lugging a canvas bag, shovels, brooms and mops, which they heaved into the back of their emergency truck. A tenant had plunged down an airshaft. No longer hungry, I spent the time sitting in Battery Park. There were to be more jumpers, but none quite so unnerving.

World War veterans, having been promised a bonus, agitated for it during the harsh days of The Depression. When my mother read that it would be paid, she wrote to Washington, the Navy, perhaps, hoping I suppose for a share in her estranged husband's windfall, the husband she had rejected. The reply was that the government did not reveal confidential information.

When pedestrian traffic was heavy in the Wall Street area, sidewalk vendors sold huge Red Delicious apples from Washington State, the very best. These were provided by the federal government. Signs on the crates read "Unemployed. 5 cents".

An Army veteran, boy-friend of a friend of my mother, Bill Elmers, bedridden, had been poisoned in France by mustard gas or phosgene. We all knew that his days, to borrow a phrase from a popular song, that his days "narrowed down to a precious few". On a visit to Bill in his nearby apartment on Eastern Parkway, I was touched; he offered me his several medals. While I appreciated his affection and generosity, I could never accept such treasures. It occurred to me on the way home that those medals must have meant a lot to his lady friend, Lucretia, who was there but who had said nothing either way.

The National Industrial Recovery Act (N.I.R.A.) became law in 1933. Soon the scope was broadened, or at least the name shortened, by deletion of the term Industrial. Detailed codes of management were drawn up, custom-tailored for each kind of business, as though The Depression could be conquered by imposed universal standards of business conduct, as though a prosperous free-market economy could be re-invigorated by dictatorial control planners, Washington bureaucrats, socialists in capitalists' clothing. Roosevelt's New Deal was on the march.

Employers everywhere displayed for public view placards bearing the N.R.A. spread-eagle logo with the legend "We Do Our Part". At Mc Caffray's we employees were required to sign weekly time sheets that spelled out in detail what purported to be each one's schedule for each day: arrivals, lunch breaks, and departures. No one refused to sign those false statements, so craven were we, so fearful of losing our jobs. The silly N.R.A. proved nothing. Indeed, how could it have been otherwise? We Do Our Part; oh yes, to serve our best interests.

From early childhood I had been in the habit of biting my fingernails. I don't know why I did; in fact I would have been quite pleased to be rid of the shame. Temperament must have played a part. Well, whatever the explanation, a short time after I went to work, the nail biting stopped, nor can I explain that either.

Smoking had no appeal for me as a school boy. Oh, there was the time that a friend invited a couple of us classmates to share a cigar he had filched at home. I went along only because I lacked the courage to say no. We passed it around; pretending to enjoy it, until common sense and coughing prevailed. I know of only one classmate who was hooked on cigarettes, Fred Grander, nicknamed "Grubber". "Hey, got a butt?" Ironically, Fred went on to become a sandhog helping to build the Lincoln Tunnel.

Sometimes on social occasions my mother went through the motions of smoking cigarettes offered to her, never inhaling, however. When Lillian and I were about ten years old, our mother having gone out on a date, I lit a Lucky Strike cigarette from an opened pack left by some guest. Just a couple of puffs and we were coughing and in danger of vomiting. The experience taught me a lesson I'd not forget, not until puerile fantasy crowded out common sense.

When I was barely seventeen years old, I decided to adopt a manly trait: smoking a pipe, just like Cousin Ed Foley in Vineland, NJ. Smoking as well as wearing long pants was a sign of manhood, as everyone could see, and working full time, wasn't I now a man? And so I bought a cheap briar pipe at Walgreen's drugstore across Broad Street. With it a widely advertised rough-cut tobacco, Granger.

I stubbornly persevered with the infernal instrument in spite of the constant coughing and sore throat, in spite of the bad taste, in spite of the pain to the tip of the tongue that comes from breaking in a pipe, in spite of the mess. Obviously manhood came at a price.

After Granger, I tried another brand, then another and another, delighted to discover that every one of them was so much milder. Sir Walter Raleigh, Revelation, Prince Albert, Rum & Maple, Bond Street. etc.

Wally Frank's, a shop at Nassau and Fulton Streets, stocked a great variety of pipes from around the world, some carved, some expensive, all beautiful. Also exotic tobaccos, domestic and imported, custom blended to order, like the coffees and teas at nearby Callinan's on the site of the World Trade Center. Luxuries for the affluent gourmet.

Cigars come in various shapes, sizes, and of course prices. Phillies and White Owls, for example, sold for a nickel. Optimo Blunts, two for a quarter. Coronas, in individual tubes of glass, one dollar.

One self-indulgence leads to another. It wasn't long before I was addicted to cigarettes. Popular brands sold for two packs of twenty for a quarter. Camel, Old Gold, Chesterfield, Phillip Morris, Lucky Strike etc. Kool had menthol added. Salisbury, a strong Turkish blend, was oval not round. Mr. Hosford smoked Sweet Caporal.

In those early 1930's, even though cigarettes were called coffin nails, half in humor, and were so obviously habit-forming, and known to cause shortness of breath, nevertheless most men smoked, few, if any, being aware of the serious threat of emphysema and cancer. Yes, we were living in a fools' paradise, like the first-class passengers on the Titanic.

Indeed smoking cigarettes had become a mark of sophistication, of social grace at parties, like sipping cocktails or champagne while nibbling at hors d'oeuvres. It was fashionable everywhere. Gentlemen, however, refrained in elevators. A common advertising slogan advised "Be nonchalant. Light a Murad". The spread and perpetuation of this myth must be traced in large part to the example of glamorous movie stars, especially on-screen chain smokers such as Charles Boyer, for example.

I remember well with what disgust I crushed most of a pack of Chesterfields and hurled them into the gutter on Exchange Place, so vexed at being their slave. Yet it was only during Lent that I managed to summon enough willpower to give up tobacco for long, at least until noon on Holy Saturday.

Wednesday, June 27, 1990

Among my mother's friends at National City Bank, the head of the Out-going Mail Department, Andy Murphy, rented a summer bungalow at Rockaway. On his recommendation, she leased a small one in the same cluster, Georgian Court, on the west side of 109th Street, between the boardwalk and Rockaway Beach Boulevard. Occupancy ran from May 1st to October 1st 1934.

That was many years before Shore Front Parkway and high-rise apartments altered forever that charming community. The boardwalk stretched at ground level from 116th Street, a busy thoroughfare, east to about 110th Street, were a slope at right angles joined the raised main portion that lay closer to the shore. Just west of that ramp: the summer home of a Brooklyn orphanage, St. John's Home. Just east of the ramp, nestled in the corner, fronting on the boardwalk, and alongside 109th Street: Krueger's Restaurant, popular not so much for dining as for drinking beer, singing, camaraderie and gaiety, especially on weekends.

West of 116th Street, Belle Harbor and Neponsit even then were the sites of conventional all-year homes, many luxurious, whereas Rockaway Park and Seaside were crowded with humble wooden summer bungalows, favored mostly by ethnic Irish from all parts of the city, with the probable exception of Staten Island.

Indeed Irish Town, as we dubbed it, 103rd Street between the boardwalk and the Boulevard, was monopolized by beer halls, shoulder-to-shoulder, with Irish names, Irish management, Irish musicians, and Irish clientele. Sligo, Innisfail, Healy's etc. On Friday, Saturday and Sunday evenings they had four or five piece bands – not yet corrupted by electronic enhancement – blessed with rich repertoires of both Irish and popular American dance music, with which they enchanted usually full houses. Teenagers congregated on the sidewalks until the band began to play, where they'd march in and dance until the next break, not spending a dime all evening.

Georgian Court consisted of about a dozen bungalows huddled on a patch of sand perhaps seventy-five feet long and fifty feet deep. Each stood on piles a couple of feet high, were sheathed in tongue-and-groove pine boards, and covered in white clapboards. Gabled roofs. Narrow porches. Semi-detached; thus a tenants rooms were a mirror image of his neighbor's. They came in three sizes, the differences being mostly the number of beds and cots. Those in the rear were so close that in walking to the curtained shower on the duckboards between them, one had to be careful not to scrape his shoulders.

To the typical tenant – the elderly were remarkable for their absence – his bungalow was merely a convenient place to eat and sleep, most daylight hours being spent sitting or lying on the beach improving on his tan, and so the Spartan furniture was taken for granted. Indeed we were glad that only linens, kitchen utensils and dishes need be lugged in suitcases from home. By the way, the icebox had no pan to be emptied; a pipe drained into the sand. Of course we were free of telephones. Everyone had a radio, ignored excepting on rainy days, of which in July and August there were few.

Unlike vacationers at other resorts and cruise ships, who by custom were fashionable, we Rockaway denizens lived in bathing suits, modest in design I must add. Only to go to Sunday Mass at St. Camillus Church did we dress up. Men wore sport shirts, jackets, trousers, socks and shoes. Women and girls donned dresses, hats, stockings and shoes. All just as at home. Heat and humidity made no difference. But of course as soon as we got back to the bungalow,............

No one we knew in Rockaway had a car, or at least brought one to the beach. I met a young lady, Aleen, in a deluxe bungalow closer to the boardwalk, whose father owned and managed a parking garage in midtown

Manhattan. Even he commuted by train. Only one motor vehicle do I recall seeing on 109th Street. A local bakery, Duddy's, hawked its pies and cakes, knowing well that none of us ever lit an oven in the same spirit in which we never washed a window. It was bad enough, surely, that some of us had to jackass blocks of ice.

The Long Island Rail Road provided service between Flatbush Avenue, Brooklyn, and the Rockaway terminal at 116th Street, with stops at such colorful places as Aqueduct Race Track and a mysterious gaggle of shacks that hovered on piles over Jamaica Bay with the quaint name "The Raunt", said to have sheltered rumrunners during Prohibition, an unlikely allegation it seems to me, in view of its isolation. Fishermen maybe, but rumrunners?

The Green Bus Company offered alternate service, crossing the Bay through Broad Channel and Howard Beach to the subway. Slower than the train; yet cheaper.

To accommodate overnight guests, our Kelly cousins from Darby for instance, I moved my cot out to the porch, where I lowered split-bamboo shades. Mosquitoes were rare, but during the day green flies on the beach were wicked. Incidentally, the sea air was so humid that salt shakers were always clogged.

At intervals of one-hundred yards or so the city posted at least two lifeguards during the day. One scanned the surf from a bench on stilts, while his partner usually patrolled in a catamaran, beyond which swimmers were forbidden.

When the tide was low enough, we cavorted on a sandbar, free from undertow, broken shells and pebbles. One afternoon when Lillian, Dorothy Kelly and I were out there, unmindful of the time, and the tide had been creeping in, Dorothy became alarmed at the prospect of deep water between us and the beach, a distance I guess of no more than thirty feet. The catamaran lay beached. By the grace of God she grew calm and relaxed enough for me to slip my left arm around her as she floated on her back. While I worked the side stroke, we soon glided over the gully to shallow water. No sooner had we stood up and began to wade in surf only knee deep, out trots the lifeguard, scooping up Dot and depositing her on dry sand, thus compounding the poor girl's discomfiture, for half of those lounging on the beach had stood up to see why he was running. Do you suppose he reported a rescue?

From time to time I used to stop off at the apartment to fetch something or to empty the mailbox. On one such occasion I couldn't open the door. Maybe I had left my keys at the bungalow, or we had left a set with a neighbor or the landlord, and he wasn't home. Well, whatever the explanation, I decided to break in.

The back bedroom shared by my mother and Lillian had two double-hung windows, one of which opened onto the fire escape. In the 1930's, criminals were not yet so great a threat in New York City that such windows were screened on the inside by steel accordion-type gates, not yet. We simply pulled the shades down all the way. Each side of the square glass panes measured about two feet. With a pocket knife I began the tedious task of prying and scraping off the hardened putty and glazer's points, much of the debris falling four stories to the backyard. Afterward a friend pointed out that I could have been shot as a burglar, and should have informed the police at the nearby 80th Precinct station house.

At least an hour dragged by before the pane was excavated. Very carefully, lest I cut my hands, I tilted the pane toward me from the top and eased it up out of the frame. Then somehow it slipped and shattered on the sill.

Thursday, July 19, 1990

The firm's senior partner, Mr. Walter Peck Mc Caffray, died on May 11, 1935 at age 46. Eddie Curran, the cashier, Maurice McCormick, a fellow runner, and I took the subway together to the wake after work at the Mc Caffray townhouse on Park Avenue, our first and only visit to that regal residence.

The other partners carried on under the name Walter P. Mc Caffray Company, but alas, not for long, not more than a few months, after the federal Securities and Exchange Commission alleged misuse of customers' securities by a certain junior partner. Whether the charges were later proven or refuted I don't know, but either way they were enough to have the firm suspended from trading; thus out of business.

It happened then that in the spring of 1936 I joined the great throngs canvassing the employment agencies every day, and filling out scores of applications at personnel departments all over town. We also perused the want ads every morning in the Times and also Herald Tribune, hoping, ever hoping.

During the two years as a runner, I worked hard, not once missing a day due to illness. Let me add that in those days one didn't stay home from work just because he had a cold. Some of the blotter clerks used to tease new runners as though we walked slowly or lounged in Battery Park. As far as I saw, however, no one did either. At any rate, I left 25 Broad Street with a letter of recommendation, consoled somewhat by the prospect of claiming experience. Never again would I be vexed at being turned down for consideration because I had no experience, which I couldn't get because I had no experience. Well, at least as a runner.

Having earned sixteen dollars a week, I spent sixteen dollars a week. Had I coveted money or the things that money buys, a car for instance, or had I been just a bit prudent, I'd have been building a small savings account. Then too I'd probably have striven for promotion, but in my world money was only a means to things of value. Moreover, my needs were few and basic. Living from day to day, I gave no thought to the future.

While searching for work, I'd have taken a job as runner, yet I was not eager to stay where pursuing money was all that mattered, and not indeed through skilled craftsmanship or artistry that fostered pride in a product, but merely in garnering commissions through the humdrum and often frenzied buying and selling of certificates. Obviously I had been an alien in the world of high finance, a square peg in a round hole, and too immature, too dull-witted to care about a proper fit.

Wednesday, August 1, 1990

Although during the Depression searching for a job was tedious and discouraging, it must have been so much more so for those with wives and children to support. If the junior partners rather than the late senior partner owned their seats on the exchanges, then probably they joined other firms and resumed their careers. In either event, the breakup had to be a hard blow for both employees and partners.

Only one co-worker did I ever see again. While strolling along 35th Street, behind Macy's, I chanced to see a former runner, Neil Kenelly, now a uniformed security guard on the freight dock, as cheerful as ever.

It was probably he who told of Ivy Odsen, former margin and blotter clerk, now a New York City patrolman, a tall muscular Viking, reputed to have fractured the jaw of a suspect resisting arrest.

Ivy Odsen, by the way, used to work out in the gym' at Central Y.M.C.A., Brooklyn, sometimes sharing barbells with the body builder "Charles Atlas", who advertised "I was a ninety-seven pound weakling......" Humiliated at having sand kicked in his face by a "bully", he went on to invent "Dynamic Tension", a technique he marketed as able to build muscles without equipment, by playing one muscle or set of muscles against another.

His ad's appeared regularly in pulp magazines such as <u>Popular</u> <u>Mechanics</u>. When I was fourteen or fifteen years old, I mailed the coupon. The literature convinced me, accompanied as it was by photographs of muscular young men purporting to be clients, but the price, alas, kept the course out of reach, even months later when successive discounts were offered.

Tuesday, August 7, 1990

After a month or so of daily job hunting in the spring of 1936, an ad in the <u>Herald</u> <u>Tribune</u> led me to an employment agency on Broadway, opposite St. Paul's Chapel. Alexander's a small one I had not known, was looking to place an office boy at a weekly salary of sixteen dollars, for a fee therefore of sixteen dollars.

During the previous week I had been screened at another for a helper's job in a printing shop. The interviewer having asked the lowest salary I'd accept, I was uneasy but desperate enough to say fourteen dollars, what banks were paying new office boys, plus fringe benefits, however modest. Well, off I sped to the printers. The noise, litter and shouting were a shock. I left, for I wasn't that desperate. Oddly enough, the interviewer was not surprised to see me back. Perhaps I had not been the first.

Alexander's sent me a short stroll to Mr. Joseph Dietsch at Giegy Company Inc, just down from the Woolworth Building at 89 Barclay Street, on the north side, between Greenwich Street and West Broadway. It was the American Headquarters of John R. Geigy of Basel, Switzerland, manufacturers of aniline dyes and related chemicals, (and a major rival of Ciba.)

This New York firm occupied three contiguous four story buildings (reputed to be owned by Columbia University) buildings that evidently had been townhouses, built perhaps before the Civil War. The interiors had been gutted, of course, and remodeled, leaving the ancient cracking wooden stairs, the red-brick facade, double-hung windows, and ornate metal cornices. Doorways had been hacked out of the two interior walls. Massive steel fire doors hung ready to roll closed. It was curious that the building on the right, the one closest to West Broadway, had upper floors a step higher than the other two.

Small orders were shipped to branch offices and customers from stocks on the ground floor. Others from a subsidiary mixing plant, Cincinnati Chemical Works. Second and third floors provided for executive offices, salesmen, General and Financial Departments. Laboratories (with a solitary commode) spread through the top floor.

Mr. Dietsch, Assistant Treasurer (and bachelor from Guttenberg, NJ) managed the Financial Department: Miss Lillis, secretary; Charlie McGinn, general assistant; John Runge and Ray Wheeler, bookkeepers; Eleanor Boehm, typist-clerk; Miss Ellsman, file clerk; Harold Swenson, clerk and former office boy; Donald Crombie, clerk and my immediate predecessor; another young lady typist whose name I've forgotten. There was probably another file clerk, feminine variety.

Executives of the corporation and salesmen were not so bound, but the rest of us worked Monday to Friday, eight A.M. to four-thirty P.M., with a half-hour break for lunch at noon. Mr. Dietsch came early and left late. In fact he was reputed never to have taken a vacation. It was as though he lived only for Geigy.

The first thing I did each morning was to remove and fold up the black rubber-coated covers on the typewriters and Comptometers. Incidentally, at the end of the day, after putting them back, and having checked to see that all the account books had been stowed in the huge black safe, I closed the twin doors and then twisted the dial slightly, just enough to engage the lock. Thus in the morning it could be opened quickly.

Each of us had a desk, though seldom did I have occasion to use mine, for I was usually running errands for Mr. Dietsch among the other departments and most often on foot to the Custom House, banks, post office, foreign consulates, warehouses, shipping lines and as far away as Staten Island, Bayonne and Prospect Park NJ. A couple of times I fetched silver dollars from the Federal Reserve Bank, Maiden Lane, occasional gifts for young relatives. Incidentally, in those days there was a post office where Broadway and Park Row meet. That triangular plot is now an extension of City Hall Park.

Once I was sent close to noon to deliver an envelope to a corporate officer dining with his Swiss family at the rothskeller in the Woolworth Building. His table was in clear view, about thirty feet from the door. He had to see me coming, to recognize me. When he looked up from the soup, I stopped closer and handed over the envelope. He said nothing. I paused, expecting a reply or instructions. None came. I left. A few hours later, as we were about to pass in the hall, he stopped me to say how sorry he was that I had rushed off, for he wanted to invite me to join him for lunch. That was the same Treasurer reputed to have begged small change from employees, none of whom dared asked for repayment. I wonder whether I'd have the guts to refuse him.

When not traipsing about, developing leg muscles, I was filling ink wells, sharpening pencils, handling out office supplies on request, keeping inventory, sealing envelopes. Mr. Dietsch was all business, never smiling, never interested in small talk. I wasn't there a week before he reprimanded me for whistling. A reasonable objection I do admit; not everyone can work and listen to classical music at the same time. We in the Financial Department spoke in hushed tones, managing always to at least look busy, whereas our colleagues elsewhere were relaxed enough to chat and even laugh while working.

Mr. Dietsch worked mostly at a huge antique oaken roll-top desk near the front windows. The enclosed stairwell in the middle blocked his view of everyone but Miss Lillis and the two bookkeepers. These, John Runge and Ray Wheeler, perched on high wooden stools before ledgers spread open on broad slanted desks. The boss never called to anyone. One dash on his buzzer summoned John. Two for Charlie. Three for the office boy.

Charlie Mc Ginn and Mr. Dietsch worked late one night. Having locked the last of the doors behind them, Mr. Dietsch asked, "Charlie would you like a drink?" On the other side of Barclay, on the corner of Greenwich Street stood a tavern, below the 9th Avenue El, favored by local businessmen. To the waiter's "What'll yuh have?" Mr. Dietsch spoke up: "Two sarsaparillas".

Several times I was asked to come in on Saturday mornings. Mr. Dietsch had the whole place to himself while I was off running errands, which was most of the time. Around noon he paid me two or three dollars. I went home. He stayed.

Friday, August 10, 1990

After three months with Mr. Diestch in the Financial Department, my morale had so eroded that I finally decided to give him two weeks' notice, after which to look elsewhere, largely because I had lost hope of overlooking his fault finding, irritating criticisms that were unfair and sometimes contradictory. Not once had I missed a day's work, I always arrived on time, was well groomed, got along well with everyone, and always did my best. Even so, he used to chide me as though I had taken too much time on errands, whereas in truth I had kept a fast steady pace, avoiding distractions and interruptions. Indeed, here I took professional pride. Then too he'd instruct me in a procedure which I'd then follow, but a few days later express displeasure and direct me to do what I had been doing originally.

In retrospect I came eventually to see these petty annoyances as trifles that I ought to have taken in stride, as one of life's little crosses, just as my colleagues in the department had been doing. My failing to do so was not in fact a valid indictment of the boss, but rather of me myself, of my immaturity, chronic anger, and impatience. Oh, I was well aware of my impatience and anger, but oddly enough regarded them as natural, like the color of my hair and the shape of my nose. I was then eighteen years old, and just as my former classmates and friends were all graduating from high school, I had completed only three of the eight terms. While they had definite goals, however wise, I was only drifting, aimlessly drifting. The nagging dissatisfaction, then, that I ought to have traced to myself I charged instead to poor Mr. Dietsch, my subconscious scapegoat.

It was a Friday evening when, as I was about to leave, I finally determined to quit. Mr. Dietsch sat at his roll-top desk. Miss Lillie took stenographic notes. "Excuse me, Mr. Dietsch, but I'll be leaving here two weeks from today". I turned immediately and left, unable and unwilling to say more.

Upon my arrival Monday morning, Miss Lillis told me the boss wanted to see me. (Why had he not used the buzzer?) He asked me why I wished to leave and whether I had another job to go to. I lied, saying something to the effect that there was no future for me there, a monumental irony in view of my utter lack of ambition. To my astonishment, Mr. Dietsch said perhaps he could help, for he had many influential friends in a local Greenwich Street businessmen's association. Before the end of the week, he asked whether I'd like to work in the laboratory upstairs.

Thursday, August 16, 1990

The colors of most dyed things are achieved with blends of dyes, usually two, each ingredient having its own distinct characteristics. Makers of dyes, such as Geigy or Ciba, used to market the same products, though with differences in strengths and blends, and of course each with its own fanciful trade name and code number.

Manufacturers of textiles and leather goods, setting or keeping pace with ever-changing fashion, rely on their dye suppliers to provide the novel pre-packaged blends. From time to time, moreover, they call upon these dye makers to help solve technical problems, services offered free in the hope of continued patronage.

Meeting these needs was the primary function of Geigy's New York laboratories. Standard and seasonal color cards (sample yarns of the various fibers dyed in broad spectra) were not enough. Salesmen and branch offices submitted samples of yarns and textiles dyed with anonymous products. These we were to match, in color as well as light and washing fastness, beginning with the appropriate color cards, ultraviolet lamp, and rarely the spectrometer. Then too, just as often, they submitted a few spoonful's of unknown dyes which we were requested to duplicate, evidence of our salesmen's persuasiveness.

The laboratories comprised specialized departments, each headed by a master dyer: cotton, wool, leather, paper, miscellaneous fibers, research, and several small units hard to categorize.

Master dyers, through years of experience, had memorized all the characteristics of all the dyes used in their specialties. With a strange dye sample, the first step was to blow gently a few grains from the tip of a tapered spatula onto wet filter paper stuck to a window. The tiny particles of ingredients in the blend were thus separated. Dissolved in separate spots, they were recognized by expert eyes. Tiny drops of acidic or alkaline solutions helped confirm the identifications. Finally, proportions were estimated.

Based on this analysis, the dyer calculated a series of combinations of the ingredients, a dozen perhaps, with graduated percent's of each, in the hope that one would match the sample precisely, or at least greatly narrow the search.

For each such tentative blend, a small amount of appropriate fiber (commonly a five or ten gram skein) would then be dyed, all at the same time, all under the same conditions. This is where the lab' assistants began to function.

With the exception of leather, which tumbled in drums, and paper, which formed in pans, test dyeings were done in ceramic or Monel metal pots holding about a liter. They had flanges near the tops, permitting their suspension through a steel plate into a shallow pool filled with a strong solution of calcium chloride, like food trays over cafeteria steam tables.

The temperature of that solution, and hence of the dye baths, was regulated by a valve controlling the flow of steam through a pipe meandering along the bottom. Thus with a thermometer and a conditioned fingertip, the heat level was kept suitable to the fiber at hand, for instance low for nylon, boiling for cotton.

Suspended about three feet over each pool; a metal hood and ducts which vented hot air and steam through the roof. At several places nearby, the ceiling and roof were pierced by skylights and hinged windows. Air conditioning was unknown. The few electric fans were placed mostly close to the desks, in the building on the right.

A glass-enclosed room spread across the front of the middle building. Shallow shelves against opposite walls held glass bottles topped by tapered glass stoppers an inch wide, row upon row, like a library, each containing about a quarter-liter of a single dye. Reserved for each department was a glass-enclosed apothecary-type balance, complete with metric weights and tweezers.

In accordance with the worksheet drawn up by the department head, or an assistant, a two-hundred c.c. water solution of each putative ingredient was prepared, all of the same concentration. Likewise a solution of the same strength of the anonymous sample. Then with the aid of a graduated glass pipette of appropriate size, the precise number prescribed of cubic centimeters of each was drawn and deposited in a pot. Added clear water completed the dye bath. Incidentally, each assistant had his own set of pipettes as well as a rosewood-handled spatula.

The skeins, prepared by the ladies in the ground-floor yarn room, each of precisely the same prescribed weight, were distinguished from each other by the number of tiny knots where the strands were tied together. These allowed a skein's special blend to be identified during subsequent comparisons.

Each skein, hung over a glass rod about the size of a pencil, was immersed in its bath, the rod left lying across the rim of the pot. Thus a small portion of the skein was suspended out of the bath. Because the dye had of course to be distributed evenly throughout, skeins were rotated around the rods four or five times a minute, during the course of a half to three quarters of an hour. We used to tease each other with "Get 'em even!"

This turning could have been done with the help of a second glass rod, while the first held the skein dripping above the bath, but that tactic was slow, and ran the risk of pushing the skin off the end. Moreover, two rods for each pot was clumsy. Hence we almost always relied on thumb and forefingers. Efficient, but at the price of skein stains that had to be bleached out, before we went home, with a stripping agent such as sodium bisulphite.

In the final moments of the dyeing process, the dye was set often by the addition of a ten percent solution of either common salt or Glauber's salt. After the last rinse, in cold water, the batch was spun in a centrifugal pump, spread on a wooden rod or rods, and then hung to dry like spaghetti, but in a steel cabinet heated by coil steam pipes.

Thursday, August 23, 1990

Executives and salesmen went off somewhere to lunch, with customers perhaps or Kiwanis. The rest of us brought sandwiches from home, or splurged at a lunch room across Barclay Street, a small place run by a Greek couple, two sons and a daughter. We in the lab' used to take turns fetching coffee. They'd fill a ceramic dye pot, about a liter, for a nickel. In hot weather a new rival of Coca Cola, Pepsi Cola, was hawked day and night by this singing radio blurb: "Pepsi Cola hits the spot. Twelve full ounces; that's a lot. Twice as much for a nickel too. Pepsi Cola is the drink for you. Nickel. Nickel. Nickel. Nickel".

Al Ezratty's one-man lunch counter huddled next door to us on the west side. Al was a voluble, cheerful naturalized Turk who had driven an American ambulance in France, in the war against Kaiser Wilhelm. A bowl of rich home-made soup and a kaiser roll with butter cost a dime. Where else could we get a meat-loaf sandwich? Where else could we get credit until payday? To strangers the pinball machine was only for amusement - to strangers.

Some unknown labor union began picketing the Greek family's place, hoping evidently to expand a local. The signs announced a strike, even though the sons and daughter were in fact content, and all the dozen or so pickets were only strangers. We and the other customers ignored the picket line, not that we were anti-unions, but a fraud is a fraud. After a few weeks the would-be organizers gave up.

Once in a while Jerry Jerold would drive his car to work so that at noon a carload of us could dash up to nearby Chinatown for chop suey or chow mien. Occasionally one of us would run down to Callinman's on Fulton Street for cold cuts and hard rolls.

Roy Ferris, head of Miscellaneous Fibers, was the trouble-shooter most in demand at dye houses needing help. Company policy required its representatives to stay at the best hotels, to entertain, customers at the best restaurants, and to submit to Mr. Dietsch an itemized account of expenses.

Now Roy's breakfast every day was no more than a cup of coffee at Al Ezratty's. Upon returning from his first rescue mission, his "swindle sheet" listed for breakfast only the price of a cup a coffee. Somehow word got around to the salesmen, whereupon one of them argued that in the future Roy ought to claim, as they did, the price of a full meal. Why make them look bad? Was he convinced? I hope not.

Dyeing was done in the middle and left (west) buildings. Each had spacious double sinks of soapstone, presided over by a full-time pot washer. Kept busy with brushes and Sap olio, a strong cake soap containing a grit like pumice, Charlie Koehler was stationed on the left side. A memorable likeable character, he had unfortunately not learned to read or write, which is not to imply low intellect. Thus he pronounced words just as they sounded to him, "pension" for attention, and "polio" for Sap olio, etc. In his youth he had played semi-professional baseball with minor league teams, such as the Bushwicks and maybe also the House of David. A hard dependable worker, in slack moments we'd get him to reminisce about famous ball players he had known, such as Honus Wagner.

On rare occasions we'd get a length of fabric that needed a large pot in which to remove the sizing before dyeing in swatches. For such jobs we had several gas burners. These served also whenever we obliged anyone downstairs, or at home, who asked that a garment be stripped and re-dyed. Then too, just before St. Patrick's Day, March 17, we got requests, mostly from ladies in the General Department, for satin ribbon dyed bright Kelly Green, of which we managed also to bring home a bit. Incidentally, these off-the-record projects were called "government work" whenever anyone asked "What are you doing?"

Walter Strobach and a helper, Rudy (whose last name I don't recall, though I remember his moving to La Jolla, California) either ethnic Swiss or German, comprised the Research Department.

One night we went to see a German film on 86th Street, Yorkville, with no subtitles, I went along, and sat between them, while they whispered running commentary. Hitler and his National Socialists had been festering; yet the romantic story ignored politics, a quality appreciated, for Nazis were an embarrassment to Walter and Rudy. I was impressed by the beautiful autobahns and the charming star fräulein, Heli Finkenzeller. How could I forget such a name?

When the mother of a lab' assistant died, several of us in Miscellaneous Fibers went after supper to the wake uptown. The coffin lay diagonally in the corner of a small parlor, blanked by potted palms. No flowers, no candles, no cross, no crucifix, no kneeler, no memorial cards. We, and her only son, sat in a circle, all the while making small talk, much as we would have done in a tavern, for instance, or someone's kitchen, not, however, smoking or sipping beer. No clergyman came to pray, nor even the funeral director. Nor did any of us mourners have the grace to speak up, an omission that I soon came to regret. Surely the poor soul deserved some ritual. Sad. Very Sad.

The remnants of dye samples left over – a few grams of this, a few grams of that – were accumulated until they filled a barrel. After thorough mixing at Cincinnati Chemical Works, the potpourri was sold to dyers of reprocessed wool or anyone else looking for a cheap all-fiber brown. Of course fastness to light or washing was an unknown variable.

Victor Dubois, head of the Shipping Department served on occasion also as <u>de facto</u> building superintendent, in as much as he regularly put out poisoned bait for the few rats that shared our quarters. It was curious that they favored only the top floor, where at night they gnawed at book spines to feed on the glue. Only rarely did on scamper across the lab' 'floor in daylight, from one hole to another. One Friday afternoon I was last to leave the lab'. Down on the first floor I recalled leaving something of value in my locker, something I'd want over the weekend. As I tramped back up the venerable wooden stairs, I made lots of noise. The effectiveness of Victor's cuisine was proclaimed from time to time by a foul odor, offensive enough to warrant his ripping up floor boards.

On Fridays the head of the laboratories, Mr. Swanson, handed me a manila envelope, about the size of a playing card, holding cash: a ten-dollar bill, a five and three singles, making it possible for me to indulge a weekly vanity. A barber shop with four or five chairs lay between us and West Broadway. A haircut was twenty-five cents plus a ten-cent tip. At first I used to sit in whatever chair was vacant, until I observed that Tony was the only one who did not bombard customers with non-stop chatter. He had the soul of a Trappist; after the polite exchange of greetings, he was lost in contemplation. Amen.

Budd Pitts was an assistant in the Cotton Department, under George Wilson. Nephew of a salesman, Mr. Schrieber. His father's mother was a full-blooded Cherokee, married to a white man. Bud's mother was probably an ethnic Swiss or German. Thus he was one-quarter Cherokee. While he was a youngster, he used to spend part of the summers visiting Grandma on Oklahoma. One of the local attractions was watching the daily train come and go.

With the exception of two young women, clerks at desks in the right-side building, the laboratory staff was male. On hot summer days, most of July and August, we tended the dye baths stripped to the waist, for the heat and humidity were infernal. Bud did not relish the distinction, but he was the only one with no hair on his chest or arms, and almost none on his chin. For what he lacked in fuzz, however, he was compensated by brawn.

In the absence of ladies, our diction was frequently coarse, earthy, if not also bawdy. A warning shout went up, however, on the rare occasions when our cloister was violated, for we were not utterly depraved.

It's fair to say that staff morale was high, that warm camaraderie helped relieve the inevitable tedium born of repetition. Conversation, good-natured kidding and humorous repartee kept minds alert while we stood tending the dye baths or performed other routine tasks. Nevertheless, at least once that I recall clearly, someone took offense and invited the offender up to the roof. There in privacy they exchanged punches, returned to work, and that was the end of it.

One day Bud Pitts said something disparaging about the Irish, no doubt needling me and John Morey, the nylon specialist. At the time, however I was blind to that. Whereas I ought to have laughed it off or countered with some quip about the Cherokees, I was stupid enough to invite him up to the roof. Now this may sound like some foolery dreamed up by Woody Allen, but it's the plain truth. Because it was close to four-thirty, and Bud, who commuted from Union New Jersey, might miss his train, he asked if I'd postpone our engagement, and so we agreed to come fifteen minutes early next morning.

It would have been less traumatic for me, as it turned out, had we not put it off, for in the interval I learned what may have inspired Shakespeare's observation (expressed by Caesar) that "Cowards die many times before their deaths." (though I challenge his correlative: "The valiant never taste of death but once".) Bud was built like a football player, and outweighed me by about forty pounds, and I was as much a fighter as a concert pianist. A beating was certain; tumbling off the roof a possibility. There was no guard rail. What a fool I'd been.

We were first to arrive at the lab'. As we started up the stairs to the roof, my heart pounding, Bud said something to the effect that he had intended no offense and that we ought to shake hands and forget it. By then I had already come to see my indignation as unfounded; nevertheless something deep inside goaded me on to the challenge, pigheadedness perhaps or stupidity or the shameful memory of trembling in panic before bullies long ago in St. Joseph's School.

We squared off then and traded perfunctory punches for several minutes, until it was obvious to us both that neither had the stomach for violence, and so we shook hands and went down to work, friends again. But the best part was that I had exorcised an old devil.

Monday, August 27, 1990

When I began working in the lab', there was an elderly gentleman, probably in his late seventies or early eighties, who, though retired from the company, used to come back once or twice a week. We called him George "Pickles", a pun very likely on his surname. After hanging his coat and hat in a locker, he'd sit in a chair reserved for him in a remote corner of the building on the right side, and soon nod off to sleep. Once in a while when he woke up, he had to hurry to the toilet, a single seater in the far rear corner of the left-side building. Ladies had ample accommodations, as did others, downstairs. Whenever George found the door locked, he'd pound on it while wailing pitifully that he was about to foul his pants. His diction, however, was more earthy. Yet as it happened, his fear was always unfounded. Thank God.

From my beginning at Geigy's, I formed a warm friendship with Ray Wheeler, one of Mr. Dietsch's bookkeepers. Single, a few years my senior, Ray commuted from Carlstadt New Jersey, where he lived with a middle-aged Polish-American couple who had no children. Had Ray been their son, he and the Lewandoskis could not have had greater mutual love.

All three loved movies, so much so that they had built in the backyard at 324 Third Street what they called The Whoopee House, appearing on the outside to be a small bungalow, but fitted out for entertainment. A projection room on the right concealed Ray's movie projectors, for which he rented first run films.

The Lewandoski's were gracious hosts, each time I went home with Ray on Friday. He'd drive us sightseeing, the two of us, all over northern

New Jersey, pausing to quench out thirst with local beer. On Saturday afternoon we dropped in to a movie: Rita Hayworth in "Cover Girl", the end of which we skipped. I don't recall why we had to leave early. No occasion for annoyance, however, for the film, while long on visual splendor, was short on plot and dialogue.

On Sundays we heard Mass – all but Ray, who was not Catholic, - at the nearby Franciscan church, St. Joseph's in East Rutherford, New Jersey.

The lab' had a large number of others from New Jersey, Jake Stumpf from Teaneck, for example, Jerry Boyce from Boonton and Vinnie DiPetrillo from Paterson, elder son of the owner of La Francaise Silk Dyeing and Finishing Company.

Vinnie was a graduate of the New York Military Academy and also the Philadelphia Textile Institute. Handsome, always cheerful, about my age, he laughed readily.

Knowing my frequent visits to Grandma and Uncle Eddie Foley, he invited me to go along for a weekend visit to friends and former classmates in Philadelphia. We'd rendezvous on Sunday afternoon. And so on a Friday afternoon I accompanied him home by train. After supper he would drive his car. Great Italian cuisine was served by his mother, while a sister kept refilling our glasses with an excellent dry burgundy from the wine cellar, and so by the time we set out for Philadelphia, we would surely have flunked a sobriety test had State Police pulled us over. Our guardian angels, however, were evidently proficient. Yet I must add that Vinnie was an expert, cautious driver.

Over a late weekend I was his guest at home. We went to a carnival in a nearby town, a feature of which was a tent where for a fee of twenty five cents on could get a close-up view of what purported to be the mummified remains of John Wilkes Booth, Lincoln's assassin. Well, it was a human mummy surely. A shriveled corpse like a skeleton encased in brown leather, But John Wilkes Booth? This we were asked to take on faith, despite his having been cremated alive in a barn in Maryland, or so historians believe.

Then there was the weekend that I spent as a guest of the Di Petrillos at their summer home in a mountain – lake resort. The local name escapes me, but not an incident I'd rather had not happened. Vinnie, his sister, several lady and gentleman friends and I had as usual been drinking. Thus we were feeling no pain when we came upon a huge swimming pool. Some jackass stripped to his underwear, climbed the tower, and dove off the board. Incidentally, my swimming trunks would have covered less.

Bud Pitts and I, after the episode on Giegy's roof, became even closer buddies. He too invited me home to Union New Jersey for weekends, on which occasions he ran grand parties for housefuls of friends. One Friday night we got a head start on the festivities before heading for the ferry, and so, in a state of euphoria, upon seeing two pretty smiling young ladies waiting to cross West Street, I strode up to one and in silence planted a kiss on her left cheek. She said not one word; neither did we.

There was still another memorable character in the lab', on loan one summer from our Portland Oregon office, being groomed I guess for sales. I've forgotten his name, alas, though we worked together and the fraternized after hours.

At first he roomed at the Y.M.C.A. Sloane House in midtown Manhattan, until he discovered cheaper quarters in a rooming house across the street, within walking distance of the theatrical district and hotels where big bands played the jazz to which he was so addicted. His idol above all others was Benny Goodman, of whom he couldn't hear enough.

Whereas most of us in the lab' were hooked on cigarettes, by slavish habit, if not preference, this lad filled the air with sweet aroma (stench to some) of an aromatic pipe tobacco: Rum and Maple.

When he wasn't dreaming of Benny Goodman, he was reminiscing about a performer back home, whom he missed, "Father Heinz", or was it "Heins"? Of him I had not heard, barbarian that I was obviously, but then he probably had not heard of Lauritz Melchior, or Giovanni Martinelli, or Kirsten Flagstad.

Tuesday, August 28, 1990

My mother had a friend from the George Washington Democratic Club, Mrs. Moran, a widow. For the 1936 summer season, to save rent, they agreed to share a three bedroom bungalow on 108th Street, Rockaway Park. Mrs. Moran and a daughter (about twenty years old) would share a bedroom; my mother and sister Lillian another. One toilet for the five of us was tolerable. However, one stove, one icebox, one sink, one table and two sets of utensils demanded cooperation and discipline. Entertaining guests was of course limited. Well, even so, we managed to survive, still friends.

Our bungalow stood at the end of the row, at the back of the court, near the backs of others that faced 107th Street, all midway between the boardwalk and Rockaway Beach Boulevard.

One evening as I sat alone on the front porch, an attractive young brunette stepped out the back door onto a tiny square porch just a few feet away from me; no space was wasted. There she hung up a bathing suit. Whether she saw me in the half-light, I couldn't tell, but neither of us said anything. Though it was the middle of August, I had not seen her nor anyone else in the place before. After dark, I stretched over the low fence, and draped my swimming trunks next to her suit.

As we were leaving for Mass, the following morning at St. Camillus Church, the laundry line was bare. Later, after breakfast, I climbed over, knocked on the back door, and the second she opened it, smiling at me, like an angel admitting saints to Paradise, my heart skipped a beat, nor for a long time would it return to normal, for at once I was infatuated by the

151

prettiest, most charming young lady in all of God's wide world, a colleen whose soft brogue enchanted my very soul.

That same evening August 16th 1936, Emily and I strolled the boardwalk to the Park, a movie house on 116th Street, not far from the railroad terminal. Featured was "San Francisco", with, among other greats, Clark Gable, Spencer Tracy, and the soprano Jeannette McDonald.

On the way back, unhurried, we held hands, while we chatted, eager to know all about each other. The bench in front of Krueger's beckoned. We were alone, Emily and I, and the moon, the stars, the Atlantic surf, caressing the beach, and the distant tunes of the calliope at Playland. There we lingered, my right arm hugging her close. Intoxicated by her charm and fragrance, I drew her still closer and kissed her on the lips.

Emily Duffy was the youngest of five daughters, of whom two were married and mothers. The other three, close in age, shared the bungalow. Ruth worked for Metropolitan Life. Rose too worked in Manhattan, Girl Friday and sole employee of a Mr. Stitch. Emily, (just three days younger than I) was a clerk in St. Mary's Hospital, Brooklyn. Emily Christine Duffy was born on October 07, 1917 in Castlerea County Roscommon Ireland. The previous June she had graduated from the all-girl Bishop McDonnell Memorial High School, on Eastern Parkway, across Classon Avenue from the Brooklyn Museum. Mr. Patrick J. Duffy, a local official in Roscommon, had fled with the family from Ireland, urged by the violent troubles in the early 1920's.

During the week that followed, we saw little of each other, due to the long hours commuting and working, and yet from the morning until night, I could think of no one nor anything but Emily. It seemed the weekend would never come. Ah, but the heavenly fantasy was swept away abruptly the very next Sunday evening.

John Gaffney, an unmarried young colleague of my mother at the bank, had dropped in, as he used to do now and then. We were lounging with the Duffy sisters in their place, when one of them – I've forgotten which – discovered that a familiar car had just pulled up near the court, old friends from upstate Cornwall, they said, fellow natives from Roscommon. Would John and I please scoot out the back door!!

My wheel of fortune spun a half-turn, plunging me into deep despair, for though infatuated and credulous, the implication of that curt dismissal pierced my romantic heart. John, who earlier in obvious amusement had teased me about my silly obsession, and who I suspected – though several years my senior – had no similar experience, tried to console me and to distract my mind with the prospect of "other fish in the sea." He pointed out that I was only eighteen, with my whole life still to come. His kindness was appreciated, to be sure, but stab wounds take time to heal. John had been right from the beginning; I had played the fool. Now I must pay the price. "He who dances must pay the fiddler."

Several days later, as I sat sulking over supper, Emily called to me from the back porch. Summer bungalows had no telephones. Like Lazarus I revived at once, and casting off the shroud of despair, I stumbled out to her, alive again. It was as though I were awakened from a nightmare. Neither she nor her sisters ever again spoke of her old friends, from Cornwall, nor did I.

We became inseparable, Saturdays and Sundays, whether loafing on the beach – oh, we did a lot of that – or swimming, or ambling along the beach, just above the breakers. After dark we strolled the boardwalk, hand in hand, or sipped beer and danced at Kreuger's or Valinti's on the Boulevard, or Healy's in Irish Town, or we rode the roller coaster at Playland. (Thunderbolt was it called? Cyclone?) Afterward, when ordinary mortals were asleep, we lingered back at her place, on the front porch – mostly in silence or whispering, loath to say goodnight. Perfect bliss.

"...... my cup runneth over.

Wednesday, August 29, 1990

In the previous summer (1935), next-door neighbors, in Georgian Court, the Bickels, had as an occasional guest a tall slim pretty brunette neighbor from the Bronx. May and I made a date for a Saturday night in the fall. After supper in the Shaw apartment in the Fordham section, we were to enjoy the show at the Paramount, in Times Square. Glen Gray's band was to be featured on stage. That part of the Bronx was unknown to me, a contributing factor in my choosing the wrong subway line, and thus up on the street I was disoriented, lost in fact. May's parents and brother were gracious, as though I were on time, and the meat was not overcooked, when I stumbled in at least a half-hour late, having hiked all the while, guided by a series of helpful pedestrians. In those days it was safe to walk the streets after dark. Yes, and to ride the subways.

Thursday, August 30, 1990

It was a great joy to learn that the Duffy's lived only about a mile from us, in St. Augustine's parish. They had a brownstone townhouse (whose façade was in fact granite) at 192 Park Place, near the convergence with Carlton and Flatbush Avenues. Also they owned an apartment house, nearby, in Park Slope, on Berkley Place.

After autumn chill and expired leases eroded Rockaway's charm, I was delighted at the prospect of continuing to see a lot of Emily, or more precisely, continuing to see Emily often.

Our relationship was perfectly chaste, in thought, word and deed. Anything less would have been sacrilege.

Mr. Patrick J. Duffy was a fascinating character, a retiree, having sold Duffy's Tavern in the Times Square area. On Saturday evenings, when I called for Emily, he usually answered the bell, and invited me into the front parlor, where we'd chat until his youngest daughter finished doing whatever young ladies did before going out on a date. Often I deliberately arrived early so as to spend more time with him.

Now there was a highly intelligent gentleman! Though without the benefits of a college education, he was in fact more learned, articulate, and cultured than any of fifty college graduates picked at random. He loved to exchange views on current affairs, politics, religion, art, philosophy, the Roosevelt New Deal, Irish history, literature, etc. In every session he was more a Socrates than a Cicero, for though he spoke with wit and eloquence, he did a lot of listening too, a quality rare among the gifted. Oh, wouldn't he have made a great teacher! One night my arrival chanced to interrupt his reading of the <u>King James Bible</u>, devout Catholic though he was. He preferred its style to the <u>Douay-Rheims</u>, both of which translations he had read, because of what he judged to be the more poetic diction. Theological nuances and exegesis were not considerations, as I recall. I wonder what he would have thought, had he lived to read the <u>Jerusalem Bible</u> (among recent translations) especially its Twenty-third psalm.

After the show at the Carlton theater on Flatbush Avenue near Seventh Avenue, Emily and I stopped at a neighboring tavern for a drink, just one each. At a sign from me, the waiter brought the check, turned and returned to his post. Now I discovered that the total as written was about double what it ought to have been. At the second sign, he hurried over, and before I could say a word, stammered an apology.

To get back for a moment to Mr. Duffy, Emily once related with pride how generous and compassionate he had been toward an impoverished poet, whom he housed and helped in publishing a collection of verses. I never saw the volume, but oddly enough I recall the title:

<u>Hallroom Soliloquies</u>.

Friday, August 31, 1990

On a few Saturday nights we babysat for Emily's sisters, Rachel and Ethel. Rachel had an apartment in Park Slope, a few paces below Prospect Park West. Her husband was tall, handsome, soft-spoken, Irish, probably native. I have a blurred memory of walking alone one afternoon in that neighborhood, and approaching an open parlor-floor window. An unseen artist at a grand piano – preparing for a concert perhaps – was playing a Chopin etude. Beautiful ! Of course I had to stop and listen for a while, enchanted, like the children of Hamlin.

Ethel Duffy married Dick Molnar, an ethnic Hungarian, as I recall. They had an apartment on St. John's Place, a couple of doors west of us Dees. Emily and I minded their toddler Brian.

Emily, Rose and their father didn't smoke, but their mother and Ruth enjoyed a cigarette from time to time, never, however, in each other's presence.

The George Washington Democratic Club held an annual formal ball at Columbus Council, 126, Knights of Columbus, where Grand Army Plaza, Prospect Park West, and Union Street converge. The ballroom, entered directly from Union Street, was huge. A spacious dance floor sandwiched in between dozens of large round tables, above which, on three sides, a mezzanine fitted with theater-type boxes and tables. A stage, opposite the doors, served the dance band.

Holding court in their box were the district leader, Tom Lantry and co-leader Ella Healey. Every Democratic politician in Brooklyn (Kings

County) attended. Every would-be office holder attended. My mother delighted in such festivities, not from ambition, surely. She once turned down an appointment, in Staten Island I believe. To her the ball meant chatting with scads of friends and making new friends.

Downtown at Howard's, on Flatbush Avenue, close to the Brooklyn Academy of Music – one of a large chain competing in men's clothes with Crawford's, Bond's, and Moe Levy's – I bought a tuxedo and accessories for close to the price of a four-piece business suit, two pairs of pants, a little less than twenty dollars. Emily was gorgeous in black velvet. Afterward in the Duffy vestibule, after I complemented her on the gown, and how well it fit her cute figure, she was so ingenuous as to confide that the smooth lines were due in part to her wearing a minimum of underwear, an innocent allusion that triggered my hasty departure, for I wasn't made of stone.

On one of my Sunday trips to Grandma's in Philadelphia, I brought Emily, probably to show off my Irish girlfriend and Irish grandmother to each other. Incidentally, Grandma Foley did not have a brogue.

Wednesday, September 5, 1990

My sister Lillian was a year older than I, but because of one illness after another, she was so petite and had lost so much time at both elementary and high school, we pretended, whenever the question came up, that she was a year younger. She attended nearby Girls Commercial High School (since renamed Prospect Heights High School) 833 Classon Avenue at Eastern Parkway in the Crown Heights section of Brooklyn. Located across the street are the Brooklyn Museum and Brooklyn Botanical Gardens. She did not live long enough to graduate.

In June of 1937, my mother arranged a stay of a couple of weeks at a convalescent home in Manasquan New Jersey. I've forgotten the diagnosis. Then in July, Aunt Katie Kelly, a sister of my mother and a most generous soul, volunteered to nurse Lillian in her home in Darby Pennsylvania.

The same Dr. Boyle who had vaccinated us so long ago took Lillian under his care.

One afternoon at a tiny private hospital in Philadelphia, housed in what must have been originally adjacent townhouses, Lillian received a direct transfusion of my blood. We lay on cots separated by a small square table holding a hand operated pump. A tube from my right arm channeled blood into a glass cylinder. A physician seated between us kept it flowing into her left arm.

Our hearts ached all the more for Lillian whenever she had to eat raw liver, chopped into bits. It was all she could do to force herself slowly to swallow.

159

In time it became obvious that she was getting steadily weaker, that alas, she'd not survive. Even so, when death finally came on Thursday, August 12, 1937, feast of St. Clare of Assisi, we were all shocked, heartbroken. She had been so sweet through all the pain, never complaining, so grateful for all the attention. My mother and all the Kelly's had been with her at the end.

It was curious that, having spent most of her short life in far-away Brooklyn, she should die in Darby, and just around the corner from where she had been conceived.

The death certificate listed pernicious anemia as the cause of death. Dr. Boyle confided, however, that the choice was arbitrary, for she had several equally severe illnesses.

The wake was held in the Kelly parlor, just below the master bedroom where she had died. Bart Cavanaugh, who had buried Grandpa Foley, was in charge. There were more gorgeous gladiolas massed about the coffin than I had ever seen before in one place. Beautiful!

One evening as I stood outside on North Front Street smoking a cigarette, a middle-aged man followed and introduced himself as a neighbor and old friend of the Kellys, Foleys, and even the Dees. I thanked him for his condolences, but I lacked the interest or the wit to ask what he knew of the Dees, where, for instance they lived in California, or whether my father was dead or alive. At that moment I just didn't care. It occurred to me later that he could have relayed the sad news to California.

Sunday intervening, the funeral was delayed until Monday, August 16th 1937, when we buried Lillian from St. Clement's, Woodland Avenue, where she had been baptized and her parents married. Grandma Foley's infirmity kept her at home, and so, for her sake, the cortege to Holy Cross Cemetery, nearby in Yeadon, passed along Cobbs Creek Parkway, where Grandma could see it across the fields from her front porch. And so we buried Lillian alongside Grandpa in the Foley plot, Section 7 Range 4 Lot 23, close to the intersection of Mc Dade Boulevard and Rundale Avenue. Our lives would never be the same; part of us went with her.

Friday, September 7, 1990

During the early part of 1937, before Lillian became gravely ill, changing our routines, Emily and I dated often, on most Friday or Saturday nights. On such occasions, by the way, the universal custom was for the gentleman to bear all expenses.

Neither of us went out with anyone else. She told, however, of parties with cousins and their friends on several occasions. One such was Bernard McGreevy, a personable New York City fireman. The term firefighter had yet to be coined. He used to speak, incidentally, of a premonition that he'd not live to see his twenty-fifth birthday.

Emily and I took each other for granted, there having been neither explicit nor explicit commitment, nor talk of marriage. The closest we came to that was in her remarking – in what context I don't recall – that her first choice for a name of a son would be Paul. Moreover, we observed perfect chastity.

In this regard I'm reminded of an anecdote told by one of the Duffy sisters. A man, having decided to ask his lady friend's hand in marriage, and being, alas, neither self-confident nor well-spoken, stammered "Ah, ah let's get married or something." To which the maiden replied "Let's get married or nothing."

In the fall of 1937, Emily and I were guests at a small party in Woodhaven. A young lady who worked with Emily at St. Mary's Hospital was there, with an escort. She struck me as attractive enough to prompt

161

my 'phoning her at home a few days later. Chances are I found the number in the 'phone book. We made a date.

The next evening Emily 'phoned me, irate and demanding the return of her portrait, a graduation photograph that was hanging in my room. Evidently her co-worker had embarrassed Emily, taunting her about the date with me. She'd be right around to fetch my portrait, and would I please bring it down to her in the lobby, when she rang the bell at the front door. She'd be waiting near the mailboxes.

There I found her, sitting on the table, crying. The ever-cheerful, poised, vivacious Emily, crying. I was shaken. She composed herself after a few minutes. I offered to escort her home. When we got to the house I went in too, but I don't know why. It made no sense.

Immediately she passed through the front parlor, sobbing, through the French doors in the rear, while I stood perplexed and alone near the hall door. Just a few seconds after Emily closed the doors, they swung open, and out strode Ruth, an avenging angel, who slapped the left side of my face. Whatever she was exclaiming in righteous indignation I've since forgotten, but I do know her motive was not at all clear. It was as though her sister's distress were proof enough of an unspeakable barbarism, too heinous to spell out. I said not one word to Ruth, but turned at once and left; it was not a propitious time for discussion.

Two days later, Mr. Duffy 'phoned in the evening to say that Emily was depressed. Would I please come over; a short visit might cheer her up. The initial shock having subsided during the two days, I began to see clearly what was at stake: marriage or nothing. What was past was gone forever. Though in my puerile fashion I loved Emily, and I probably had told her I loved her, I was far from prepared to assume the grave responsibilities of husband and father. The prospect was frightening, for I was a mere nineteen year old drifter, a leaf in the wind, a mamma's boy, with no long term plans or aspirations, or even long-term vision, whereas Emily was clearly a mature young woman, ready and eager for a home and family. Well, even so, I loved her father enough to do anything he asked.

Mrs. Duffy answered the bell, and in friendly fashion ushered me into a small rear bedroom on the parlor floor. Emily was sitting propped up by pillows in a twin bed on the left, as lovely and charming as ever. The house was silent. We were alone. A normal young man would have melted. My heart and head began a fierce tug of war. We chatted amiably for about an hour, about everything, everything but what was uppermost in our minds, or at least in mine. Before seeing myself to the door, maybe I kissed her goodnight. Maybe not.

Some months later, having learned that Mr. Duffy was ill and in St. Mary's Hospital, I went for a visit the same evening. (Perhaps Ethel told me.) Emily was there ahead of me. Both were obviously glad to see me again. Had she been merely formal and civil, the encounter might not have opened old wounds, for Emily was still her old sweet self. But wounds do heal in time.

On the way home from Geigy one day, as I got to Washington Avenue, I looked north just in time to see the dirigible Hindenburg sailing west toward Lakehurst, New Jersey, just before its hydrogen bomb exploded.

On May 6, 1937, during the landing operation, the Airship Hindenburg burst into flames at an altitude of about two hundred feet and was burned to destruction by hydrogen fire. Germany's perfect record of safety had been shattered in a spectacular tragedy before the assembled media and public. The commercial airship would never recover.

It must have been in the mid 1930's that Mary McLaughlin telephoned us Dees in Brooklyn. Would someone please go to the morgue in Manhattan, to see if the body found between the piers in the Hudson River was that of James McLaughlin. When seen last, about a week earlier, he was leaving a bank with cash needed in his plumbing business. Detectives had found no identification except for a key of some sort that they managed to trace.

My mother and I took the subway next morning up to Bellevue. A futile trip because of decomposition, marine life and bloating. A few days later dental records answered the question. Yes, it was James McLaughlin. Yet the mystery remains.

New York City death certificate number 13198 indicates that James W. McLaughlin died on April 8, 1936. The place of death was Pier 60, North River, in the Borough of Manhattan. The cause of his death is listed as "asphyxia by submersion: undetermined". He is buried in Cathedral Cemetery 4800 Lancaster Avenue, Philadelphia, PA, Section X, Range 5, Lot 17, #2 North Grave.

Friday, October 26, 1990

It was probably in 1935, the second year of my running for McCaffray, that I enrolled in Brooklyn Evening High School. The Nostrand Avenue trolley car north to Putnam Avenue. One block east to Marcy Avenue. During daylight hours: Boys High School.

For no more than two terms did I persevere (if indeed I completed the second term) even though I respected the school with its small classes, serene hushed atmosphere and talented faculty. Mr. Foote (European History), Mr. Callahan (Plane Geometry) and the chemistry teacher whose name, alas, I can't recall, as well as Dr. Shachtman (English) were typical of the staff, learned men who loved to teach and did so, very well. Textbooks during their classes were tools for learning, not for teaching. Mr. Callahan, for example, was qualified to write his own textbook on Euclidean geometry. Mr. Foote I can still see sitting on his desk holding me fascinated with Monasticism in the Middle Ages.

After the long day's work, hustling around the financial district, it took willpower – more evidently than I could sustain – to get up from the supper table and to hurry off to school night after night. Moreover, I was too easily seduced by clever ads for the movies. What I lacked at the time was a powerful motive, a coveted goal. Obviously it wasn't enough merely to want a diploma for its own sake. More or less content with my life as it was, I just drifted, giving little or no thought to tomorrow. Much the same torpor prevailed when I began working as a laboratory assistant at Geigy. I never took the trouble of inquiring about night classes at Manhattan's Textile High School.

Monday, November 05, 1990

Whenever in the neighborhood, I used to drop into the Church of St. Francis on West 31st Street, near Penn Station, that great granite beauty reputed to have been inspired in part by the Roman Baths of Caracalla. One could always depend on finding several friars hearing confessions, all day, every day, and never did they give a penance without a word of encouragement and inspiration. On Holy Days of Obligation, so many Masses were said, alternating in upper and lower churches that no one had to miss Mass because he had to work.

In St. Teresa's parish we had dedicated priests, of course, such as Frs. Francis Ryan and Robert Crowell, for example, but it was the Franciscan friars at 31st Street who won my warmest admiration, because the spirit of St. Francis of Assisi had won my heart, then down-to-earth gentle poverello, who wanted nothing more in this world than to emulate in every way Jesus Christ. So well did he succeed that he even came to share the five stigmata of our crucified Savior.

The upper grades of St. Teresa's Boys School had been for several years under the tutelage of teaching brothers, the Congregation of St. Francis Xavier, from Maryland, probably Baltimore, (early friends of Babe Ruth.) The principal, Br. Charles, C.F.X., charming and charismatic, founded an alumni – alumnae association, in which I became active. Thus I grew to admire Br. Charles more and more, enough, indeed, to get me pondering a career as teaching brother, until one day it dawned on me that I ought rather to become a Franciscan priest.

It was not the first such aspiration. I recollect vaguely my going with my mother by subway up to St. Vincent Ferrer's in Manhattan when I was eleven or twelve years old. Why she chose a Dominican friary I've forgotten. The kindly white-robed friar advised that when I got to high school I take Latin.

Fr. John Damascine Janco, O.F.M., an ideal friar, who was on parlor duty when I climbed the steps at 31st Street and asked to speak to a priest. It may have been close to Easter, 1939.

Washington Irving Evening High School, a short walk from the I.R.T. subway station at Union Square in Manhattan, on Irving Place and East 16th Street, had a full program, a large student body and an excellent faculty.

Mr. Reis taught Latin, a tall handsome young man with a Phi-Beta-Kappa fraternity pendant hanging from a pocket-watch chain across his vest. A born teacher.

An English teacher asked the class one night – in what context I've forgotten – how we define success. Someone spoke of pride and recognition. Another of having enough money. But it seemed to me that the teacher must have intended to start a discussion of more fundamental goals, of values we would define or refute, and so I volunteered something to the effect that success was accomplishing a difficult task that was worth the effort. With a wave of his hand, he dismissed this at once, briefly commenting on the suggestion's being "classical" or philosophical", a reaction that made no sense to me, though I judged it imprudent to pursue the point.

On another night he assigned the reading of a well-known work of English or American literature, after which we were to write a brief commentary. The Rubaiyat of Omar Khayyam caught my attention. He did not dispute my negative evaluation of its thesis, if indeed he read my paper.

Chemistry was taught by Dr. Goldman (or Goldberg) to a small class. At the approach of the Regents exam: several times he remarked that it would be very difficult, even for his full-time day students, who were, he added, more likely to pass than we. Those gibes were designed, no doubt, to spur us on.

I recall well the morning of the Regents exam in Plane Geometry. At Nevins Street I switched to the Lexington Avenue Express that would rush me up to Union Square. With the review book in my left hand, and the overhead "strap" in my right, it happened that there was just enough time en route to read over the more difficult propositions, which, it turned out, were on the test. After the scores were listed, I could have gone back and asked, but I didn't, and so I never learned where I had lost the two percent.

Friday, October 26, 1990

In the late 1930's after supper on Fridays, payday) I often hung out at a bar on the west side of Franklin Avenue, halfway between St. John's Place and Lincoln Place, the Franklin Roundtown. Yes, there were others closer to home, on Washington Avenue, congenial places like Noonan's for instance, where, if he thought you had enough, Mike Noonan could not be persuaded to serve more. All of those bars served draft beer brewed locally, such as Piel's, Trommers, Rheingold, Schaeffer's, Ruppert's. Ah, but only the Franklin Roundtown had an excellent porter from Fitzgerald Brewing Co., Troy, N.Y., and at the same price as draft beer, ten cents, no more. (Incidentally bottled beer was sold in grocery stores, not in bars.) Then too there were free snacks on a sideboard, with hot clam broth served in demitasse-coffee cups. Ambrosia!

Usually every third of fourth drink was on the house, probably the third. By custom also one offered to buy the bartender a drink, or left a tip, or both. A certain bartender used to prefer a cigar. He'd pick one out of the box and bite open the rounded end, as though about to smoke it, before putting it aside, to take home later. He explained that otherwise the boss might, as he had in the past, put his stash back in the box.

The regular clientele included many young men with whom I had grown up (if in fact I had grown up) former schoolmates and neighbors. One night I was introduced to Danny, about my age, a sailor on leave while his ship was at the Brooklyn Navy Yard.

It was after midnight. He was finding it hard to stay awake, and so I volunteered to help him home. Fortunately, for he was almost asleep, he lived, just a few doors up closer to Lincoln Place. The house had four stories, with two cold-water flats on each floor. In the vestibule he replied that he lived on the second floor. When finally we stumbled to the top of the stairs, he indicated the door to the right. While holding him up, he leaning against the wall, I tapped gently with a key or coin on the glass window. At so late an hour, the doorbell would have been too loud. Perhaps someone was up, waiting. After an eternity – I had not tapped again – a light went on, and a little elderly lady half-opened the door. No, Danny lived on the next floor.

The three big beers in New York during the 1940's, '50's and '60's were Rheingold, Piels and Schaeffer .

Rheingold beer was brewed by the Liebmann Brewing Company. Jacob Rupert's Knickerbocker beer was brewed in New York on Third Avenue between 90th and 92nd Streets. After Colonel Rupert died, they sold to Rheingold. The Rheingold brewery was on Bushwick Ave. between Flushing Ave. and Melrose Ave. in the Bushwick section of Brooklyn. The beer's name was an allusion to Germany's great river Rhein. There was a "Miss Rheingold" pageant. Throughout New York and New England people voted each year for the young lady who would be featured as Miss Rheingold in their advertisements and make appearances all year long. The Rheingold beer jingle used the melody of a famous light-classical waltz "Estudiantina Valse, Opus 191, No. 4 (The Students' Waltz)" by Emile Waldteufel. The lyric was, "My beer is Rheingold the dry beer. Think of Rheingold whenever you buy beer".

Piels was brewed on Liberty Avenue in the East New York section of Brooklyn. Piels had an extremely successful television and radio campaign featuring Bert and Harry Piel. The made-up cartoon characters were pitchmen for the brewery. John F. Trommer's Evergreen Brewery at Bushwick Ave at Conway Street in Brooklyn was sold to Piels.

The Schaefer brewery was at South 9th Street and Kent Ave. in Brooklyn. Their advertising slogan was "Schaefer is the one beer to have when you're having more than one."

The New York World's Fair of 1939 stretched south from close to Billy Rose's Aquacade, near Northern Boulevard, down to an area now crossed by the Long Island Expressway.

Everyone I knew who had visited the Fair spoke of it with great approval. Nevertheless, I was determined to boycott it because the tallest exhibit glorified the Soviet Union. Their Red Star was raised high above its neighbors.

During the summer of 1939, our National Guard 106th Infantry Regiment was sent one Saturday afternoon to march for the entertainment of Fair goers in the New York State compound. A long fleet of Army trucks carried us from our armory. Just a few minutes after we started back home, the cavalcade drew alongside a broad vacant field, where full bladders were drained. In those days there were vast areas of Queens undeveloped.

Tuesday, October 9, 1990

In late 1937 I became fascinated somehow with West Point and the prospect of an Army career. The fact that I had not graduated from high school, and that I was twenty years old, did not, strangely enough, occur to me. Learning that membership in the National Guard could be an advantage in seeking an appointment, I decided to join. Closest to home was a signal corps unit on Dean Street near Washington Avenue. A cavalry troop was stationed on Bedford Avenue just south of Eastern Parkway. An infantry regiment occupied the block on Bedford Avenue, Dean Street, Franklin and Atlantic Avenues.

On a night in January 1938 I strolled into the armory of the 106th Infantry (the "Old 23rd") of the 27th Division. (Why I preferred the infantry over the glamorous Calvary I can't recall.) Near the door I happened to meet two men in civilian clothes, one the supply sergeant of Company C. He easily persuaded me to come back on the night that the first battalion drilled, for he would earn a small bonus for recruiting me.

The coat of arms of the regiment commemorated an historic and critical break-through in the Kaiser's Hindenburg Line in France, a proud achievement in the World War.

The division's round shoulder patch, a red field embroidered with black stars in the form of the constellation Orion, honored Major General O'Ryan.

Most of the ground level space encompassed the drill shed, ample for the entire regiment to march in formation, and large enough for Detroit automobile makers to hold annual fall "Auto Shows". (There was a rumor at that time of an officer disappearing with rental money.)

The standard infantry weapon was the Springfield 30 '06 rifle. It had a bolt (on the right side) that when pulled back, ejected the spent cartridge; when pushed forward it slid the next into the chamber. While not being used, they were stacked in round steel racks named after the inventor, Ireland. Firing pins, by the way, were removed, and put back in the bolts only as needed for target practice or to be carried off to summer camp.

Commissioned officers and sergeants carried (on occasion) 45 caliber automatic pistols. Each squad (8 riflemen) had also one Browning automatic rifle, which was in fact a light machine gun. (Light compared to water-cooled.) It featured a folding bipod under the front sight, and the ability to fire single shots from a large magazine, or to empty the magazine in rapid succession, at the time a formidable weapon.

The weekly drills were spent in a variety of exercises: marching (in squads, platoons, company, and battalion), manual of arms, marksmanship, rolling the field pack, riot control tactics, and discussing hypothetical problems in field tactics, aided by sand tables, landscapes in miniature.

Uncle Ed Foley once commented, seeing me approaching on Greenway Avenue, that I walked like a farmer crossing a plowed field, an observation I understood to mean that my stride was broad. That remark came to mind years later when I first tried to march in close-order drill. Capt. Haffey assigned me to Sgt. Zazack, who took me aside in the drill shed where together we marched up and down, up and down, until I finally developed the ability to keep in step with everyone else. It probably took me more than one week's session.

Our Springfields, while not new, were in excellent condition. Some, if not all, may have served in France, maybe in the hands of such veterans as Capt. Haffey and the First Sergeant, who, incidentally, on occasion wore a medal hanging from a pale blue ribbon around his neck, probably the Congressional Medal of Honor.

In practice "dry runs" we drilled in handling the Springfield, but never was it fired in the armory. The rifle range in the cellar served for practice with only 22 caliber rifles of similar operation. From time to time, however, we drove up in a fleet of trucks to Camp Smith, just above Peekskill, leaving the armory on Saturday morning; returning Sunday evening. On the 200 yard range we fired the Springfields, most often in the prone position.

The row of bulls-eye targets appeared from the firing line to be standing on level ground in front of a hill. Each in fact was mounted on a frame set in a pit, and raised or lowered like double-hung windows. Below each target a guardsman stood with his back to the parapet, listening for the buzz that the machine made in piercing the paper, a fraction of a second before he heard the report from the muzzle. That buzz was his cue to pull down the target, patch the hole, raise the target, and with an X atop a pole, mark the spot for the rifleman. Whenever a shot missed, the range master called by telephone "Mark 7 (or whichever)". A red flag waved across a target indicated a miss, an embarrassment that beginners soon learned to prevent.

In cold weather the pyramidal tents, holding squads of eight, were fitted with small wood-burning stoves in the center, an amenity for which, after sunset especially, we were grateful. I recall further gratitude for my mother's suggestion on a bitter cold Saturday night, as I walked sentry duty near officers' tents. A sip now and then from a crystal hip flask, a relic of Prohibition, full of bottled-in-hand, 100 proof, Old Overholt bourbon.

Commissioned officers (second lieutenants and higher) wore leather boots reaching to the knees, as though they still were mounted. (Spurs and sabers had been discarded, however.) Enlisted men (privates, corporals, sergeants) bound their legs with woolen puttees, about three inches wide, spiraling up from shoe tops to knees. Everyone wore a campaign hat, the kind still favored by boot - camp drill instructors and state troopers.

Our regiment had also an antique type dress uniform similar to that of West Point cadets, worn on rare special occasions, as for instance for a review by the division's commanding general, when the whole regiment marched as a unit, proud to demonstrate its machine – like precision.

Although our standard (general issue, or "g.i.") uniforms and equipment were furnished to enlisted men at government expense, each man paid for his dress uniform.

Incidentally, a private was paid a dollar a day. (Hence the term "buck private.") On payday, conforming to Army tradition, the paymaster draped a blanket over a table, and there counted out the cash before each man in turn.

Every Memorial Day the regiment marched in the Brooklyn parade, up Bedford Avenue to Eastern Parkway, west to Grand Army Plaza. Early in the morning we reported to the armory, marched down to a side street, and there stood waiting, waiting, waiting, always in the olive drab, never in the dress uniform. Only once (in 1940) did we march with fixed bayonets. After passing under the memorial arch in the Plaza, we broke step as we headed down Vanderbilt Avenue.

In 1939 we paraded once at the New York State pavilion, New York Worlds' Fair, Flushing Meadows, to the music of our regimental band, of course. A few minutes after leaving the fairgrounds, the caravan of trucks stopped somewhere in Queens where there were only fields left and right, fields several feet lower than the road. You will surmise why we all hurried down the banks and into the fields.

That, by the way, was the only time in 1939 that I set foot inside the fairgrounds, with its vaunted "Century of Progress", for which I had been embittered by the despicable Soviet Union, whose red star perched even higher than the American flag. The communists did not, however, stay for the second year. Hooray!

Friday, October 12, 1990

Many large corporations in the 1930's gave employees leave with pay to serve annual training periods with Guard or reserve units. At Geigy, however, where vacation schedules were set by seniority, I was grateful in taking mine when the regiment was at summer camp.

Pine Camp, near upstate Watertown, was the site of our 1938 session. (Since then it has been developed and renamed Fort Drum.) Near the gate stood several small wooden buildings, offices and an infirmary, as I recall, and a water tower on stilts. These, a rifle range, and a zillion primeval acres constituted Pine Camp.

The 106th pitched camp in a clearing where the sole amenity, the only plumbing, was running water. (Slit trenches were dug at a decent interval.)

From a hill of straw, each man packed a bed tick, not so much for comfort as for insulation, for when the sun went down, so did the temperature, a phenomenon for which we had been prepared, being issued woolen long johns and long sturdy woolen overcoats, suitable for Alaska. (Oddly enough, no gloves were issued.) At reveille we usually shivered despite all that wool, but by mid-morning, out in the field, the risen sun had turned the overcoats especially into instruments of torment. Yet not every morning were we required to wear overcoats as we marched out.

The government money allotted for rations was supplemented informally – two or three dollars a week for each man – so that we in C Company dined well, in quality, variety, and quantity. Yes, we were blessed with Irv, the company cook, a talented chef.

Training exercises in the field were conducted most often in the morning, whether in companies independently, or battalions or the whole regiment as a unit. Seldom did we maneuver in the dark. Whenever the battalion or regiment was involved, the officers played a tactical chess game, the objectives and details of which only they were privy to. Thus our being marched from here to there, whether in columns or skirmish lines, whether in tight formations or spread out, whether concealed or out in the open, and all the while sighting no other units usually, made no sense to us chessmen, limited as we were by a kind of tunnel vision. Our battalion commander, moreover, preferred to commit Companies A & B, holding C in reserve. Afterwards all commissioned officers would huddle away from their units for a "critique", the fruits of which they hoarded.

If these maneuvers were intellectually sterile for the enlisted men, they were indeed physically challenging, sometimes close to exhausting. On one occasion, following an especially grueling morning, we city boys being unused to strenuous outdoor activity, as soon as we got back to camp, Capt. Haffey poured a couple of bottles of whiskey into a large pot of hot black coffee. God bless him!

Back in January, upon enlisting, I was issued shoes (used) that were a bit loose. Had I been less eager to get into uniform, had I been smart, I'd have waited for a proper fit. At Pine Camp my stupidity reaped its harvest of blisters, water sacs on both heels, making every step agony.

At morning sick call, while I stood in line, hoping for relief but fearing that only new shoes would do, an enlisted medic passed along the line, asking no questions, saying only "Open your mouth" and then tossing in a "C-C" pill, on the tacit premise that whatever the complaint, cascara would help. As I waited my turn, I observed a dentist working a foot powered field drill. Crude compared to conventional office machines. Which was worse, heel blisters or tooth ache? After the application of medicated powder, back I trudged to active duty and to aggravating the condition.

Regardless of how much we ached, how much we longed to lie down after field exercises, the first duty was always to clean the rifles. Though the company provided ramrods, brushes, patches and oil, many of us brought our own; we took better care of those Springfields than of our own personal grooming, shaving, for example, only when ordered. At night they were suspended by cords under the cots, handy, high and dry.

Incidentally, while we were required to shave, moustaches were allowed, as Lt. Tassetano demonstrated. During the two weeks, I did not shave the hair above my lips. It happened that on the way home from the armory afterward, on Sterling Place I met Regina Sullivan, who had been one of my sister's dearest friends. During our chat she made no mention of my moustache. The following morning I shaved it off.

Monday, October 15, 1990

In the summer of 1938, while the regiment was training at Pine Camp, it was probably on a Sunday afternoon that the first battalion – if not the whole regiment – enjoyed several hours of recreation at a state park near the Thousand Islands Bridge. Two things I remembered especially well.

As the fleet of trucks rumbled alongside the jail in Watertown, a score of arms waved through the bars, as though greeting their rescuers.

While we were lounging under a tree, my buddy, Henry Hasenpflug, and I decided that the opportunity to stand for the first time on Canadian soil must not be wasted.

At the bridge approach, the first car we signaled to, thumbs up, stopped. Maybe the driver mistook us for Customs officers or members of the Border Patrol, although we were not armed.

The driver was allowed to proceed at the Canadian checkpoint. We however, were refused entry because we were in uniform, the official explaining, half in earnest, that American troops had not set foot on Canadian soil since the War of 1812. Henry and I had expected to get a bit farther into Ontario, but we were not annoyed, for we had in fact done what we had set out to do. Back among our comrades in the park, we didn't share our secret. Prudence. Prudence.

One night in Watertown, the city proud of the first Woolworth five and ten, a handful of us were sipping beer in the bar of the Hotel Woodward when a comrade announced that a cab driver at the front door knew a lady devoted to erotic hospitality.

In a silent neighborhood of similar houses, separated by narrow side yards, it was a one-family white frame bungalow. A porch ran along the left to a door near the middle that opened into a dining room. On the opposite side: a buffet between two closed doors. At the right: a shallow center hall affording a view of the front room, a parlor most likely.

No radio. No phonograph. No voices. The house was as quiet as a funeral parlor, until the door on the right squeaked open.

A woman about thirty, clutching a faded blue men's bathrobe, slouched against the left jamb, her face deadpan as though she were not quite awake, obviously a stranger to cosmetics.

A few seconds after she closed the door behind Sgt. X and herself, a light went on in the front room. A man paced slowly from side to side, an infant nestled in his arms. I stepped out to the porch, the side yard, fresh air and the stars, Corporal Carlucci close behind me.

Afterward Sgt. X became the butt of teasing because he seemed to have had only enough time to open his fly. He only smiled. Perhaps he had his own little secret.

Another comrade next day rhapsodized about surrendering his virginity in the back of a cruising sedan. A medic, incidentally, stood ready back in camp to inject a germicide in to the urethras of all such adventurers.

While Pine Camp pampered no one with creature comforts, a phenomenon that may well have been a deliberate contrast with Camp Smith, our officers were evidently concerned with our health. For example there was "short-arm inspection". Enlisted men stood in double ranks, their pants down, hands holding up shirt tails, while a medical officer strode by looking for symptoms of venereal disease.

On other occasions, walking along the same formation, an officer carrying a bottle of "c – c" pills asked each man (in earthy terms) whether that day his bowels had moved.

Raucous laughter drew our attention to an enlisted man in Company B, our next door neighbors, so to speak. The poor fellow was sitting on his foot locker in the entrance to his tent, shaving his pubic hair, while his buddies roared in amusement. He was infected with lice. Shaving and kerosene had been prescribed. Though he appeared to take the kidding in good grace, I pitied him. In his distress and embarrassment there was no privacy, a fact true for the whole operation, from the moment we put on the uniform, yet more poignant in this instance surely.

We got along well enough without flush toilets, but we did have cold showers, in a square enclosure about twenty feet on a side, set on a wooden platform with broad sides surrounding a score of showerheads. Wearing only raincoats and shoes, the company marched in double file. They were ushered in, squad by squad.

Under military discipline, smoking on duty was forbidden, except when expressly allowed temporarily. The conventional formula being "Smoke, if ya got 'em". Several of us cigarette addicts bought "Red Man" chewing tobacco. Having so often to spit, however, guaranteed short life to the fad.

Before retreat every evening, the company stood for inspection by Capt. Haffey, Lt. Tassetano or Lt. Tyler. Not only did the barrel have to shine, as though the rifle had never been fired, and the rest of it spotless, but shoes had to shine also, despite whatever abuse they may have endured hours earlier. Ideally we would have had two pairs, one worn only for inspections and parades, but in the real world we were saved by "Dyanshine", a liquid cordovan-colored polish that worked miracles, sold by neighborhood shoemakers.

Before we marched back to the New York Central coaches, we made sure we were not about to carry home Canadian coins, which up there, close to the border, were used interchangeably at par.

Tuesday, October 23, 1990

After the rigors of Pine Camp, we were primed to appreciate the luxuries of Camp Smith during the summer of 1939. Tents on wooden platforms. Permanent wooden buildings for mess halls, px, guard house, and latrines with flush toilets and concrete floors.

Half of each company's tents faced the other half across an unpaved "company street", each pair separated by just enough space to accommodate the tent pegs and stays. Slightly more space was allotted between the backs of neighboring company's' tents. As a regular practice, when a company was at mess, two men were assigned (one left, one right) to stand guard at the rear corners of the first tents, there to keep watch against possible sneak thieves from other units, for every man was held accountable for all equipment issued to him. To lose an item was to pay for it. Incidentally, the Springfields were never at risk; each had a recorded serial number.

Just as at Pine Camp, C Company dined well, in fact even better, sheltered in the comfortable mess hall. Even so, we had that year a new member of the squad who bemoaned our having always "delicatessen", never "dairy".

Tables, assigned to squads, seated four on each side. That man's table manners were so primitive that the rest of us competed for the three places on the side with him, so as to avoid having to look at him, with his arms anchored like flying buttresses, and his chin hovering close to the mess kit.

Infantrymen were required regularly to "qualify" on the rifle, to achieve a prescribed minimum score. With normal vision, sighting and firing were simple enough, and the precise range was known, 200 yds. Critical variables were, first, one's ability to hold the weapon steady, then the wind, and lastly the peculiar characteristics of each rifle. The test was taken with the rifle each man had had chosen at random from the rack in the Brooklyn armory. Like cars of the same year and model, Springfields all looked alike, and yet, like cars, there were individual differences, so that several rounds had to be fired before the rifleman learned how best to aim, to compensate. "Marksmen" those with consistently good scores. Excellent scores earned "Sharpshooter" medals.

When the first sergeant called for a man for a chore, such as k.p., corporals assigned squad members in turn, equitably. At Camp Smith that year our squad had a corporal and one of his younger brothers. Lest he be suspected of favoritism, the corporal sent the brother about half the time. Yet the lad was always cheerful.

Every summer session included several days on bivouac, away from the amenities of base camp, (such as running water,) sleeping on the bare ground under two man pup tents formed by buddies combining their "shelter halves".

The PX stocked bottled beer, of course, and yet while officers and sentries chose not to see, at night a few of us used to sneak down the cliff and to hike into Peekskill, as though we needed the exercise.

In the course of daily field maneuvers, infantrymen became conditioned to respond at once to aggressive or defensive commands. Perfect teamwork was essential to success in military operations. Late in the second week, at the order "Hit the dirt", I landed in poison ivy. This I deduced a day or two later when my hands and forearms swelled up, itching painfully.

First Lieutenant Tassetano knew just what to do. With yellow laundry soap and liquid ammonia from the cook, he would bathe away the scourge. It was like treating a headache with blows from a club.

As I passed close to the colonel's tent on the way to the ambulance, a voice boomed out "Button that collar!"

The post hospital at West Point was truly first class, excellent in every respect. (Yes, my dream came true; I got to West Point.) Two or three ambulatory enlisted men shared the handsome ward, professionals stationed at the academy, one of whom eager to gripe about the drudgery and boredom of his daily routine under a lieutenant he held in contempt. His discontent was, I guess, owing in part to his ailment.

Meals, served in restaurant-style china, were great. When we were not in the mess hall, or receiving treatments, we were free to lounge or to roam in handsome bathrobes.

Frequent applications of calamine lotion and later of a weak solution of potassium permanganate served me well.

Only once were peace and quiet disturbed, and then only briefly, when a military escort passed the hospital with a visiting Cuban general.

After three or four days I was discharged, given back my uniform, driven down to the Peekskill railroad station, and handed a ticket to Grand Central Station. It happened that I had no money for the subway to Brooklyn, not even a nickel to get me home. At St. Francis Friary on 31st Street, near Penn Station, the brother porter gave me a nickel, saving me from a long hike. Oh, he wanted to give me more, but the nickel was all I needed.

Thursday, October 25, 1990

In August 1940, under First Army commander Lieut. Gen. Hugh A. Drum, the 27th Division joined the professionals and reservists in maneuvers for three weeks in St. Lawrence County, N.Y., along the Canadian border. Equally involved were the five Guard divisions of Massachusetts, Connecticut, New Jersey, Pennsylvania and Maryland.

The "Blue" and "Red" armies contended in "war games" while referees roamed the fields observing, judging, assessing, and finally designating "casualties", combatants ordered to retire for so many minutes before rejoining their units. Just as in the smaller operations at Camp Smith and Pine Camp, here too we riflemen followed orders, ignorant of over-all tactical goals, not to mention the underlying strategy. My mother, incidentally, kept me informed about the maneuvers through newspaper clippings, most from the <u>Brooklyn Eagle</u>.

Our first platoon, having marched without incident across streams knee-deep, over hills, and through the woods, was ordered to take cover as we marched close to a clearing. We had been in single file along a path just wide enough for a farm wagon. While we were standing hidden by the foliage on the edge of a broad meadow, off to the left, at a range of about five hundred yards, a long line of infantry, shoulder-to-shoulder, appeared at the crest of a hill. Whether comrades or enemy, I'll never know. Our Springfields and B.A.R.s were loaded with blanks; yet we fired not one shot as the unknowns passed out of sight. If enemy, they evidently had not discovered us, nor did we see them again. What impressed me to remember the incident were two reactions.

At the order "Take cover!" I jumped to the left among bushes hiding a rail fence where a chipmunk was perched atop a post. So startled was he that he stood motionless, a chipmunk, for several seconds, not two feet away. He had nothing to fear from me, of course, but he couldn't have known that. Then, a moment later, when skirmishers appeared, for a second I was frightened, as though I were about to be fired on, a mindless reflex, to be sure, for we were boys playing soldier, but a reflex to make me wonder afterward whether in the real world I'd have acted with honor under fire in spite of terror.

On bivouac one night we marched in the moonless dark, each man, in silence, guided only by a small strip of white cloth dangling on the backpack of the nearest man in front.

Conditions in the field were rugged, and yet at our DeKalb Junction base camp we had enough drinking water, hanging from tripods in "Lister bags". We always set out with full canteens, of course. Even so, I'll not forget the afternoon that we were tormented more by thirst than fatigue, the every-day morale tester. As we were trudging past a farmhouse, I chanced to recognize a well in the back yard, the kind with a cast-iron pump on the ground-level cover. By the grace of Providence, a few minutes later we were ordered to the side of the road for a short rest. The farmer was kind enough – God bless him – to allow my buddy, Henry Hasenpflug, and me to fill the squad's canteens.

Water was too precious to use for anything but drinking, and so shaving regularly was not ordered. There happened to be, however, a marsh close by, between our tents and a herd of cows. Stagnant water was better than none at all, and it did serve the purpose, at least once.

Whereas in Pine Camp we had made do with slit trenches, and in Camp Smith had been pampered with flush toilets, up near DeKalb Junction we had temporary privies, long wooden boxes, with rows of oval holes on top, covering deep pits, the amenity surrounded by a wooden fence.

Regardless of where in St. Lawrence County we happened to be, we in Company C were provided three hot meals every day. Our esteemed cook, Irv, managed to find us every time, in a truck loaded with large double-walled cans and bottles. Once, on a forced march, we eluded him until late in the evening, but rarely were we hungry for long.

The company, or at least the first platoon, lay stretched prone along a ridge, overlooking a small detachment of enemy infantry lying near the base of the hill. While we all lay still, until referees could assess the situation, no shot, incidentally, having been fired, we and the enemy identified our units, for we were close enough. They were from the Massachusetts National Guard, the "Yankee" division.

Then there was the time I was posted alone at the intersection of two country roads through a wooded area. I've forgotten whatever instructions I was given, but no doubt to "guard" the crossroads. As usual, my Springfield was loaded with blanks. While I lounged in a dry drainage ditch, the peace and quiet were disturbed by a canvas-covered Army truck churning up dust and gravel as it sped by. Whether theirs or ours, I couldn't tell before it disappeared. Nevertheless I ought to have fired, but I was too slow to react. Before writing this, I have never confided the incident to anyone, not anyone.

Being scout often for the first squad, I stalked "point" for the company, an assignment I saw as an honor, a testimonial, although that did not blind me to the fact that in the real world I'd have been most vulnerable, easily the first casualty.

We were laboring up a steep hill, partly wooded, the rest of the squad in single file about thirty yards behind me. Nearing exhaustion but required to plod ahead, for one stopped to rest only on orders, at the crest I stumbled among a small detachment of enemy lying concealed. Of course, they jumped up and surrounded their "prisoner". I was embarrassed, to be sure, and yet I did welcome the pause, for I was so worn out, so out of breath, that for several minutes I couldn't speak. The rest of the squad came charging up close behind me, arrayed then in a skirmish line, halting just a few yards from the top. Corporal Johnnie Cates boldly demanded my release just before he bellowed "Fix bayonets!" The enemy, no gamblers, and more prudent than foolhardy, chose to retreat quietly. None of us asked Johnnie what the next command would have been; we didn't want to know.

It happened during the maneuvers that President Roosevelt, having conferred somewhere near the border with Canadian Prime Minister Mackenzie King, was due to return to Washington in a motorcade that would pass close to the base camps of the 27th Division. In anticipation, the entire division was arrayed in close formation in a gently-rising meadow, facing the road linking Canton and DeKalb Junction. Fortunately we were not burdened with the usual backpacks. We waited for what seemed like three or four hours, although it was probably not more than two. Roosevelt's open touring car sped by so fast that I did not get a glimpse of the president "neutral" in favor of the English, with his "Lend-Lease" giveaways. But then we were not there to see, but rather to be seen.

Tuesday, November 6, 1990

Holy Name Province had a minor seminary – four years of high school and two years of college – in upstate Callicoon, a tiny village on the Delaware River.

The three-year enlistment in the National Guard was to expire in January 1941 (or was it February). Even so, having heard of precedents, I requested discharge effective on or before September 1, 1940, after our return from First Army Maneuvers in August. The date was critical because I had been accepted for admission to Callicoon for that fall term. Captain Howard Dicker of Company C assured me there'd be no hindrance. Had there been, I'd have had to wait until September 1941 to enter the seminary, losing a year.

Shortly after that request, which was months in advance of the anticipated discharge, I was demoted from Private First Class, with no more explanation than had accompanied the promotion. Standard procedure I presume. Incidentally, when finally the discharge paper was mailed to me upstate, the reason given was "for the good of the service". Now, make sense of that! Of course, I could have asked for clarification from Capt. Dicker, but by then it didn't matter; I had risen into another world.

Thursday, November 15, 1990

The rector of St. Joseph's Seraphic Seminary (Seraphic here being a synonym for Franciscan) mailed a brochure spelling out requirements, programs, fees, goals, spirit, rules, etc. This aspirants approved for admission got a fairly good picture of what to expect, a prospect to most alluring. It was my good fortune in the spring of 1940, moreover, to enjoy a preview of the seminary.

On Mothers' Day the friars of Holy Name Province used to sponsor a bus ride from 31st Street to Callicoon, filling four or five buses with families and friends from the metropolitan area. Of course my mother and I were delighted by the opportunity.

The main building, joined to the chapel by an enclosed bridge at the west end, perched near the top of a hill high above the village and the Delaware River. From the top floor (third) dormitory windows, one could see several miles down toward Cochecton. The square granite tower in the middle held a water tank kept full by springs higher on the hill in the back, that hill surmounted by a life size crucifix. Crowning the tower was a clock with a dial on each side. When the wind was favorable, one could hear the Westminster chimes a mile away. The bells, by the way, were silenced after dusk.

Apart from the walk in front of the building, the only level area in the seminary grounds was the path around the man-made lake (fed by an uphill spring) a round pond about twenty-five yards across, behind the chapel and close to Route 97 as it climbed up to Hankins and Hancock. By the grace of Divine Providence, the lake was never called upon to serve its primary purpose: to provide a reservoir for fighting fires.

A red-brick gymnasium (with basketball court, game room, two bowling lanes, and showers) stood a few paces from the back door, at the southeastern corner of the ball field that sloped gently uphill. A path east of the field and the gym, and close to a small grove of very tall pines, led up to cow pastures and the crucifix, from which site one could enjoy a vast panorama. God's country indeed.

Among the points of interest was the shrine path, along the west side of the ball field, leading to a spring and the handball courts. Then too there were the gym, library, and the chapel, that Romanesque beauty which served also Holy Cross parish.

Friday, November 16, 1990

The children's encyclopedia that Lillian and I had loved, The Book of Knowledge, I shipped (incidentally, in the original wooden box that I had used to hold tools) to the seminary's librarian, Fr. Barnabas Abele, O.F.M., who later donated it to the Holy Cross parish elementary school, staffed by Franciscan sisters from Alleghany, New York.

Railway Express Agency in those days would for a modest fee pick up heavy baggage, such as trunks, from home and ship it to the baggage car of the train one was to ride. A priceless service for those living in high-rise apartment houses.

The Erie Railroad scheduled two trains daily from Jersey City to Callicoon and beyond, the first arriving around noon, the other about six o'clock. The earlier was slow, stopping everywhere, even where there was no station. Yet to this newcomer it offered the more prudent choice. Thus it happened that I labored alone up that steep hill about a quarter mile, in each hand a loaded suitcase, the laundry number twenty five sewn on all my clothes. Lay brothers with a farm wagon would fetch all the trunks the next day.

Saturday November 17, 1990

The program, non-elective, of the four high school years, stressing liberal arts, led to a New York State Regents diploma, which program included four years of Latin, and two each of Greek and Public Speaking. Academic standards were high; getting into the seminary was easier than staying in. Those failing to keep pace would not return the following year, Latin being the most troublesome challenge. How ironic it was that the patron saint of parish priests, St. John Vianney, Cure of Ars, could not have survived at Callicoon. God does work in mysterious ways.

The two college years (under the charter of St. Bonaventure College) stressed for Latin, Greek, German, English and Public Speaking. There also were no electives.

Daily Schedule

6:30 A.M. We were awakened by a friar clanging an infernal brass bell.
7:00 Mass
7:45 Breakfast
9:00 – 12:00 Classes
12:00 Dinner
1:00 – 2:00 Study Hall
2:00 – 3:00 Class
3:00 – 5:00 Free time
5:00 – 6:00 Study Hall
6:00 Supper, followed informally by the rosary

7:30 – 8:30 Study Hall
8:30 Night Prayers
9:30 Lights out.

Wednesday and Saturday afternoons were free until 5 o'clock. No classes were held on Sundays, holy days or "free" days.

Monday, November 19, 1990

Access to the dormitory was forbidden before 4 o'clock, at which time one could wash, shave, change clothes. At no time was talking permitted there. Most of us observed this rule in both spirit and letter, with rare exception, for instance to borrow soap. One classmate, however, Mike Barbarossa, was so conscientious that in an emergency I believe he would have hesitated before shouting "Fire!" Mike, by the way, had served a hitch with the regular Army in Pearl Harbor's Scofield Barracks, site of the novel From Here to Eternity.

Thursday, November 22, 1990

Up in the rolling hills of Sullivan County it never became oppressively hot, because of the typical low humidity. Although winters were long – from the first snowfall the ground was hidden until spring – the dry air mitigated the harsh Arctic bite that at home we had come to expect.

None of us ever swam in the lake, nor do I recall anyone ever falling in. After it froze, however, and the ice in time became at least a foot thick, it served for skating and, of course, hockey, the sport favored especially by our Eskimos from Massachusetts, many of whom were skilled players.

About a mile upstream from the truss bridge to Pennsylvania, on the New York side, was a place suitable for swimming, and isolated enough to provide privacy among the trees on the bank while we donned or doffed our trunks. By September the weather was too cool, but when spring finally returned, bringing robins, red-winged blackbirds, and warm breezes, we'd ask permission to swim on Wednesday and Saturday afternoons. The Prefect, or his assistant, usually consented, but not before the first thunderstorm of the year.

The Delaware River froze over, of course, at least the top, a thick jagged mass in narrow stretches, a natural pedestrian bridge for the adventurous, and the occasion – or so it was rumored – for a pool among the people down in the village. The pot went to the one whose guess came closest to the day and hour that the river began to thaw and the ice to break up. The cracking was loud enough.

Wednesday, December 5, 1990

As aspiring seminary students and would be Friars Minor, we at St. Joseph's, overlooking the pristine valley of the Delaware in remote Sullivan County, enjoyed a priceless insulation from the distractions, the cares, the vulgarity, the frivolities of the mundane world we had turned our backs on. It was virtually a year round retreat. Of course we missed in varying degrees such indulgences as beer, cigarettes, bacon and eggs, scrapple, toast, marmalade, whipped cream. Yes, and we kept count of how many days there were until the next vacation, Christmas or summer. Thus when a classmate scrawled a number on a blackboard, we cheered; no one had to ask what it meant.

Nevertheless, we were a happy fraternity, Catholic gentlemen bound together by the same values, the same heroes, the same aspirations, the same loyalties, the same challenges, bound by mutual respect, mutual love. Indeed it is not exaggerating to say that after a couple of years we were closer than most blood brothers. Hence it was a sad blow whenever anyone dropped out, especially a classmate. There was, for instance, in the first year, Larry R., for whom Latin proved an obstacle. Ah, but then there was the mysterious lad who arrived at Callicoon, for the first time, around noon, climbed up the hill, looked around, and marched back down again in time for the four o'clock train. What do you suppose he had hoped to find?

Snow on the hills made it difficult or impossible for visitors, whether traveling by train or car. In early fall, however, and after Lent especially, hardly a weekend passed without some student's asking permission to dine with his family or friends at George's Restaurant or the Olympia

197

Hotel, down near the Erie station, or even up to the Hancock House. The Olympia, by the way, small but excellent in food and service, stood so close to the tracks that, as my mother reported, during the night the whole room rattled whenever a freight train thundered by.

George's was famous for great food, especially pecan pie. From there if you trudged about one hundred yards up the steep curved road above the hotel, up to Route 97, and turned right, very shortly you'd come to a large stone Victorian house with huge windows and oaken woodwork, the home of the two Halliday sisters, transplants from New York City, ladies who shared two or three bedrooms for a small fee, as a favor to the Franciscans. Their Sunday breakfasts were a gourmet delight.

On the far side of the Erie tracks there sprawled a block of single-story commercial buildings, side-by-side. A newspaper, The Sullivan County Democrat, stood on the end near the mouth of Hortonville Creek. A small bank and the A. & P. crowded the other end, separated from the post office by the short road to the bridge across to Wayne County, Pennsylvania.

In about the middle of the row, Larry Milk (Mayor of Callicoon) had a shop, part luncheonette & ice-cream parlor, part "candy store". In the back he also had a small unpretentious movie theater. Several times he invited the seminarians to a private showing on Saturday afternoons, at no charge. Evidently he was generous and thoughtful; he had nothing to gain from us, for there was no way we could repay his kindness. Indeed, his place was off limits normally, not that we had any money. One of his treats I've not forgotten: The Pride of the Yankees, a biography of Lou Gehrig, starring Gary Cooper and Teresa Wright. I must confess to being more impressed by the charming Teresa.

Thursday, December 6, 1990

Although our lives were regulated twenty four hours a day, seven days a week, the only dress requirement – other than when serving Mass – was that we wear traditional clerical black suits on Sundays. White shirts and black ties, of course. At other times we seminarians looked like typical college students throughout the Northeast. Newcomers wore out whatever suits they brought. Only then were they replaced by black. So too with shoes, overcoats, fedoras, etc. Thus before he graduated, everyone had made the transition. The same formal black was worn on the infrequent occasions when the choir – more often only a part of it – sang at funeral Masses in any of the outlying mission chapels, whose pastors taught and lived at the seminary, those in Hankins, Cochecton, Narrowsburg, Pond Eddy, and Jeffersonville.

The large room in the basement, under the library, where our trunks and luggage were stored, and where wooden lockers clung to the walls, had a scent all its own, not like any other anywhere, and not unpleasant. Indeed, we savored the aroma each time we got back from vacation, as though rejoining an old friend, happy to be home again. "Ah, doesn't that smell good!' In this it was just as I remember Grandma Foley's house, a delight every time, every room breathing its own unique fragrance.

"Latin One and Two Special" was the specialty of Fr. Flavian Colligan, O.F.M., whom we came to admire for both scholarship and humility. Engelmann's Latin Grammar and he resolved almost all knotty problems. Whenever a doubt remained, a rare occurrence, he held the matter in abeyance until he conferred with Fr. Cuthbert. When, years later, several of us thanked him for a solid foundation, he brushed off the praise with something to the effect "Oh, I was only a chapter ahead of you all the time".

Fr. Cuthbert Cotton, O.F.M., older and more experienced in teaching, was, like Fr. Flavian, very good at it, though in style more flamboyant. He used to tell us "You won't be a Latin student before you've worn out your first dictionary."

Tuesday, December 11, 1990

The faculty at St. Joseph's had a young scholar whose major field was history. Fr. X was well grounded and especially interested in the history of our republic. With no need to refer to notes or texts, he could discourse for an hour in detail the philosophies of Jefferson, Madison, Hamilton, Franklin, etc. He could well have agreed with Thoreau that the best government is that which governs least, meaning of course that it provides only the barest essential services. Consequently Fr. X held in contempt Roosevelt's "New Deal" with its proliferating bureaucracies, its creeping socialism.

Wednesday, December 12, 1990

In late 1940 or early'41, when the Selective Service, the draft, was initiated, the friars and their charges registered with the local draft board, which met in an upper room of the firehouse, alongside the Erie tracks and close to Larry Milk's place. Subsequently we were all classified as "4-D", a designation the clergy and seminarians shared with patients in mental institutions, or so it was reported. "4-F" identified those with physical disabilities. "1-A", those likely to be called up and assigned as needed to the various armed forces.

Candidates so classified were at the risk of course of being shipped to branches of the service that they would not have chosen. Hence to volunteer for the Navy, as many did, was to avoid the Army. But then to volunteer for any branch was to avoid the others. Similarly, volunteers with special skills had a good chance of having their choices respected.

A cousin, Eddie Kelly, of Darby, Pennsylvania, classified "1-A", volunteered for the Army, promised a place in the Air Corps. Following basic training, off he was sent to the infantry. The irony stings: had he waited for the draft, he could have been sent to the Navy. What is more, when he preferred the Army, he could as easily have chosen the Navy or Coast Guard.

Around 8 o'clock AM Hawaiian time (2 PM New York time) on Sunday December 7, 1941, the Japanese bombed the American Naval Base at Pearl Harbor and drew the United States into the Second World War.

The Japanese attack on our fleet at Pearl Harbor was to us in Callicoon a stunning blow. In our rural seclusion, American involvement in the war that had dragged on for over two years in Asia and Europe seemed unlikely, in spite of President Roosevelt, England's not-so-secret ally.

I was torn between going back to Brooklyn and staying in the seminary. Did I owe it to my former comrades in Company C to re-enlist? After supper that same Sunday December 7, 1941, I decided to open my heart to Fr. Gregory. I'd follow his advice. At his office door I found Jack Doyle waiting his turn. Presently a line formed behind us. Fr. Gregory's position – indicated to us all in turn presumably – he stated about like this "You've registered for the draft. If and when the country needs you, you'll be called to serve, at which time you'll go with my blessing".

Early in 1942 local Civil Defense men built a tiny wooden shack on the upper edge of the slope between the seminary's lake and Route 97, where it climbed toward Hankins. That site afforded a clear view down the Delaware valley, and easy access from the village, standing close to the side entrance to the seminary grounds.

Equipped with binoculars, silhouettes of civilian and military aircraft, telephone, and kerosene burning heater, it became an observation post manned all day, every day, by seminarians and local civilians in turn. On the few occasions when a plane was heard and seen, the observer reported its type, altitude, and direction of flight. In those days, by the way, all planes were propeller-driven, none of which was fast enough or high enough to escape recognition, though identifying the type was difficult.

Before the war we used to see and hear the Erie's giant black steam locomotives, at all hours, dragging scores of boxcars and tank cars up and down the valley, familiar welcome elements of local color. After Hitler made the fatal blunder of declaring war on us – to the delight of Winston Churchill – we began to see trains of flat bead cars heading south, toward the Port of New York, their bulky loads concealed under brown tarpaulins.

Sunday, January 13, 1991

The seminarian, on the way to an awesome lifelong commitment, can't escape reviewing his prospects and motives from time to time. Do I in fact have a vocation, or rather have I been deceiving myself? Have I stayed despite my doubts because I'm afraid to face an uncertain future elsewhere? Do I have what it takes to become a holy Franciscan priest?

The apostles, having been called explicitly to become "fishers of men", had no occasion for such doubts; to be sure, an enviable advantage. My confessor, Fr. Barnabas Abele, O.F.M., once pointed out that in the church's view, when a bishop, just before ordaining, calls out a candidate's name, then he has a vocation.

I chose to lay bare my soul, so to speak, to the visiting confessor, to whom I spelled out the doubts that had been harassing me. Those sporadic slides into depression – now infrequent and brief – I did not see as impediments. At the core of my quandary, however, lay only chastity. Was it reasonable, or was it foolish, to aspire to a chaste celibate life?

The friar advised that I enter the novitiate as planned. The cloistered year of meditation, conferences, and liturgical exercises is ideal for assessing one's fitness, guided by the Holy Ghost. Indeed that is high among the goals during the year as a religious novice.

Tuesday, January 15, 1991

My mother had a friend living upstate in the rural hamlet Willow, about fifteen minutes northwest of Kingston. We planned to accept her invitation to spend a few days after graduation on Monday June 12, 1944.

On Friday, August 4, 1944, the feast of St. Dominic, our class, all twenty-eight of us, was to report for induction into the Order of Friars Minor at the Franciscan Monastery, 174 Ramsey Street, Paterson, New Jersey. The schedule called for a retreat until Saturday, August 12, 1944, the feast of St. Clare, when we would be received formally as novices.

Tuesday, January 29, 1991

In a neighborhood of modest mostly one-family houses, the monastery and its garden occupied all but a small part of a city block which it shared with the red-brick parish church of St. Bonaventure – attached on the west side – and also a handful of neighbors on the north, beyond the garden wall.

Ramsey Street sloped down from the church on the corner of Danforth Avenue. The monastery's oaken main door, level with the church and the intervening Shrine of St. Anthony, stood above high granite steps. Consequently, shops for woodworking, bookbinding, tailoring, etc. and also the St. Anthony's Bread dining room, though in the so-called basement, were in fact at ground level. A handsome cloistered chapel wing jutted into the garden in the back.

There in the novitiate we were insulated from every day cares and concerns, from radios, from telephones, from newspapers, from mail, from stultifying popular music. Our professors back in Calicoon were so right: "Enjoy the novitiate; it's going to be the most carefree year of your lives."

Towards the end of the retreat Fr. Gerald called us one by one to his room to choose our new names. Following the traditional protocol, we went in class order. Jack Eustace came out after choosing or accepting Alexander, my second choice. Then it was my turn. "John?" "Oh no," says Fr. Gerard, "We have too many Johns already". I had known there were a dozen or so in the province, leading me to suppose there'd be no objection to another. My mother's father had been John Andrew Foley. Fr. Gerard stood firm not that I was much of a salesman.

Luke Dee sounded too much like a Chinese laundry. A silly reason to spurn the name of an evangelist.

"We haven't had a Severin since Fr. Severin died about eight years ago". I agreed to Severin, but alas not for long. At that time there was a frequently-aired radio commercial for Savarin brand coffee that ended with "Man, that's coffee". This phrase several of my classmates found amusement in repeating for my benefit. Looking back now, I don't know why that annoyed me. At any rate, once again I demonstrated my immaturity when a day or two later I trudged back to Mickey's room and asked for a change. We agreed readily on Pualinus Joseph. Incidentally, there were notable instances of alliteration in the class: Cajetan Campbell, Norbert Norton, Owen Ormsby, Dominic Dean and Cassian Corcoran.

Friday, February 1, 1991

All religious take the vow of poverty, forfeiting the legal right to own anything. Each member owns nothing at all, not even the habit. The community, however, in some orders and congregations, does collectively own its houses and furnishings. But Franciscans – except for the Conventuals, - and hence the name – own nothing either individually or collectively. If like our Holy Father Saint Francis, a candidate fully embraces the virtue of poverty, the vow adds no perceptible burden.

The vow of chastity is in fact a misnomer. More precisely it ought to be vow of celibacy, forfeiting the right to marry. To view it from another perspective, a religious is not bound more by the virtue of chastity then he had been as a layman. The Sixth and Ninth Commandments are equally grave matters for everyone everywhere, though the matter of scandal may add to the gravity.

The vow of obedience is the least burdensome, and the one rarely offended against, because it obliges the religious to comply with a direct order of a superior imposed expressly under the vow. "Under the law of obedience I order you to..." or words to that effect. Occasions for such formal commands seldom arise, but when they do, superiors are reluctant to act, to place the subordinate in a position to incur grave penalties. Of course the virtue of obedience is another matter, for while vows are instruments, means to goals, virtues have intrinsic value in themselves. As the adage has it: Virtue is its own reward.

Monday February 4, 1991

Grace having been said, the community seated at table, and I had just begun to read when Fr. Patrick, who happened to preside, rang the bell, calling for silence. He announced that President Roosevelt had died at Warm Springs, Georgia. It was Thursday, April 12, 1945. His failing health had been public knowledge for a long time. Few however were aware of how grave the illness had been, for he had hung on to power.

May 8, 1945 was V-E Day (Victory in Europe), celebrated by the United States and the Allied Nations. The day before Germany had surrendered unconditionally to the Allies and Russia in a ceremony at Rheims France.

Toward novices under his tutelage Fr. Gerald affected a serious humorless manner, a facade of hiding a big heart, as he demonstrated to the would-be visitor at the door of the monastery.

Bells Goskowski – his name may have been John – got the nickname up in Callicoon, in the oblique reference to his amateur boxing. It was he, by the way, who at Holpp's Lodge had been a kitchen helper. By the late spring of 1945, we had been out of touch, of course, with fellow seminarians left behind, as well as those who had gone ahead. What a pleasant surprise then to have Bells drop in at the novitiate, where outsiders were as rare as English grand opera stars.

On the left side of his olive-drab tunic he wore several decorations including one new to me: Combat Infantryman's Badge, all of which he had earned in Belgium, France and Germany. We strolled and sat in the garden for perhaps an hour. Though cheerful, he appeared tense, a bit on edge, a condition understandable for one back from Hell. Yet he wasn't so nervous as another veteran I would meet near Albany. Discharged and back home it took him weeks to stay calm on hearing an airplane.

In Belgium Bells saw a Franciscan once. Our troops in trucks were passing through a village when it overtook the friar pedaling a bicycle.

A comrade and friend had been killed in battle, a man with a wife and two small children. Bells was en route to the family in Detroit, probably carrying personal effects. We never saw him again. Someone claimed, as I recall, to have gotten a letter after Bells married the widow.

While our class was at the Novitiate, Franciscan Monastery, Ramsey Street, Paterson, New Jersey, we were joined by the admission of a veteran priest, a Ukrainian who for many years had served a rural parish deep inside Brazil. In middle age he was called to become a Franciscan.

He said Mass each morning in the tiny chapel set between rooms set aside as an infirmary, (a function not needed in our time.) I don't recall how it came to be, in a class of almost thirty, but I used to serve as his altar-boy.

The cruets of wine and water stood on a small white table that had a single drawer. One morning after Mass I opened the drawer. To my amazement there lay a tiny reliquary whose labels in abbreviated Latin identified a speck as "Ex Cinertis S. Franc". (From the ashes of St. Francis of Assisi) and another speck "Ex Ossibus S. Clarae". (From the bones of Saint Clare of Assisi). Not "touched-to" but genuine first-class relics of the two Franciscan founders. I was as awestruck I daresay as had been Carter and Carnovan on first peering into the tomb of Tutankhamen.

The infirmarian, Brother Amadeus Schiffhauser, O.F.M., explained that these relics had been brought back from Assisi by the late Brother Andrew Wenning, O.F.M., on pilgrimage celebrating fifty years in the order.

August 6, 1945 was the day a single bomb dropped on Hiroshima Japan, wiped out the city. Such devastation and that suffered by Nagasaki three days later on August 9, 1945 led to the unconditional surrender of Japan and ushered in the Nuclear Age.

Our class entered the monastery on or about August 4th 1945, when we began a retreat, prior to receiving the Franciscan habit. That retreat took about a week. And so, on or about August 12, 1945, we took simple vows of Poverty, Chastity, and Obedience. It was at that time that hydrogen bombs destroyed Hiroshima and Nagasaki, Japan.

At the conclusion of the novitiate one took what were called simple vows, binding for three years, after which he took solemn vows, binding for the rest of his life. Clerics could then be admitted to Holy Orders. The profession of vows, as it was called, bound the religious also to adhere to the rule, constitutions and ordinances of his order or congregation. Clerics, moreover, were further bound, even before Holy Orders, to the recitation daily of the Divine Office, if not in choir, then privately.

Because our class was invested on August 12, 1944, the novitiate, extending by canon Law for a year and a day minimum, should have brought us to the next August 13th for simple profession. That normally would have been the day following investiture of the succeeding class. In 1945, however, August the 12th fell on a Sunday. Consequently both classes were one day late. That was how we made simple profession on Tuesday, August 14, 1945, a few hours as it turned out before Japan surrendered, ending the war, V J Day (Victory in Japan).

Still another event made that day August 14, 1945 especially memorable for me. Following the profession ceremonies in the church, Brother Amadeus presented me with the precious relics of St. Francis and St. Clare as well as the official certificate of authenticity from the Bishop of Assisi.

Saturday, February 9, 1991

A chartered bus was to have ferried the class, as in past years, but on the first morning after the war ended, none was available. Or was it that no driver was available, following a night of celebration? At any rate we were lucky to find seats on a scheduled route. In such a state of euphoria we'd have been content with a hay wagon.

The tiny rural hamlet of Croghan, in Lewis County, lies surrounded by dairy farms about twenty five miles east southeast of Watertown, and perhaps ten miles north of Lowville. The most impressive buildings were St. Stephen's Church and friary, wooden like all the others. Then the parochial school. Across the main street: a small but comfortable hotel, Lewis House, a welcome convenience for visiting relatives, the few hardy souls who found their way so far north.

The faculty at the house of study that shared the friary numbered six priests. Scholastic Philosophy, Hebrew, Greek, English, history and sociology. Some instructors ministered to mission parishes in such neighboring hamlets as Belfort, Indian River and New Brennen.

The cloister had a small chapel where clerics said the Office in choir through the day, as in the novitiate.

The course in Hebrew involved principally translating parts of Genesis into both English and Latin. Similarly, St. Luke's Gospel in the original Greek, or parts of it, was translated into both English and Latin.

The second-floor room assigned to me – like the others apparently at random – had been used in previous years to store blankets etc. This proved a disadvantage. Classmates found complete sets of textbooks left by predecessors, whereas I lacked a key text in Hebrew. Consequently I had to work in the library from its copy. Moreover, the others were beneficiaries of course outlines, lecture notes, translations, graded test papers, etc. left for them in the desks, accumulated by God knows how many earlier occupants. One set of lecture notes even had marginal inserts of puns, jokes, digressions of the instructor.

Not all of us smoked. Those who did were allotted several packs a week. Phillip Morris brand I recall. There may have been others too.

Fr. Robert O'Hea, O.F.M., who taught English, was the only one in the house with pets. (We don't count Br. Bernardine's chickens.) After dinner on clear days he sat on the steps behind the kitchen holding on his lap an open cigar box. Nearby, stacked under the porch, lay a long line of cord wood, home to a couple of chipmunks. Somehow they knew when he was there, for they'd scamper out through the lattice to feed on nuts, raisins, bread, and chunks of apple, whatever. One was so tame that he sometimes climbed into the box.

A new – and I suppose larger – hen house was being built by the friars for Br. Bernardine's flock, a project with which some of us clerics helped. It happened that a local farmer cut down a large cherry tree, and had the sawmill in the village slice it into boards. These he donated to the friars. Cherry, as you probably know, is among the most beautiful hardwoods, the delight of cabinet makers and carvers. What use do you suppose the Guardian made of that treasure? You're right; the floor. Sad. Maybe Noah would have approved.

Winters were so severe that well insulated garages were not enough. They had to be heated. Kerosene burners served nicely. The pastors of St. Stephens and the mission churches needed cars of course, and so the wooden garage in the back was wide, broad enough for an extra bay. That space on the end housed a chicken brooder. By spring the chicks were strong enough for the range.

Summer and fall, with warm days and cool nights, were pleasant in the North Country. Winter, however, arrived early and stayed late. Some wag characterized the seasons as "winter and August". My mother ventured up for a visit around Christmas. Fr. Eugene Serafin, O.F.M. was kind enough to drive me down to the railroad at Lowville. The thermometer at the window of the station master registered minus 14 degrees F. Yes, we were wearing trousers under the habits.

In the early weeks at Croghan we used to swim, weather permitting, in an isolated clear mountain lake in nearby Adirondack Park. We'd drive for an hour through primeval woods, passing streams, beaver dams and ponds. The only sign of man: the dirt roads. Awesome. God's country.

One afternoon I was deaf by the time we got back. In both ears. A physician in the village, a tall man probably over eighty, suggested a specialist in Watertown. While his nurse held a kidney-shaped pan under each ear, the doctor, using a bulky instrument like a grease gun, flushed out clots of wax.

One afternoon at breakfast, as soon as the Guardian said <u>Religiose colloquameer</u>, nine classmates at the table burst into spirited speculation about "the fire" during the night. At once I suspected an elaborate conspiracy in a practical joke, such as a tenderfoot often finds at summer camp. (Remember the snipe hunt?) It turned out, however, that with the exception of Frater Boniface Hanley and me, everyone in the house, and maybe in the village, had been awakened when the sawmill caught fire, a short stroll from us. Fire engines and residents hurried from miles around. Fr. Neal Mac Donald, O.F.M. used to bring Holy Communion on Sundays to an elderly parishioner too infirm to go to Mass. On hearing the sirens he rushed out to the mill. There she was.

We provided the choir for St. Stephen's Church and an occasional procession too, as for instance in devotions honoring the Blessed Mother and on Corpus Christi. As many as could fit in a car sang at the funeral of a young farmer in Belfort. The poor man had been run over by his own wagon. Afterwards a generous neighbor treated us to home-made layer cake.

Friday, February 15, 1991

Clerics in the Holy Name Province attended summer school at St. Bonaventure College. In 1946 those interested in mathematics and sciences were free to choose Siena College. A handful of us picked Siena.

St. Bernardine of Siena College, about four miles north of Albany on Route 9, had built by the summer of 1946 the first two permanent buildings: Siena Hall (Georgian Colonial Style) and the gymnasium. Students were men commuters, but evening classes were open to women.

Recently discharged war veterans formed a large part of Siena's student body, as indeed at many colleges around the country. The Federal government, in gratitude and to compensate for the interruption of civilian careers, paid their college expenses: tuition, textbooks and such supplies as slide rules etc. All under what came to be called informally "The G. I. Bill".

During the war the college prepared small classes of Naval cadets in the Naval Reserve Officers Training Corps. (N.R.O.T.C.). Their temporary barracks, essentially a large room with steel bunk beds, - the friars dubbed it Navy House − became at the close of that program summer home to clerics from the Holy Name Province.

The aggregate of properties north of Spring Street, formerly broad fields and farms, which were being converted slowly into a campus, still had standing several old frame houses close to Loudonville Road. In the absence of a proper friary, they were made do as substitutes. Thus the Franciscan community was scattered − if so dispersed the friars could still be called a community. Yet there was one small compensation: three priests had dogs sharing their rooms. Two of the pets I used to take care of on weekends, when their masters were helping out in parishes.

Fr. Raymond Beane's Boston Bull readily demonstrated legendary "Bulldog tenacity". One need only wave a towel or rag in front of him, and then let him bite it. He'd hang on even while being swung in the air. Never was he first to let go. Fr. John Weaver's Cocker Spaniel, Buttons, he of the silky golden coat, was not so scrappy or vocal; yet he was just as lovable.

I took care of them out of love for them as well respect and admiration for their masters, nor would I have done less if Fr. Raymond had not invited me to listen to his classical music albums. Especially enjoyable were contemporary Russian composers Sergei Prokofiev and the Armenian Aram Khachaturian.

A lay student had a through-bred white female Poodle. He hoped to breed her with a sire equally patrician. At a basketball game he brought her on a leash. Chico, a small short-haired male of plebian lineage, part Chihuahua, had the run of the campus; yet he was never far from his friar master, even in classrooms. On the night of that game, however, he chose to wait just outside the gym. Afterwards, as the fans filed out, the Poodle was let off the leash. By the time her owner got to the front steps, there was Chico answering the call. "The best laid plans of mice and men......." But all the puppies were beautiful and white.

A small flock of noisy geese was the special concern of another friar. Unlike the docile chickens, they were ill-tempered enough to peck with vigor at those with the temerity to walk close, as though to repel intruders. Eventually they had to be banished from the campus.

Frater Zachary O'Friel was the only cleric that I recall taking a course in the evening. Normally by noon we were finished with lectures and lab work in mathematics, chemistry, physics and biology. There was of course lots of "homework". Even so, we still found time a couple of times a week for walking or swimming.

A lake several miles east of Troy, surrounded by summer bungalows, had a narrow public area with a bathhouse to which we were escorted most often by the Master of Clerics.

Some of us liked to swim across, maybe 300 yards. A hornet or wasp one day kept landing on my bare head. I ducked each time, suspecting its intention, and, unlike our holy Father Saint Francis, unwilling to give it the benefit of the doubt. A couple in a canoe, evidently fearing I was drowning, rushed over, whereupon the bug lost interest. Maybe the canoe was a better resting place.

Frater Thaddeus Reuter and Frater Demetrius O'Friel shared my love of walking, the only clue to our clerical status being the black shoes. Among local points of interest was an old cemetery east of the campus on the south side of Spring Street. Ornate old – fashioned carved monuments were everywhere, many adorning the graves of Civil War veterans. American history in granite. It may have been named Albany Rural Cemetery. Out toward the northwest we hiked along deserted country roads to an airport so small that not once did we see a plane take off or land.

The Navy House, an appendage to the back of a Victorian farmhouse off Loudonville Road, had windows in the front room whose sills, like narrow French doors, were level with the floor. Someone had set up in the cellar – perhaps Frater Dunstau Dooling – a lathe. Several of us made use of it with maple bowling pins discarded because of cracks in the necks. Canisters suitable for cigarettes or pipe tobacco were popular. I was lucky to turn a pair of identical candlesticks. Recesses were bored on a drill press in the college's workshop.

My mother was pleased with the gift. At sunset on Christmas Eve 1949 she lit a blessed candle, as had been her custom, and her mother's before her, "to light the Christ child into the world". Upon returning from Midnight Mass at St. Teresa's, there on the glass-topped coffee table stood only the base, a charred stump, and a mound of gray ash, as fine as talcum powder. By the grace of God nothing else had burned.

We were lucky to have in the Navy House in the summer of 1946, a primitive television set, one of the first to be mass-produced. The small black and white screen was viewed best in the dark, as with motion pictures. There may have been other channels. I recall only one, from Schenectady, a pioneer project of General Electric no doubt. On a narrow and shallow stage, against a plain backdrop, performers could be viewed above the waist, talking, reading or singing. Broadcasting was limited to a few evening hours. One memorable feature was a contralto, evidently amateur, who rendered old English ballads to the accompaniment of a stringed instrument, a lute most likely. Typical early programs were mere curiosities, far from habit forming.

Part of Siena Hall's attic served as the chapel, where priests said Mass every morning and clerics recited in choir the Divine Office at the conventional times during the day. If the gabled roof had been insulated, the wadding was inadequate, for under the summer sun the chapel became a foretaste of Purgatory. The few narrow dormers provided no evident ventilation. In that inferno we wore the same woolen habits that in Croghan had kept us from freezing.

The Cardinal Archbishop of Havana honored us with a visit one summer. He was reputed to be uncle of a young Franciscan, an eminent Marion scholar at Catholic University. A witty friar referred to the prelate as "Cardinal Manuale Precum" (Manual of Prayers). Having endured that attic oven, he probably never returned. Not in summer at least.

A cafeteria designed for students, on the ground floor at Siena Hall, was run by Mrs. Simmons, wife of the chef, John Simmons. He and an equally able Navy veteran managed the kitchen very well. With the friary then only in the planning stage – as well as the library and other major projects – the friars appropriated for their refectory the dining room intended eventually for the lay faculty.

Before the 1946 summer session, we clerics repainted the cafeteria's ceiling and the walls above the tiled wainscot. That, by the way, was my introduction to rubber-based paint. It was too early to judge other critical qualities, fading for example, but obvious were some advantages: absence of fumes, fast drying, and water solubility, which made cleaning up easy.

Although clerics could not go home to visit – only death in the immediate family would have occasioned an exception – our relatives were free to come to us, not that we could put them up. Loudonville and Newtonville neighbors, in private homes only, were few and scattered. Adjacent to the campus on the north side, however, Mrs. Westphal (Harriet was it?) in a rambling old frame house, would rent rooms to visitors referred by the friars. She and my mother grew to be friends to the point of sending Christmas cards.

To quote her own expression, my mother was "a regular Judy Friendly". It did not surprise me, therefore, when Mr. and Mrs. Simmons invited us one year for a Sunday afternoon drive to Bennington, Vermont in their huge black Cadillac.

Tuesday, February 28, 1995

After the 1946 summer session at Siena College, we stayed there until early September, when we rejoined most of our classmates, (those who had been studying at St. Bonaventure College,) at St. Anthony's Monastery in Butler, New Jersey, there to begin the second and final year of Scholastic Philosophy. Of course those clerics in the advanced classes (1947, '48, and '49) returned from Siena to Holy Name College, Washington D.C., to continue with theology.

Fr. Berard Vogt, O.F.M., taught most of the courses in philosophy. His mind was such that he could not easily make categorical statements, because defining terms was so critical. He'd not have been comfortable with generalities such as "All men are created equal". At once he'd require a precise definition of men, created, and equal. Even those would lead to still other questions.

One of the friars in Callicoon – perhaps Fr. Cuthbert Cotton – in an informal chat remarked that after we'd studied philosophy, the way our minds functioned would be profoundly changed. We'd be more analytical and more perceptive, more precise.

The Master of Clerics in Butler, analogous with the Prefect of Discipline at Callicoon, was Fr. Edmund Christy, O.F.M. (known throughout the province by the nickname "Junior"). He had taught us Physics at Siena. In Butler he taught Advanced Public Speaking. The course required each of us to address the class from the raised pulpit of the parish church, adjoined to the monastery. There was no public address system in those days in

220

Franciscan or other churches. Thus each of us had to strive to project his voice to the classmates spread among the rear pews, while Fr. Edmund stood even farther back.

Our mentor, in blunt terms, called a spade a spade. As I recall after so many years, he found fault in my failure to enunciate clearly and to project my voice well enough, a valid assessment in view of my trepidation through the ordeal. His stern demeanor at all times and in all places was hardly conducive to fostering relaxation and self-confidence.

Even so, he was in fact a good teacher.

When the weather permitted, we indulged in hand-ball in a court in a side yard beyond the church. Monastery and church took up so much of the land that there was no room for gardens or secluded areas, luxuries that elsewhere we had taken for granted. A small pond down the hill from the high school provided space enough for neighborhood youngsters and some of us to ice skate. As we had done in Callicoon and Croghan, and yes in Siena too, those of us who liked long walks on free afternoons, explored surrounding communities, preferring, of course, little – used roads.

A motion - picture executive lived nearby in Kinnelon used to treat the friars to first-run movies that were showing in New York. Maybe three or four that year. He and a helper brought in reels, projector, and portable screen. All state of the art equipment. Let me add that during the 1940's films that were morally offensive were not seen in the large first-run or even neighborhood theaters. And so we saw only the best of the best.

About six or eight of our class of 1950 were trained choir singers, of Gregorian Chant and four-part polyphony, thanks principally to Fr. Raphael Adams in Callicoon and his successor Fr. Angelus DeMarco, excellent organists and choir masters.

There being no parish choir – nor for that matter a conventional parish – at St. Francis on 31st Street in Manhattan, we in Butler served on Sundays and during Holy Week, accompanied on the organ by their Brother Philip Egan, O.F.M. Early in the morning we'd pile into the house car, our habits crammed into suitcases, and head for the Lincoln Tunnel. Usually we got back for supper at six o'clock.

This Sunday schedule allowed several hours free, time enough to meander up to St. Patrick's Cathedral and Rockefeller Center in pleasant weather. Needless to say, perhaps, we wore clerical black and white Roman collars on those jaunts. On one such afternoon Frater Demetrius O'Friel and I climbed up to the choir loft, hoping to meet Maestro Pietro Yon, at least one of whose polyphonic Masses we had been singing for years. Ah, but we were too late.

On one occasion, probably in Holy Week when we had more time, we took the subway (7th Avenue line) to Brooklyn to visit my mother. It just happened that a classmate of mine in St. Teresa's school, John Savage, whose family lived up the street, was home for a visit. He had been ordained a Vincentian and assigned somewhere in the Caribbean, as I recall, Cuba perhaps. We had not seen each other since graduation in June 1932, nor have we ever met again.

One afternoon during Holy Week we stopped of to sing Tenebrae at St. Joseph's in East Rutherford. Afterward, before we set out for Manhattan, there was time enough to telephone Ray Wheeler in nearby Carlstadt. Ray had been a co-worker and a dear friend at Geigy's. He hurried over to the friary, where we had a brief reunion.

The management of Radio City Music Hall had a policy in those days of admitting at no charge anyone in black clerical garb. Nor was the guest required to stand on the lengthy line. One classmate – I've forgotten which – and I took advantage one afternoon. I can't recall the program.

On Christmas Eve, 1946, we sang a midnight Missa Cantata and Christmas Carols in harmony at St. Catherine of Siena Church, Glenwood Lake, New Jersey. What was most memorable there was the breakfast that followed. In her charming cottage, warmed by logs in the fireplace, a gracious parishioner served us a rare treat: bacon and eggs.

At the close of the academic year in June 1947, most of the class left Butler for the summer session at St. Bonaventure College. The following for Siena College: Fraters Alexander Eustace, Cassion Corcoran, Demetrius O'Friel, Paulinus Dee and Thaddeus Reuter.

Monday, June 17, 1996

After the summer sessions of 1947, the few of us clerics at Siena, and the many at St. Bonaventure, left for Holy Name College, a short walk from Catholic University of America in the Brookland section of northeast Washington, and adjacent to the Commissariat of The Holy Land's Mount Saint Sepulcher.

Our two storied building, like a square donut with a cloistered rose garden in the middle, has a tower that affords storage space for the library below it, and a pedestal for a statue of Christ the King, which on the evenings of special feasts, is brilliantly floodlit. Spacious grounds allow a broad setback from the private homes that snuggle together on tiny lots.

Just as elsewhere through Holy Name Province, clerics' rooms are small, just big enough for the Spartan furnishings: steel desk, gooseneck lamp, steel wardrobe, steel cot, crucifix, small double hung window, square asphalt floor tiles, painted walls, hook on the back of the solid wooden door, high enough to hang one's habit. No shade, curtain, drapes.

It may have been Frater Juvenal Ellis, class of 1948 – May he rest in peace – who got me interested in Gallinger Municipal Hospital, a vast complex, near the Anacostia River and district jail. Each cleric chose a floor to visit regularly, at least once a week. Juvenal and I, among others, favored the Medical building.

One afternoon as I made the circuit from bed to bed, a teenager in a black ward asked to be baptized. A nurse had told me the boy was critical – in our terms "in periculo mortis" – in danger of death - although he could perhaps recover. I knew of course how to administer the Sacrament validly. Even so, I deemed it wise to refer to Frater Juvenal, an ordained deacon. He wasted no time. On our next regular visit to Gallinger, we learned that the patient had died on the day of his Baptism.

The wards and other rooms of the hospital were segregated. Whites at one end of the floor, coloreds at the other. And of course men and women were assigned to separate wards and rooms. Only on the doors of the toilets were there signs: "Men White, Men Colored, Women White, Women Colored". During one of my visits, my bladder having signaled stress, I stepped into the nearest facility. A nurse – all the staff was white as I recall – was waiting for me in the hall, for she felt obliged to point out my faux pas. The door was marked "Men Colored".

I've long since forgotten what occasioned my visit to Pediatrics, but I'll not forget seeing a new-born with six digits on each hand and each foot, all perfectly formed and well proportioned. Thumbs and big toes seemed normal. A nurse confided that surgery was scheduled to remove one finger on each hand. For the feet no change was planned, at least not at that time. She pointed out that the child could grow up wearing conventional shoes, yes, but gloves would have been a problem. Then too, there was the prospect which surgery would forestall embarrassment in public.

The kitchen and laundry at Holy Name College were staffed by a small community of Franciscan sisters, many of whom, if not all, had come from Germany long before the war. They kept in touch, of course, with relatives back home, many of whom had endured hardships under Hitler's tyranny. With his defeat, as to be expected, poverty remained. Now it happened that I had a sturdy winter coat of thick black horsehide that reached almost to the knees. The full lining was of woolen plaid. From the first winter in Callicoon it had served me well. No scratches, no scuff marks, no blemishes at all. Shoe polish got it looking new. Master of Clerics, Fr. Benedict Ballou, having given permission, I gave the coat to Mother Superior. I'd like to think it continued to serve through many German winters.

The four year program leading to priestly ordination was designed to furnish us with the requisite knowledge and sound judgment to administer the Sacraments and to counsel the laity and each other. And so Moral

Theology, Dogma, and Cannon Law were studied thoroughly with abundant citations from cases both historical and hypothetical. These were supplemented by appropriate quotations from Sacred Scripture as well as from eminent scholars' commentaries. Thus on beginning his ministry, the young priest and friar could draw from a vast store of principles and precedents, both in the confessional and in counseling couples and individuals. Then too he'd be confident of guidance, by the Holy Spirit, as he kept in mind the Biblical Dabitur vobis. It will be given to you.

All texts were in Latin only, or to be more accurate, none was in English. Written assignments were frequent, as indeed were examinations, written or oral. Once each year a panel of several faculty members tested orally all the clerics, each one privately. The tester stood alone before the seated panel who required answers in the language of the questions, whether Latin or English. The range of subjects covered was limited of course by the testers place in the four year sequence. Thus the further advanced he was, the broader the scope of the questions, and the greater demand on his memory of highly technical fine points.

Although we Franciscan clerics were not matriculated at Catholic University, their library's reference room was open to us to browse, if only out of curiosity. Our own library and the even older more extensive one of the friars at the Commissariat, to which we enjoyed access, had all we needed and even more. Both Franciscan libraries are treasuries of priceless volumes, many of ancient origin, hand-written and illuminated in parchment. Then too there are the complete works of the early Church Fathers, as well as Doctors of the Church, all in Latin. Commentaries in English, those written originally in English.

The Drama Department at Catholic University used to offer – perhaps it still does – special performances on Saturday afternoons, free to any and all in religious habits or Roman collars. One such program I recall after so many years. Yet there were probably others. The entire production was superb. Acting, stage settings, lighting, writing, pace, all were of professional quality.

A movie theater close to the campus had a similar generous policy. A movie starring Henry Fonda and J. Carrol Naish was especially memorable.

Fonda played a Mexican Catholic priest persecuted and pursued by militant atheists. The Fugitive was based on the Graham Greene novel.

We clerics at Holy Name College used to provide a choir when needed up at Mount Saint Sepulcher. Gregorian Chant, polyphony, or both, to fit the liturgical function. We also had occasion, four of us with the class of 1950, to take the train down to the Marine base in Quantico, Virginia, where the chaplain and the other officers were most hospitable. They put us up for the night before we sang in the base chapel.

Just as it had been from our early years at Callicoon, walking was a popular recreation. Usually in pairs, never alone, classmates strolled in our habits through the Catholic University campus and the nearby veteran's home. Often we dropped in uninvited at the chapels – those visible from the street and not locked – of the orders and congregations of men all around. Incidentally, we had an Augustinian cleric studying with us. Evidently his people preferred us to Catholic University.

Sometimes when we had several hours free in an afternoon, we were permitted to visit in haste museums, galleries, etc. in the heart of the Capital. Admission in those days was free everywhere. And so, off we'd hurry in black suits and Roman collars, a single token in each one's pocket for the uphill return trip. There were of course many places for which we had too little time, alas.

Archbishop Amleto Cicognani, the Papal Nuncio, was especially fond of Franciscans. He'd drop in; when he had a little free time, to chat informally with any of us free to stroll the grounds with him, as though we were all old friends. I stood in awe of a prelate who could one day succeed Pope Pius XII as Vicar of Christ. When he ordained the class of 1948 at Mount Saint Sepulcher, it was my privilege, kneeling before him, to hold open the book.

Monday, June 24, 1996

To recapitulate: at the end of the Novitiate, Franciscans took Simple Vows, binding for three years. Clerics- as distinguished from lay brothers – went from there to two years of Scholastic Philosophy, followed by four years of theology.

At the end of the year of introductory basic theology, the cleric was free to leave the Order, reverting to the lay state, or to take Solemn Vows, binding for the rest of his life. Shortly after Solemn Vows, he'd be ordained to the Minor Orders: Acolyte, Exorcist, Lector, and Porter. Soon following these there would be ordination as Sub-deacon, first of the three Major Orders. A year or so later he'd be ordained Deacon. Then having completed the third year of theology, the Franciscan cleric would be ordained priest, or more precisely "Simplex" priest, which is to say one qualified to offer Mass, but not authorized to hear confessions or to perform other priestly functions. Canon Law did not permit this early ordination below a certain age.

Toward the end of the 4th year, the new priest (or younger ordinandus) would be asked to submit his first, second, and third preferences for assignment in the Province, whether parish ministry, foreign missions, etc. Wherever he was sent, the new priest was obliged to pursue advanced studies privately for several years, in the course of which he was subject to testing by a board of examiners.

Tuesday, June 25, 1996

In the fall of 1948 our class was ordained to the four Minor Orders, and then to the Sub diaconate, by Bishop Patrick O'Boyle, local ordinary, in the crypt of what would become National Shrine of The Immaculate Conception, on the campus of Catholic University. At that time nothing had yet been built above ground, and much more was still to be finished below. Notable were the side altars, each flanked by a pair of magnificent marble columns, each quarried in a different part of the world. I recall no evidence of work in progress, due probably to lack of funds.

In those days the Minor Orders served no practical purpose, being mere relics from centuries deep in the past, except for Exorcist, which function was, and still is, reserved by local ordinaries and those they delegate. The sub-deacon did serve in the celebration of the <u>Missa</u> <u>Solemnis</u> of the Tridentine Latin Mass. He chanted the Epistle. Also he held the paten under the chin of the communicant at the altar rail while the celebrant distributed Holy Communion. Insignia of his office was the maniple, a kind of short stole, whose color matched the chasuble; it was draped across and pinned to his left forearm, reminiscent of a waiter's napkin. Both the priest – celebrant and the deacon wore the maniple also, each with own peculiar stole as well.

Wednesday, July 19, 1996

I am convinced that in the Divine plan each of us, beginning with Adam, is called to serve in the same way, in at least one role, and so is endowed with those talents appropriate to success, whether we are prince or peasant, rich or poor. Who taught Michelangelo to carve the Pieta? Who taught Shakespeare to write Hamlet? Who taught Rachmaninov to compose Symphony Number Two?

Are we all not tiny tesserae in Providence's grand mosaic? However lavish or modest one's talents, success can be reached only through hard, persevering work. Even prodigies must sweat.

Moses, the prophets, John the Baptizer, The Blessed Virgin Mary, St. Joseph – all knew without doubt what roles God had assigned to them. So too did the Apostles, called to become "fishers of men". After His Ascension, in assigning duties to Saul of Tarsus, Christ was no less explicit, although perhaps more dramatic. They all know that, as Christ put it: "You have not chosen me; I have chosen you."

Ah, then there are many more numerous – Augustine of Hippo for one – who waste years drifting aimlessly, ships without rudders, before coming to see what they ought to be doing with their lives. Christ does not address them directly. As theologians say, God works through secondary causes.

Now contrast them with the few who early in life know somehow just what plans Providence has for them. St. Therese, The Little Flower, is a perfect example, with her heart set on entering Carmel. Our dear daughter

229

Patricia, while still in elementary school, aspired to become a nurse. Such self-assurance is in itself a great blessing.

From the day in 1939 when I applied for admission to the seminary, I was never fully confident of my vocation. During those early days at Callicoon, I was troubled now and then by brief bouts with depression; moods swung from elation to apathy. I spoke of this matter with no one. By the grace of God that melancholy was short-lived. Nevertheless, misgivings did not vanish.

We newcomers were advised to choose a confessor to whom we were to make confession every week. This, of course, I did. After half a century more or less, my memory is not always reliable.

During the nine years as a Franciscan seminarian, I must have grown visibly pensive, if not glum. One day in Holy Name College – I can't recall what may have prompted him; we were alone – Frater Dunstan Dooling (May he rest in peace) exclaimed "What's the trouble? Are you frustrated?" Well, I was too stunned to answer. Dreading embarrassment, I could not confide in "Tex" the dilemma that haunted me, and the root cause of it, the virtue and vow of chastity: whether to stay in the Order and become perhaps an unchaste priest, or to leave and contend with an unknown future, from the frying pan into the fire perhaps. As Lawrence Olivier said of Hamlet, in his introduction to the film (1948): "This is the story of a man who could not make up his mind". I was like the fabled donkey tethered between two stacks of feed, unable to decide whether to turn right or left.

My torment would perhaps have ended, had any confessor along the way advised me either to persevere, or to leave the Order. But that decision was always left to me, and in my view the options were equally charming and equally hazardous. I do recall now the special confessor who came to Callicoon in June 1944, just before our class graduated. He advised me to enter the one-year novitiate as planned, at the end of which I could choose either to leave, or to take simple vows.

Principles of Moral Theology were taught through texts and lectures reinforced with historical and hypothetical precedents, anecdotes and commentary. Now these left little to the imagination.

In matters concerning the sixth commandment, De Sextu, I had to guard against undue curiosity; I recognized danger, drawing me again to wonder whether I were on the wrong side of the communion rail. There was a priest I read of somewhere who, when a seminarian, had studied De Sextu, in the chapel, kneeling before the tabernacle. Perhaps I ought to have done so too. (Could he have been the priest who, on parlor duty, was reputed to have averted his glance so as never to look a woman counselee in the eye?)

St Paul's candor comes to mind:
(Romans VII, 22f)

> "For I am delighted with the law of God
> according to the inner man, but I see
> another law in my members, warring
> against the law of my mind and making
> me prisoner to the law of sin that is in
> my members."

I stood one afternoon alone in the library of the Commissariat, either in November or December 1948, reading some volume of De Sextu. It was clear at last that the priesthood and the Order were not for me. Without delay I sought my confessor, and then the Master of Clerics, who agreed to initiate a petition to Rome for a dispensation from solemn vows and a reduction to the lay state. The document from Rome would arrive in a few weeks, I was told.

Thursday, July 18, 1996

After that conference with Fr. Benedict Ballou, Master of Clerics, probably the first thing I did was to write my decision to my mother. To no one else did I confide, for while I waited to hear from Rome, it seemed prudent to continue with my studies and the other regular activities as usual.

One day early in 1949 a classmate, who had become editor of the next revision of the <u>Franciscan</u> <u>Almanac</u>, came and asked if I'd write an article on vocations. Of course I could have done so, conforming to his editorial vision, but because I expected any day the dispensation from Rome, and thus could not be sure of enough time to finish the essay, I had to decline and explain why. He agreed to keep my secret.

On Tuesday after supper, April 26, 1949, The Guardian, Fr. David Baier, sent word that he wanted to see me. He handed me the Papal dispensation and fifty dollars. The document dispensed me from the vows and also reduced me to the lay state "sine spe read missionis ad statum clericalem" (without hope of readmission to the clerical state). I don't recall, but probably I informed my confessor, Fr. Alban A. Maguire, after which I confided in one other friar, Fr. Juvenal Ellis, then a fourth – year "simplex", with whom I had been commuting to Gallinger Hospital.

It seemed to me fraudulent for a layman to travel wearing a Roman collar, and so with Fr. David's permission I went downtown hoping to buy a necktie, but by then all the stores were closed.

Fr. Juvenal (May he rest in peace) very kindly offered to say Mass for me the next morning at five o'clock, when the rest of the community was still asleep, after which I slipped out of Holy Name College carrying the two leather bags that I'd lugged all over Holy Name Province. In one: the rosary beads that had swung at my side for almost five years. Now as I look back, I wonder why I did not leave the beads with the habit, but take the sandals, custom-made to fit my feet. It would have made more sense. Incidentally, those Franciscan beads have been hanging in my bedroom closet for all these many years. When it occurred to me at last some time ago that I ought to return them to the province, rosary beads were no longer with the habit.

At Union Station I bought a ticket to New York with a stopover at West Philadelphia, planning to beg the loan of a necktie from cousin John McLaughlin, who lived on Greenway Avenue at the corner of 70th Street, in a combination house and grocery store.

John and Rose (nee Caserta) were most hospitable. Not only did he give me a black tie, but twenty dollars as well, and they were not wealthy. It did not cross my mind at the time, but there I was setting out on an entirely new life, a closed book, just a short stroll from the hospital where I'd been born.

Thursday, July 25, 1996

While I awaited the dispensation from Pope Pius X II, I confided my secret with Fr. Pat Foy. We had been fellow members of St. Patrick's Clerical Students Club back in New York. Generously he invited me to enjoy the hospitality of his rectory in Alabama, until I cleared my head and decided what I'd do with the rest of my life. I did appreciate his kindness and indeed loved him the more for it. Now in looking back I wonder whether it would have eased the transition had I accepted. A moot question, of course, and about as pertinent as asking whether I ought to have left the Order sooner. Or indeed whether I ought to have stayed.

The about face hit my mother hard, a source of embarrassment. "What'll I tell my friends?" The dear soul had come close to being the proud mother of a Franciscan priest, but now her son was a sad disappointment, a nobody. What some Irish Catholics would call a "spoiled priest". Well, time heals all wounds, or at least it helps us to bear the pain gracefully.

It was probably she who made an appointment with Catholic Charities in New York, across the street from the Cathedral, for career counseling and testing, a service well designed to advise those with goals and ambition, but unsure of how best to achieve. The professional staff was kind, competent and patient, while I evidently was unsuited for everything but what I had just rejected. My presence was like asking them to fit a square peg into a round hole.

On weekdays I went to the seven o'clock Mass at St. Teresa's. Whenever the celebrant came out alone, as happened now and then, especially during the summer, I'd fill in as an altar boy. Thus I came to meet those curates appointed while I was away. Frs. Joseph Daly, Richard Chichester, and Francis Mendler, all great assets to the parish.

There was a corporation, new to me that advertised for college graduates expert in English language skills. Their East – side office in midtown could well have been adapted from tycoon's townhouse: marble and bronze everywhere, graceful curved stairs, high ceilings, crystal chandeliers, lush carpets.

For several hours I was interviewed by three members of the staff in turn, given tests written and oral, in a manner courteous and serene. I left elated by the self-assurance that I'd done very well, very well. I was to be recalled in a few days, or so I was told. Yet despite my euphoria, I was not qualified, for whatever deficiency, because I was not called back, nor did I see fit to ask questions. It certainly could not have been lack of English language skills. Was I perhaps over qualified?

Brooklyn Law School beckoned as an open gateway to a fascinating new world. Of course I was penniless and so the law was out of reach. I'd have to pay my own way along whatever path I took. Then too I was not at all comfortable being supported by my mother. Her paying my tuition was out of the question, in law school or anywhere else.

Monday, July 29, 1996

Early in the summer my mother learned of a novel program that the Board of Education had just introduced, accelerated courses to train college graduates to qualify for licenses to teach in elementary schools. Not it happened that registration had closed just a few days earlier. With powerful friends, however, among local Democratic politicians, she asked someone to persuade Professor Crowe at Brooklyn College to accept my late application.

The plan called for a summer session followed by two or more semesters leading to a bachelor's degree and a teacher's certificate. There may have been five sections, all in the same program, the same schedule, and using the same textbooks, but of course each with its own instructors. Classes were held weekday mornings only, and so I kept the job in East Harlem. About a third of us were men. All the faculty but one were women.

Courses covered methods of teaching, arts and crafts, Philosophy of Education, History of Education, Child Psychology etc. The unspoken premise underlying the curriculum was that we all needed instruction in pedagogy, but all were well enough founded in the subjects we'd be teaching.

Most lectures on methods, record keeping, and psychology were practical, down-to-earth. Ah, but elsewhere the approach was eclectic, secular and shallow-minded, as though from Classical Greeks to the American Revolution stretched one vast intellectual vacuum, with John Dewey, father of "Progressive Education", the patron saint of "educators" spawned at Teachers College, Columbia University, where no one gave serious thought, if any, to religion.

236

It soon became obvious to me that with rare exception my classmates, regardless of their secret convictions, were keeping silent or saying what they thought the instructors would be pleased to hear, hoping thus to guarantee passing grades and entry into a professional career.

To me that was intolerable. I could not trade away self-respect and a clean conscience. Indeed, had I been disposed to do that, I might have persevered as a Franciscan. And so I evolved as a solitary gadfly, always courteous, I hope, but often seething inside.

During breaks between classes, now and then some of my classmates, potential colleagues, even graduates of (Catholic) Fordham, shook my hand and congratulated me, mummies revived until the next class. A Jewish girl – I guessed from her name – paid me a compliment as we sat in the subway on the way home. "Have you ever thought of becoming a priest?" I did not see fit to open my heart to her; silence is golden. "Oh, yes, I have considered it".

All the faculty had doctorates, an accomplishment I had equated with high intelligence in the service of scholarship, but as days multiplied to weeks, I began to wonder whether I were naive, or rather were there on campus a lack of intellectual honesty. How could so many have been misinformed about so much? Were some doctorates inflated? Is the adage true that a little bit of knowledge is a dangerous thing?

One morning as I walked with one of the instructors, I asked what the requirements to earn a doctorate were. He answered with a bit of whimsy only: "STICKTOITIVENESS".

That same gentleman, as the final day drew close, assigned a paper spelling out "What you've gotten from the course". That was precisely what he asked for. That from a nominal teacher, whose academic rank I can't recall, one who had been no more than a neutral referee, skilled at proposing questions but in the end offering no judgments, no insights.

"Raise your hand if you feel that....... Ok! One, Two, Three,....... Now, raise your hand if on the other hand....." It was as though there were no objective truths, nor standards. Can you believe it? My paper came back with no comment on its substance, but two grades: "A for candor. F for content." If I wrote as requested, by what measure could my paper be graded F? Or for that matter be graded at all? Guess what final grade! Oh, yes, I had been a thorn in his side, but at such a price.

In that same class, by the way, I had been assigned (or volunteered) to present a paper summing up Plato's and Aristotle's philosophies, and to be prepared to answer questions from the class. During the brief pause that followed, the master of ceremonies made no comment at all, as usual. Then time ran out; the bell rang. While others filed out, two young ladies asked if I'd mind answering a question: "Has your shirt been washed yet?"

An instructor in history remarked one day – in what context I've forgotten – that ancient Hebrews did not believe Moses had written the Torah. It occurred to me that a search of the texts would find explicit or implicit references to Moses as the author. No one in the class commented, not even those with Jewish names. The following day I got to the room early and cited passages that refuted her error. She muttered a few words of annoyance, and then shuffled her papers.

Perhaps she had read somewhere that sometimes Moses dictated to a scribe or scribes who then wrote his words verbatim. But her statement implied that Moses was not the author. She never again addressed the question, nor did I or anyone else.

Then there was the instructor who strode into the room sometimes after us, often wearing glossy black shoes, and a long black boa draped like a priest's stole. Having arranged her oversize matching handbag on the desk, she'd push back in the chair, fuss with the boa, cross her legs and the ask: "Well, what'll we talk about today?" Woe to any of us who failed to study on his own the subject outlined in the printed brochure, for she did not design the final examination. In a large lecture hall we all en masse took departmental tests for each course.

About halfway through the fall term, the prospect of a happy career in the public schools gradually ebbed away. The scholarly pretensions, smug self-assurance, condescending lofty pose of so many "educators", many of whom were not well-rounded in the liberal arts, who appeared to be accustomed to timid classes, to students unable or unwilling to pose probing questions, all had the cumulative effect of eroding away my morale and my respect for the school system. If, as it seemed, I was out of step with almost everyone else, who was at fault? Obviously I was a misfit. My future lay elsewhere. Dr. Darcy, the only one deserving of my admiration, the only one to whom I had laid bare my soul, tried to persuade me to hold on. She even telephoned me at home, but I had had all I could stomach. I wondered if I could find a way to pay my way through Fordham. In looking back after forty six years and more, I ask whether Dr. Darcy was wise and I foolish and lacking "STICKTOITIVIENESS".

Despite the vows and ordination and all the years I had spent in preparing for the priesthood, deep in my heart I was not content. It was not as though I knew, or even suspected, what I ought to do with my life. No, I was haunted by neurotic fears, fears that had no logical cause. Maybe a physician would have diagnosed psycho-neurosis. Well, at any rate, in April 1949 I was granted a dispensation from the vows and a reductio ad statum laicum. My mother was baffled, and began at once to assume command, as though I were a naughty boy.

I found a job as a messenger with Bankers Trust Co., Wall Street. It dawned on me that I ought to go into teaching, and so I applied to St. Francis Prep, hoping to teach Latin. Just a little later it happened that one of the Franciscan brothers took ill, one who taught Latin. While there, I worked at Fordham for a master's degree in Education, and thus for a state teacher's license that would open the door to work on Long Island, a license in English, Latin, and Mathematics.

Recently discharged war veterans formed a large part of Fordham's student body, as indeed at many colleges around the country. The Federal government, in gratitude and to compensate for the interruption of civilian careers, paid their college expenses: tuition, textbooks and such supplies as slide rules etc. All under what came to be called informally "The G. I. Bill", a great boon obviously to veterans who could take advantage of it, but as it was to become clear in time, a mixed blessing at best for many small Catholic colleges and even prestigious universities. Coveted dollars from Washington became addictive. More and more were sought and accepted at the price of less and less autonomy, for they always come with strings attached, dragging along secular bureaucrats. Thus little by little over the years, many Catholic institutions bartered away their souls.

Friday, August 2, 1996

The friends I had before leaving home for the seminary were scattered by the time I got back from Washington. Charlie McNally was in business for himself in New Jersey. DeForest Billyou had a law practice in Manhattan. Jimmy McCusker, George McCaffrey and Jess Bennett were God knows where. Charlie's sister Jerry had married Bill Quinn. They lived with their babies in a Quonset hut near Fort Hamilton.

Bill's family still lived in the apartment on Lincoln Place. All the Quinns were most hospitable. On many weekend evenings I shared their new television and refreshments. A jolly bunch, with a keen sense of humor. Oh, did we laugh !

My Leggett cousins came back to City Line after the war, Bill, Stanley and Eddie, but by 1949 John and family were in Sheepshead Bay; Bill in New Jersey. They welcomed me most cordially, as though I were a brother. They were great company; I visited often, until a certain lady had me hobbled.

Eddie's wife, Rita, had a sister in the neighborhood, Peggy, who had been a close friend of Chloe, and whom I remembered meeting at a party my mother gave. Peggy was gorgeous and charming. She used to wear a scent that enhanced her allurement, one that I did not recognize, nor have I smelled it since. Perhaps I was deceiving myself. At any rate, I sensed that the attraction was mutual. Ah, but there was one enormous obstacle blocking the road to romance: Peggy was a wife and mother, and so I kept the friendship formal and my conscience clean.

240

Then there was the friend of Rita Leggett and her sister, Helen Redmond, a pretty Italian girl in Sheepshead Bay. I phoned one afternoon inviting her to a movie that evening. But there wasn't time enough to get her hair done ! As though I had invitations to a swanky ball at the Waldorf. Yet the damsel may have set her sights on big game.

Having turned my back on Brooklyn College and a career in elementary schools, I began to consider teaching on the more challenging high – school level; I saw myself as better suited by temperament to working with more mature minds. A license to teach in secondary schools in New York State required specialized graduate courses and a master's degree. Fordham had a suitable program, with classes on weekday late afternoons and on Saturdays. Whereas I paid no tuition at Brooklyn, Fordham's rates presupposed either full-time students supported by others, or part-time students supporting themselves. The graduate-school schedule was obviously designed to accommodate those already teaching, who were free for advanced study after school hours, and also those in other fields working nights.

Shortly after dropping out of the elementary school program, I found a full-time job as a messenger at Bankers Trust, where Nassau Street begins at Wall Street. Oh, my mother was not at all happy with me. I was self-supporting, however, and not too proud to run errands for the time being. It was the fall of 1949.

One morning before finding the job on Wall Street, I served as an altar boy for Fr. Chichester. Afterward in the sacristy he invited me to join his lay helpers in the Confraternity of Christian Doctrine classes on Friday nights.

Fr. Chi, standing on the auditorium stage, conducted lessons for about forty-five minutes. The public-high-school kids sat six or so to a table, while volunteers lent moral support, standing scattered about at random. Afterwards the class chatted or danced to records, all the popular hits.

Following the lesson, the students would dance to phonographic records, the most popular at the time. We adult volunteers then sat together, enjoying small talk. Among those was a young lady of boundless charm, an angel incarnate, sent obviously to rescue me from mindless drifting. She was Mary Daniels, a bacteriologist – chemist. I fell in love with her at first glance, even though another volunteer, Frank Hurley was so attentive that I supposed they were romantically tied. And so I kept a polite distance.

Nevertheless, I couldn't get her out of my mind. After a week or so it occurred to me that maybe I still had a chance. If I asked her to go out with me, she'd either accept or gently make some excuse.

Father introduced the new man to his helpers: Mary Daniels, Mary and Anne Maxwell, Marilyn Miller, Mary Dugan, Frank Hurley, Jim Brennan, and John Kennelly. All about the same age, 25, all single, all devout Catholics. The new man was 31.

After we locked the auditorium, Father "Chi" went back to the rectory, we often strolled the block to Lewnes' ice cream parlor on Washington Avenue, more to enjoy each other's company than to indulge appetites. Not once did Charlie usher us out when we had taken an hour or so to finish a sundae or a coke. All very pleasant.

Of all those attractive young ladies, one I found especially fascinating: Mary Daniels. When we first shook hands, I was smitten by her touch, her smile, her sweet voice. As the evening wore on, however, and other evenings in later weeks, I sobered up; my ardor cooled slowly, as I noticed the warm attention that Frank was paying to her, and only to her, suggesting to me a romantic relationship. Despite this troubling suspicion, hope held on.

It occurred to me finally to propose a date with Mary, for if she were involved romantically with Frank – or anyone else – or if she found me a bore, being kind, she'd make up some excuse to turn me away gracefully. Baby-sitting. Working overtime. Hairdresser. Visiting a sick friend. Whatever.

The Daniels family lived in a townhouse on St. Marks Avenue (#666) near Nostrand Avenue, the kind commonly called brownstone. Theirs however, was faced in granite.

One night after an early supper I hurried to a bar near their place, where I 'phoned, pretending that I happened to be in the neighborhood, and asking if she were free, and if so would she like to go out with me. Since that historic turning point in my and her life, I've forgotten where we went. Oh, was I ecstatic!

Wednesday, August 7, 1996

Bankers Trust was good to me; wages were enough to pay for room and board at home and to save a little each week. Indeed as the spring semester of 1950 drew near, the bank agreed to transfer me to Maintenance as a night porter. Thus I was able to enroll at Fordham, No, my mother was not comfortable with a son a mere porter.

The foreman, a pleasant man, assigned me to a floor, or floors, where alone from midnight to seven in the morning I emptied wastebaskets, swept floors, swept and washed restrooms, sinks and commodes, waxed and polished terrazzo hall floors. Once each night he walked the circuit, inspecting. Very soon the work became so routine, so mechanical, that my mind was free to savor the silence and solitude, to plan for the future, to meditate. Of course we did get a thirty minute lunch break, where all the porters, men and women, gathered to eat what we had brought from home.

Most of us were hard workers, foreign born, judging from their accents, supporting families, salt of the earth. A notable exception to these humble souls was a man who in his native Ukraine had been a college professor. Dr. Wasil Lencyk invited me to his Uniate church in Greenwich Village for the Easter Sunday liturgy. The church was almost full when Mary and I arrived. We found seats on the left side. During the Mass we noticed that only men were on the right side, and women on the left. The last I heard from "Bill" was that he found an opening to teach at St. Basil Seminary in Connecticut. Stamford perhaps.

Fordham's School of Education occupied a building on Broadway, a short walk above City Hall Park. My guess was that it had been designed originally for commercial offices.

Dr. William Kelly, having evaluated my transcripts, told me I lacked undergraduate courses, which I'd have to make up, after which I'd need thirty graduate level credits. As a part-time student I'd be held to a maximum of six credit hours per semester. And so, between the spring term of 1950, and the summer session of 1953, by the grace of God I managed to reach graduation, and all the while self-supporting.

Friday, August 9, 1996

On the beautiful spring Sunday morning of June 11, 1950 my class was ordained to the priesthood in the elegant chapel of Trinity College on Michigan Avenue, Washington D.C.

The Pullman porter was kind enough to wake me up at Union Station in time for me to visit the class at Holy Name College while they were getting ready. It happened that I was the only former classmate there, although it's unlikely that I was the only one invited. Frater Comrad Schomske, class senior, gave me a memento: a small black and white crucifix.

At the chapel I recognized some of the jubilant families. Chances are they recognized me too. We did not speak; it would have been awkward for them.

As I saw ordained my Franciscan brothers, with whom I had toiled and prayed so many years, did I regret leaving? No, I did not. On the contrary, in looking back to that April morning the year before, if I regretted anything, it was taking so long to make up my mind.

Tuesday, August 13, 1996

Shortly before the fall semester of 1950, I asked to be transferred from night porter to night watchman. While the hours were much the same, there would be time to read, to study, to write term papers, later at home to be typewritten. Also the work was not so physically demanding.

There were two of us who started work at 12 midnight, alternating through the night between two jobs. The more active duty was to patrol at regular intervals through all the banks offices; not through those of the tenants. (They filled the highest floors at 14 Wall Street.)

The patrol began at the uppermost of the bank's offices, through which a through circuit was made. At key places en route the watchman sent an electrical signal down to a recording device in the guard room that noted time and place. Then spiraling down floor-by-floor, he followed the same routine to the lowest sub-basement. He then rose to the street level where he stationed himself inside the massive locked bronze gate at the main lobby, until time to begin another patrol.

These were – I ought to say are – four floors below street level, A to D. Impregnable vaults are at floor D, huge, concrete, steel re-enforced boxes standing on concrete pillars with spaces well lighted below and on all sides. Mirrors at corners allow unobstructed lines of sight. Sensitive microphones and alarm triggers occupy strategic places. Any sound, however faint would be relayed to the guard room.

The man on duty in the guard room below ground, while his partner was patrolling or keeping watch at the gate, was there to monitor, alone and in utter silence, all the visual and auditory safety devices receiving signals from key places throughout the whole building. It's impossible for any employee, tenant or intruder to move out undetected, not, that is, during the night.

Bankers Trust stands between two subway lines: I.R.T. and B.M.T., yet we heard no sound at all, nor did we feel vibrations. And so I got lots of schoolwork done, while keeping alert by sipping coffee, generously supplied by the bank.

There was another advantage to my working nights, besides being able to study at Fordham: I could assist at early morning Mass before going home to breakfast and to bed. I learned somehow that in what had been the home of St. Elizabeth Anne Seton, on State Street, across from Battery Park, Mass was said every morning shortly after seven o'clock. And so I raced down Broadway, usually in time to serve as altar boy. All of us in the chapel could have been counted on two hands.

Wednesday, August 14, 1996

My mother from time to time took occasion to say things in praise of Irene Egan. "Oh, I met Irene this morning in the subway. What a lovely girl ! So sweet ! So poised !" An assessment for which I fully agreed. Indeed I had drawn much the same judgment long, long ago, when she, Regina Sullivan and my sister Lillian were closest friends, neighbors and classmates at St. Teresa's. Yes, Irene deserved well my mothers' admiration. Other young ladies must have looked with envy at her lustrous red hair, shapely figure, and stylish clothes. It was obvious that my mother would have been delighted, had I shown interest in her, but isn't there a critical difference between intellectual admiration and romantic magnetism? Irene had always stood on the same pedestal as had Lillian, my sister. Then too, God had other plans for us.

Later on, my mother reported that Irene had married a Merchant Marine officer. They were living on Staten Island. Was the name George Kilackey?

Thursday, August 15, 1996

In those early days of television there was a popular comedy: "Your Show of Shows", broadcast live from studios on Columbus Circle. Starring were the famous talented comics Sid Caesar and Imogene Coca.

My mother got four tickets, two of which went to an engaged young lady on the first floor, Virginia Dewey.

While Mary Daniels and I were en route in the subway, I showed her the tickets, and then put them back in the front breast pocket under the topcoat. Well, that's what I thought I had done, but when we got to the door, they were gone. "Oh, stop the kidding;" says Mary, "we'll be late."

The antique show at Madison Square Garden proved a poor substitute. Virginia raved about Sid and Imogene.

The Brauhaus on Third Avenue in Midtown Manhattan boasted an ensemble of strings and grand piano, entertaining with light classics. All very romantic. We came upon the place by chance as we window – shopped the antique dealers on 3rd Avenue under the elevated tracks, all closed at night. It was just as well; we had no money for the extravagances.

Long ago my thirst for beer had tapered off; a glass or two was enough, or none at all. Mary, however, was challenged to finish even one glass. We had dropped in because there in solitude we could chat and enjoy each other's company, just we two.

We sipped beer at The Brauhaus. The wooden tables were embellished with initials carved with initials of earlier patrons. Of course I added ours, with the pocket knife that my mother had given me many years ago. I wonder whether the place is still there. As I recall, a small triangle enclosed the initials M and H. And that was our first date.

It was probably my first visit to the Daniels' summer place on Fairfield Beach, Connecticut, on Long Island Sound. Mary's friend Rose Salerno Fernandez, also of Brooklyn, was a guest too. At bedtime when I retired to my room, I found that the bed had been "short-sheeted", which is to say that the sheet, instead of being tucked in at the foot, was folded back, giving the appearance of a bottom and a top sheet as usual. The practical joke would be discovered only when the guest tried to slide his feet in.

Now it just happened that I had neglected to pack pajamas, and so I had to sleep in my underwear. In the meanwhile Mary and Rose, in a room close by, were expecting to hear me laugh, and then to offer to remake the bed. But rather than embarrass them and myself in my underwear, I quietly set things right and went to sleep. If I had had the wit to put my trousers back on, the girls would not have lost sleep, wondering as Mary put it in the morning: "Will he ever finish his prayers?"

Fr. Joe Daly, (who was to marry us, or perhaps had already done so) gave us a pair of tickets in the Dress Circle at the Metropolitan. That was, of course, before Lincoln Center, when the Met was on Broadway below Times Square, where standing room cost only a dollar, where seats at the highest level, (the Family Circle?) were equally inexpensive.

Wagner was on the program, Siegfried, perhaps. Certainly not Tristan and Isolde, nor Tannhauser; I'd have remembered.

Well, the stars, the chorus, the orchestra, the staging were superb as always. Even so, in a light-hearted mood, I could not resist making Mary chuckle with an occasional whispered parody of the dialogue. Not, that is, until an impatient patron behind us voiced her displeasure.

Sunday August 18, 1996

While I was working nights full-time at the bank, and studying days part-time at Fordham, a friend suggested I apply to teach Latin at St. Francis Prep in downtown Brooklyn. I did, late in the summer of 1951. God does indeed work in mysterious ways, for shortly after the fall term began, Franciscan Brother Patrick became so ill that he could not continue with his classes.

Brother Charles, the Principal, assigned me to teach first and second years. Salary was ten monthly payments of $230, September to June. Compare that with the $54 that the bank had been paying every week, along with regular contributions to a "Profit Sharing" fund, set aside to be paid in a lump sum upon leaving.

In addition there would be priceless advantages at the Prep. The state in granting a teaching license would probably accept full - time experience in lieu of the college course: "Student Teaching". Also, I'd get back to sleeping at night. Moreover, having my weekends fall on Saturdays and Sundays again would help my social life.

From the day I left the Order, there grew a certain friction between my mother and me, in large part because I was so great a disappointment, in part because I worked at such menial jobs, and in part because, having a mind of my own, despite my initial aimlessness, I was not always submissive in taking directions. Oh, she loved me certainly, and was generous to a fault, but somehow she still saw me as her little boy.

The day came in the fall of 1951 when we weren't even talking to each other, my cue to look for a rooming house. On Duffield Street, close to Fulton, with its many department stores, Miss Kay had a tea room catering to lady shoppers who came to chat and have their tea leaves read.

On the two floors above, she had six or so rooms fitted with gas stoves, refrigerators, and kitchen sinks with ample hot water. The men tenants – of whom I saw only one, and heard none – supplied their own linens, tableware, and cooking utensils. Clean, well-maintained, and after dark as quiet as a tomb. A shared bathroom. Ideal for me.

By the grace of God I enjoyed good health; in fact I lost not one day at the bank. While at the Prep, however, I became so sick that I had to find a doctor. At random I picked Dr. Walter Auerbach, on Henry Street, Brooklyn Heights, diagnostician extraordinaire. He saw I had what he called viral pneumonia, for which he prescribed tobramycin and frequent doses of yogurt. The antibiotic was easy to get down, but the insipid yogurt, intended to replace the necessary bacteria that perished with the invaders, called for unwavering purpose.

The good doctor, on hearing that I taught Latin – he himself with a Liberal Arts education in Germany – quoted from memory passages from Horace. Had there been time, I suspect he'd have recalled Greek Homer too.

In discussing diagnosis, he recounted a chance encounter on a trolley car, where on the face of a woman sitting across the aisle, he detected symptoms, portents of serious illness. He waited for her to get off, and then followed her to the sidewalk, where he advised her to see a doctor. Cumberland Hospital was blessed indeed to have such a physician, scholar and gentleman. After so many years, he may today be talking shop with the Apostle Luke.

Monday, August 19, 1996

From that first date in the fall of 1949, Mary Daniels and I saw a lot of each other, and only each other. To use an idiom current in those days, we were "going steady", or again we had a tacit "understanding". It took a couple of years of work and study before I became confident that soon I'd be able to provide for her, and – God willing – children.

The summer session at Fordham would close about the middle of August 1952, a good time for a wedding.

It was Saturday afternoon, December 8, 1951, Solemnity of The Immaculate Conception, when we knelt alone in the Lady Chapel at St. Patrick's Cathedral. We prayed for the Blessed Mother's special care for our years to come. Then I slipped on the engagement ring. Oh, what bliss!

I must add that while kneeling there in God's house, I was fully confident in the wisdom of what we were doing. Somehow I knew in the depths of my soul that I had found my vocation that God meant us for each other, that in due course the day would come when our bones would lie together until Gabriel sounded reveille. Yes, it was one of those rare days-of-decision when I was not haunted by neurotic doubts..

Julia and Jane Boden, old friends of my mother, shared an apartment at 115 Ocean Avenue, at the corner of Lincoln Road across from Prospect Park, with easy access to the B.M.T. station of the Brighton Line, and a short walk to Ebbets Field, home of the Brooklyn Dodgers. Knowing that Mary and I were soon to be married, Julia phoned my mother in the summer of 1952 to say that a friend in the same house, Gladys, had just died suddenly. Perhaps we'd be interested in her apartment.

I signed a one year lease at a reasonable rent for a top-floor apartment, six F. One large bedroom; a small, narrow kitchen not twelve feet wide; sitting room. Windows on Lincoln Road. Doorman twenty four hours. Some might say we were lucky, very lucky. I'd say we were blessed, very blessed. What did the Psalmist say of "the Lord our maker"? "....... we are his people, the flock he shepherds."

Shortly before the wedding, Fr. Joe Daly one evening held the usual rehearsal, after which we all were guests at Mary's home for a lavish dinner. Afterwards he and I walked back together. At the door of the rectory, before he went in, he said to me in all seriousness: "Be good to Mary, or I'll beat your bowl in." Now after forty - four years, I'm happy that not once has the good priest been provoked to assault my bowl.

A classmate who had left the Order shortly after I did, Joe Reuter of Newark New Jersey, agreed to serve as best man. My mother invited us to spend the night before the wedding as her guest. As I've said earlier, she was most generous. A limousine got us to the church, in our tails and top hats, with time to spare. A wedding scheduled ahead of ours, however, was running late, and so Mary, the bride, and her party had to wait a bit in their limo.

Our wedding proceeded smoothly as planned. While we knelt before the altar, I was fully relaxed. Even so, for a moment I felt a twitching in my right knee. Those I asked afterwards said they hadn't seen any leg movement. The baritone soloist we had preferred sang brilliantly the numbers Mary had chosen. Incidentally, Because, not being "liturgical", he was not allowed to sing. What a pity. Compare "Because" with the awful stuff that fills our hymnals today ! Ah, but he did enchant us with "On this day, oh beautiful Mother........." Now how could anyone prefer a mere tenor? OK Because isn't a hymn.

The Hotel St. George, Brooklyn Heights, in those days was comparable to the fine competitors in Manhattan. The Pennsylvania, for example, or The Astor. The wedding reception was a huge success. Evidently everyone had a great time. At the height of the party, Mary's Uncle Willie Meehan, her deceased mother's brother, ordered champagne again and again for everyone. Mary and I must have been the first to leave, in fact to slip away quietly, even though we had enjoyed the celebration too.

The banquet manager must have sensed that we were about to leave. Quietly he offered me a quart of Imperial Brand whiskey, adding that there was still much of it untouched. How could I refuse?

Mary's father's sister Libbie Daniels, lent us her car for the honeymoon. We had hidden it the day before in a garage near the hotel. If there were practical jokers hoping to ambush us, we managed to elude them with the help of Rose and Joe Fernandez, who spirited us out the back door via a freight elevator.

Our honeymoon plans were to spend the first night in whatever attractive hotel we'd find in Stamford, Connecticut. Then to wander like Gypsies through New England to Quebec. No reservations. No fixed itinerary. Of course we'd have to be back in Brooklyn before the end of Mary's vacation from the laboratory, and in time to begin the fall term at St. Francis Prep, and Fordham.

In most places we stayed just one night, but in Sacco, Maine, we chose a cute cabin over a room at the lodge. We fanned out visiting the area over several days. Our cabin was like bungalows in Rockaway Beach; walls were sheathed on the outside only. Similarly, partitions were bare on one side. The bottle of Imperial whiskey we'd carried off from the St. George, of which we'd drunk very little, I hid behind a mirror hanging on a stud. Why tempt the chambermaid? We may have reached Augusta before I remembered. What are the chances that it's still hidden there?

In heavily wooded Jackman, Maine, close to the Canadian border, we chanced to find a cozy cabin with fireplace and a good supply of firewood. Temperature went down with the sun, from cool to frigid. Hoping to find snacks and marshmallows to toast, we drove to the nearby general store. While Mary browsed, I took a bottle of beer from the cooler and put it down on the counter. Seeing this, the clerk, scowling at me, scooped it up and announced with gusto: "Not on Sunday!"

Oddly enough, in Quebec the next day the weather was balmy. It was like going from Northern Maine to Florida.

Rates at the picturesque Chateau Frontenac were outrageous, as though tourists would willingly pay. We dined there twice, as I recall, even so. But just a bit down the street we were quite happy for several days at Hotel St. Louis. The manager addressed Mary as "Madame". She liked that.

The City was charming. We left the car and roamed about enchanted. We had, of course, to drive up to the Shrine of St. Anne de Beaupre. Unlike many others there, we were not so devout as to climb stairs on our knees.

En route home we drove down on the Canadian side of the St. Lawrence, crossing into New York near Alexandria Bay. In Truxton Sadie Wallace invited us to stay a while, but the next morning we had to set out for the "Libbie D" on Fairfield Beach. The honeymoon was over. Yet Mary and I were still euphoric.

Saturday, August 24, 1996

While I was teaching Latin full time at St. Francis Prep, Brooklyn, I studied part-time at Fordham, aiming for a master's degree in Education, the key to a state license to teach at public high-schools. In due course I was issued a certificate permitting me to teach Latin, English and Mathematics.

A Franciscan seminary classmate, Father Boniface Hanley, then serving a parish in northern New Jersey, telephoned to ask if I could and would teach Latin to a small group of young men who aspired to become priests. Their schooling had not included Latin. All were working full-time in business careers. No seminary would accept them without the ability to read and write Latin. (Reading was especially critical.)

One of the would-be priests taught business courses at a small school several floors above Radio City Music Hall, The School of Business Practice and Speech, Dan Tierney. He hoped to enter St. Joseph's in Callicoon. Then too there were Hank Clarence, Andy Drew, Joe Lakis, Tom Mylott, and Tom Reed.

Hank Clarence went on to become a Passionist, (or was it Benedictine?) In time he left the order and the priesthood, married, and settled in Berkeley. Andy Drew persevered to become a Capuchin and a dear friend even to this very day. Today he serves in Springfield, Massachusetts.

Another dear friend, Joe Lakis hoped to become a Jesuit priest. In the seminary he learned that upon ordination he was to be assigned to a parish in Syria, due to his Syrian ancestry, his fluency in Arabic, and despite his Baptism into the Roman Rite, and his exclusively Roman Catholic education, from grade school through Fordham University. The Order was adamant. Joe dropped out. Later, Mary and I asked Joe to be Chris's godfather.

Monday, August 26, 1996

After graduating in June 1953 from Fordham, I had a transcript sent to Albany to support my application for a secondary school teacher's license. A permanent certificate was issued on July 8th 1953 authorizing me to teach Latin, English and Mathematics.

With the towns and villages out on Long Island growing rapidly, because so many young families were leaving the City, suburban school districts were forced to expand. New schools, both elementary and secondary, were needed. The small districts that used to farm out their high-school kids to nearby towns – Farmingdale, for instance – were compelled to grow. The mother hens needed the room for their own chicks.

By the grace of God I soon found a job, to begin in September, teaching English and Latin in the one year old Bethpage High School, then sharing space in Broadway School. The annual salary was $3,800. (Incidentally at the Prep my salary for the second year was $2,400.)

The manager – owner of the employment agency in Rockville Centre kindly agreed to my paying his fee in installments, the first of which would be due in September. (Total: $380)

Shortly before the first day of school we bought a new two door Ford Customline sedan. eight cylinders. "Timberline Green" The dealer arranged a loan through Commercial Investment Trust, a.k.a. "C.I.T.", with twenty four monthly installments. Now, that burden, combined with all other expenses, kept us scrimping from payday to payday for two years. And yes, that '53 Ford was a wise investment. It served us well, with no serious problems of maintenance, for seven or eight years. We got our money's worth. Style changes in following years were in my eyes no improvement.

In the summer of 1954, while Mary and I were guests for a few days of Sadie Wallace in upstate Truxton, Mary's father phoned to report: "There's been a fire in your house; you'd better hurry back to salvage what you can." Oh, no! Salvage!

The fire marshal concluded that a short circuit in the complex wiring between the top - floor ceiling and the roof had sparked the fire. It had begun above our apartment and the two that flanked it. Damage was extensive, due both to the flames as well as the water used to put it out, seeping down to the cellar six floors below. A total loss were books we had stored down there, among which were Constitutions of The Order of Friars Minor, and others irreplaceable.

Well, that was the bad news. Here's the good news. Good for Mary and me at least. The large apartments between which we were sandwiched suffered severe damage, from both fire and water. Mary and I, however, lost a lampshade and two small scatter rugs. Now, what was I saying about our being blessed, very blessed? Four lines from Psalm 91 come to mind :

> "Upon you no evil shall fall,
> no plague approach where you dwell.
> For you he has commanded his angels,
> to keep you in all your ways."

Thursday, August 29, 1996

Severe damage to some of the top floor apartments, and perhaps to some below, forced tenants to find another place to stay while repairs were being made. We decided to look out on Long Island, close to Bethpage. Our furniture, other belongings and we ourselves found refuge at the Daniels home at 666 St. Marks Avenue.

Libbie's friend and fellow teacher, Agnes Cleary, living in East Northport, invited us to stay with her while we scouted the area. May she rest in peace.

The large frame house at 62 Penataquit Place, Huntington, had the second floor converted into a small one bedroom apartment, accessible from the back. Furnished. One bedroom. No linens, cooking utensils, or dishes etc. Neighbors had similar houses, similar lots. The landlady, Mrs. Pritchard, lived on the first floor that she shared with Mrs. Pineo, another widow.

West Neck Road was a short stroll away; Main Street was no more than a quarter mile south, and on it St. Patrick's Church and school, the original red-brick church, on whose site there is now a parking lot. Mary and I used to walk to church and the shops, Sears, for instance and the A. & P. But not in fowl winter weather. Even closer was the office of Dr. Douglas Harrington on Central Street, who took care of us until he retired not long ago, alas. On occasion he even came to our home ! Yes, we do miss him.

Distracted one afternoon by a toothache, and recalling a dentist's shingle on West Neck Road, I walked in. The doctor said he specialized in orthodontics, but if I'd like, he'd phone a colleague nearby.

Off I hurried to Green Street and the office of Dr. Fred Kornblueh. Even with a client waiting, he sat me in the chair at once. With mock annoyance, he pretended to chide me for not having made an appointment, while he probed around in my mouth. It may have been that first visit when he proudly showed his brand new high-speed, water-cooled drill. Indeed, I may have been the first one on whom he used it. What will Mary and I and Chris do when Dr. Fred retires? What other dentist plays classical music on the stereo while he works? None of that "elevator music" for him and his patients.

Mrs. Pineo had a huge beautiful gray male cat, Buttons. She fed him only frozen cod fillets. He had been born in a fish-processing plant. When not in the house, he was tethered on a long laundry line at the back door. On occasion he liked to climb our stairs for a visit. A lovable, gentle pet. The squirrels seemed to know just how far that tether reached.

Frank and Naomi Daniels had a young puppy for which they were hoping to find a home. Mary and I presumed that the landlady would not object. A day or two later we had to bring Pogo back.

On the other side of our street, close to Clinton Avenue, several kittens were up for adoption. Our landlady gave permission, and so with a shoe box, Mary and I walked over early one evening to fetch one. The owner had one of her children bring a kitten in from the back yard. A cold rain had been falling. The poor thing was soaking wet. "Oh," says Mrs. Bauer, "they like it outside".

It was a tiny black and white male. All four broad paws had an extra claw. Mittens or Snowshoes would have been fitting names, but we called him Spookey, because it was Halloween.

After he gobbled up his first meal, we covered the kitchen table with newspapers. With the kitten lying quietly between us, using tweezers we picked off fleas that we killed in a shallow dish of rubbing alcohol. Fleas, fleas and more fleas on every square inch of his body. In the end they hid the dish. He lay all the while like a rag doll. Thus with few interruptions he slept for about twenty-four hours.

The veterinarian we found in Syosset found a respiratory infection for which he wrote a prescription. The pharmacist across from St. Patrick's, seeing the small dosage, exclaimed "Oh, a preemie!" But then he read the patient name: "Feline Dee".

I almost forgot. The morning after we adopted Spookey, we happened to look out the kitchen window across to the garage roof. The rain had stopped. There atop the gable lay Spookey's mother, looking at us. Now, how did that cat know where her kitten had been brought? Maybe she sensed that he was in good hands. She never came back.

Saturday, August 31, 1996

When we rented the apartment, the landlady offered garage space for an additional five dollars per month. It happened that both bays of the two-car garage were filled, like an annex to the crowded attic. Assured that space would be made for us, I paid in advance one month's rent for both apartment and garage.

On the day that the second month's rent came due, no change had been made. I was still parking out on the street. And so I paid for the apartment only. A couple of days later, Mrs. Pritchard had taken all the stuff out of the right bay and compacted it with and on top of the potpourri in the left.

One night I swatted a mosquito against a wall in the bedroom. Daylight showed the red smudge to be so ugly that I washed it. Only then did a clean circle draw attention to the grimy appearance of the rest of the wall. There was nothing to do but wash that entire wall. In spare time I got to work. The improvement was so dramatic that I went on to scour all the other walls in the bedroom. Not long afterward the landlady was easily persuaded to supply enough paint to do the whole room. Of course, my labor cost her nothing. I can't recall whether it was Mary or she who chose the color.

Our landlady's driveway lay on the west (right) side of the lot, while the next-door neighbor's lay to his left. Only a low wire fence separated them.

That stretch of wire wasn't always there, or so we were told. Mrs. Pritchard and her neighbor, Mr. Elsworth Johnson, were sister and brother who, years ago, had a falling out, leading to neither speaking to the other.

After snowstorms, Mr. Johnson – Uncle El, as Mary and I came to call him – used to shovel his driveway to the street, maybe six car lengths. His sister parked her car behind her house, from which place, after heavy snow, she would shovel the shortest distance to his driveway. After the dispute that led to the breakdown, Uncle El put up the fence. Incidentally, as long as Mary and I were tenants, it was I who shoveled her driveway. And yes, we got along very well with Uncle El and Aunt Belle, a lovable couple. No children.

Tuesday, September 3, 1996

During my second year at evolving Bethpage High School, at Broadway School, I carried a full program of classes, plus homeroom and cafeteria duty. In addition I served as moderator of the fledgling student newspaper. The principal, Ernie Secrest, promised to relieve me of one of the classes the following school year. In June, he informed me that he could not keep that promise.

It happened that a fourth grade teacher would leave at the close of the school year to become an assistant in Plainview to the Supervising Principal. Art Bunce asked if I'd like to go with him; he'd recommend me.

What was becoming Plainview-Old Bethpage High School shared space in Jamaica Avenue School. In September 1955 I began a long teaching career with Algebra and Plane Geometry. In due course I added combination of Mathematics, Latin and English. In the first couple of years I taught also eighth grade mathematics.

Wednesday, September 11, 1996

As I was about to leave for home one afternoon in Bethpage, one of my ninth grade English students burst into my room. She had received her report card showing a failing grade for the marking period.

School policy was to assign no grade lower than sixty, minimum passing grade being sixty-five. In my judgment it was wise only in calculating <u>final</u> grades. We teachers, however, were held to the policy all through the term.

That young lady was irate because of the grade sixty. She demanded to know how she could have been given a failing grade. Just when had she failed? During the marking period, she pointed out, she had been absent often, she had been away for <u>every</u> test, she had turned in <u>no</u> homework, and she had turned in <u>no</u> book report.

The same minimum sixty policy was imposed in Plainview as well. Another – with which I had no objection – was that to pass the final Regents examination was to pass for the course for that term. Consequently if anyone had been failing all along, but in the Regents had scored at least sixty one points, the teacher had no choice but to grade the paper as sixty five. Official records showed sixty five in a circle. Report card showed sixty five without the circle. It happened that a boy in one of my classes, who had not earned a single passing grade during the term, not even in the Regents examination, was passed <u>for the year</u> with that artificial sixty five.

In addition to several classes of English at Bethpage, I was assigned one in First Year Latin. No more than fifteen boys and girls. All very bright, well disciplined, motivated.

One of the brightest dropped out of school suddenly in midterm. Rumor had it that she had become pregnant, and so her parents had quietly spirited her away to something like The Good Shepherd, where her schooling could continue while she awaited the birth of her baby.

In those days, you see, becoming a mother before becoming a bride was a disgrace and a scandal. To the family an embarrassment. Moreover, in those days causing a baby in the womb to die was regarded everywhere as unthinkable barbarity. In those days.

Saturday, September 14, 1996

Shortly after the school- year ended, probably in 1954, I was enticed by an advertisement aimed at teachers to be trained to sell during the summer <u>Compton's</u> <u>Encyclopedia</u>. Those interested were invited to report to a conference room in the Hotel Commodore, Manhattan.

Except for an hour's break for lunch, we spent from early Monday morning until late afternoon listening to animated lectures and pep talks by several men introduced as highly successful salesmen and former teachers. "As we did, you too can make lots of money. All you need to do is follow our instructions".

All the special features of <u>Compton's</u> <u>Encyclopedia</u> were spelled out in great detail, as was to be expected. Much more time was given, however, to numerous clever sales techniques. The strategy was a prescribed, minutely detailed and memorized sales pitch that anticipated all sales resistance. We were to be like actors reciting their lines committed to memory verbatim from a script. Even the timing and the manner of spreading open a large, full color display poster were precisely choreographed.

Following the introductory standard presentation, came the "closing", designed to persuade the prospect to sign the contract. Then, if necessary, we were to proceed to plan B and closing B. Then as needed to C, D, E, F, etc.

We were instructed to canvass the districts where we taught, going methodically from house to house, street after street, beginning in early morning, breaking for lunch, and then returning until late afternoon.

Finally, in the evening we were to report by telephone to a local agent of the publisher.

On the following morning I chose at random a street in Bethpage, and beginning at the corner, went from house to house in the manner prescribed. That day, Tuesday, I sold not one set, nor on Wednesday or Thursday.

In looking back, I see my failure as due to a temperamental deficiency; I have no talent for selling. Then too, the set was expensive. In fact, I myself could not have paid the price. And so, when fathers and mothers confided the same limitation, it seemed to me a waste of my time and theirs to press on with further selling points. It was obvious that those blue-collar workers, whose homes were furnished modestly, were striving to raise children on low incomes. And so it was fruitless to persuade them intellectually of the value of the encyclopedias.

After supper on Thursday I phoned as usual the publisher's agent in Laurel Hollow, at which time he proposed to take up on the next morning where I had left off. He would do the selling, while I in silence would observe and learn, being introduced as his "associate".

Early on Friday morning I led my mentor to the house next to the last one I had canvassed the afternoon before. Through all morning and afternoon, except for the lunch break, we went systematically from door to door, street by street. By late afternoon Compton's agent had made not one sale.

Wednesday, September 18, 1996

After the failure of the revolt of the Hungarian people against the Communist Russian occupation, in 1956, put down by overwhelming force, Mary and I learned of Hungarian babies in New York Foundling Home (or was it Hospital?). After four years, our hope of conceiving a child was getting fainter and fainter. We wrote to Cardinal Spellman offering to adopt one of the babies. Of course we'd have been overjoyed to have more than one, for brothers and sisters ought not to be separated.

The Cardinal answered, saying that none of the Hungarian babies was up for adoption. Whether we had applied too late, or whether they were to be re-united with their parents he did not say.

Whatever the rationale, we were greatly saddened. Yet we could not see that God had other plans for us. It wasn't long afterward that Mary conceived. Christopher Joseph had begun his pilgrimage.

Friday, September 20, 1996

After Chris was born, it became evident that the apartment was no longer big enough. And so we began to search for a house at a price we could afford. On Saturdays and Sunday afternoons we used to cruise through residential neighborhoods for miles around. Real estate advertisements in newspapers we studied. And of course we sought the help of local brokers.

Month after month the places we could afford were unsuitable for various reasons. The bungalow, for instance, on Northern Boulevard in St. James had only one fault: the kitchen was much too small. Those houses that seemed ideal were priced out of reach for us. Take for example the red brick one with Spanish – tile roof on Taylor Avenue in Greenlawn.

During all the time we did not tell our landlady nor neighbors of our searching. Without a lease we could have been asked to leave before we were ready. Yet in the summer Mrs. Pritchard informed us that with the baby, we'd have to get out.

A real estate broker, on one of her excursions, drove us to a new listing. At first sight we loved it. Perfect ! Beautiful ! Somehow I knew in the depths of my soul that here at last was the place we had been looking for, the home that God had prepared for us. Chris was not quite a year old when we moved in.

Saturday, September 21, 1996

At Hempstead General Hospital's delivery room, Mary was in labor with our second child. Down in the lobby on the main floor, I waited, anxious to know whether it would be a son or daughter. It was Friday June 26, 1959.

Chances are that I was smoking too much, and drinking more coffee than was good for me, when Dr. James Heffernan – the same obstetrician who helped Chris into the world – came down to me, still in his pea-green coveralls, to tell that the baby, a girl, had been born dead, for she had strangled on the umbilical cord.

God works in mysterious ways, as we know. It is not for us to ask <u>why</u> some babies are born dead, some perfect, some cretins, and some come into the world with all sorts of other handicaps. The strong, mature father says, of such a child, as did the Biblical Job in his afflictions: "......if we have good things at the hand of God, why should we not receive evil?" But I was neither strong nor mature; I stood in a corner, face to the walls, crying.

Bad enough that Mary should suffer that loss, losing a daughter she had not even seen, but that she should then suffer through the funeral, would have been piling burden upon burden. And so in haste I made arrangements with M.A. Connell Funeral Home in Huntington Station. Then I hurried off to the rectory at St. Philip Neri's in Northport, where I asked to buy a grave. There was space among the babies along the fence on the west side, to the left of the tool shed.

One of the O'Connell sons, Peter, escorted me to a room the next morning where the baby lay in a tiny, white, velvet-covered casket. I did not open it, nor did I ask Peter to do so. He closed the door behind him. Margaret and her father were alone for a few minutes, while I struggled to regain poise.

With the casket on my lap, I rode alongside Peter in the limousine. A grave digger was waiting at the open grave. And so we three buried the casket, and marked the grave with a temporary aluminum sign.

Years later, when we could afford it, we had a carved stone monument made set in flush at the head:

"Margaret E. Dee
June 26, 1959"

Lillian G. Foley Dee - 1915

Leonard Dee and Lillian Dee - 1915

Leonard Dee -1918

Thomas Dee and Leonard Dee - 1918

Harry Dee & Lillian Dee in front of the Brooklyn Museum - 1925

John Andrew Foley and Catherine Boyle Foley - May 1925

Lillian Dee July 1934

Lillian Dee - Summer of '34

Harry Dee – National Guard - January 1938

Harry Dee – June 1944

Harry Dee & Lillian Foley Dee – June 1944

Harry & Mary Dee – August 16, 1952

1 John Andrew Foley (Grandpa) born Ireland 1851 died September 12, 1926

1 Catherine Boyle Foley (Grandma) born Ireland May 14, 1854 died February 01, 1939

2 Mary Foley McLaughlin (Aunt Mary) born May 10, 1875 died May 6, 1936

William A McLaughlin (Uncle Will) August 05, 1874 died August 12, 1935 married 1901 in Philadelphia

    3 Catherine McLaughlin Gibney born 1902 died July 08, 1952

    3 James W McLaughlin born 1904 died April 08, 1936

    3 Margaret McLaughlin born June 15, 1906 died July 31, 1906

    3 John McLaughlin born May 16, 1908 died January 6, 1956

    3 Mary McLaughlin Mahon born July 31, 1910 died November 07, 1990

    3 Anna McLaughlin Donahue born July 13, 1913 died September 22, 1986

    3 Margaret McLaughlin Shannon born March 05, 1915 died April 21, 1984

    3 William A McLaughlin (Billy) born July 07, 1916 died September 09, 1998

2 Frances Foley Swift (Aunt Fannie) born 1882 died December 31, 1938

2 Rose Foley Leggett (Aunt Rose) born 1888 died December 24, 1924

Henry Stanley Leggett (Uncle Harry) born December 18, 1884 died January 6, 1962

    3 John A Leggett born August 11, 1910 died May 24, 1969

    3 William Leggett (Bill) born October 10, 1911 died January 07, 1960

    3 Chloe Leggett Paulstich born 1914 died November 29, 1948

    3 Henry Stanley Leggett Jr. (Stanley) born March 3, 1916 died September 20, 1982

    3 Edward Bernard Leggett (Eddie) born March 29, 1920 died February 16, 2000

2 Catherine V. Foley Kelly (Aunt Katie) born June 07, 1890 died April 1, 1955

Edward J Kelly (Uncle Ed Kelly) born April 15, 1891 died August 30, 1954 married February 12, 1916 St. Clement's R.C. Church Philadelphia

    3 Dorothy Kelly Ballas November 17, 1916 died September 15, 1982

    3 Kathryn G Kelly McCrory (Kass) born April 27, 1919 died April 23, 1984

    3 Helen Marie Kelly Schaefer born March 03, 1921 died January 05, 1994

3 Edward Kelly Jr. (Eddie) 1923
3 Jack Paul Kelly born August 06 1925 died September 15, 1987

2 Lillian Gertrude Foley Dee born January 24, 1891 died December 29, 1975
   Leonard J. Dee born April 27, 1889 died August 24, 1967 married October 10, 1915 St. Clement's R.C. Church Philadelphia
      3 Lillian G. Dee born October 12, 1916 died August 12, 1937
      3 Harry P. Dee born October 4, 1917 died January 10, 2000

2 Edward Bernard Foley (Uncle Eddie) born December 1, 1892 died June 18, 1947

John Francis Dee born April 2, 1866 died April 28, 1957 married June 10, 1887 St. Agatha's Philadelphia PA

Ellen Mary Leonard born May 1, 1870 died November 04, 1944
John and Ellen had eleven children.

1 Leonard J. Dee born April 27, 1889 died August 24, 1967
2 William J Dee born August 12, 1890 died March 20, 1961
3 Anna Marie Dee Stover Parker born June 26, 1892 died August 13, 1986
4 Mary A Dee Callahan born January 26, 1894 1894 died August 13, 1976
5 John F Dee born July 1895 died September 28, 1903
6 Thomas Leonard Dee born April 24, 1897 died December 7, 1973
7 Ellen Dee born 1899 died November 19, 1901
8 Christopher J Dee born December 25, 1901 died July 30, 1986
9 Maurice Dee born January 29, 1905 died August 6, 1984
10 Catherine Dee Palma born December 17, 1907 died March 12, 1962
11 Frances Julia Dee Brooks born June 25, 1910, died March 29, 1993

"Cousin Ed"

Edward J. Foley April 08, 1889 – November 16, 1953

Married October 01, 1913 Most Blessed Sacrament Church Philadelphia PA

Mary Margaret Davis October 01, 1888 – April 21, 1953

They are buried in Sacred Heart Cemetery Vineland NJ - Sec. H, Lot 69B

Edward and Mary had five children.

1 Joseph Patrick Foley October 05, 1914 – April 14, 1970
2 Mary Margaret Foley September 01, 1916 – March 24, 1984
3 John R Foley - around 1918
4 Isabella Agnes Foley Steinborn February 05, 1920 – October 26, 2005
        Sacred Heart Cemetery Vineland NJ - Sec. H, Lot 69B

5 Edward John Foley Jr. January 05, 1931 – January 10, 2007
Married Florence Saussy November 01, 1927 – January 02, 2007
They are buried in Highlands Memorial Park Maron County NC

Edward J. Foley April 08, 1889 – November 16, 1953

His Mother - Rose Boyle
Born October 27, 1859 Donegal Ireland
Died June 07, 1923 Philadelphia PA

His Father – Patrick Foley
Born March 27, 1854 Worcester MA
Died March 05, 1922 Philadelphia PA

Rose and Patrick are buried in New Cathedral Cemetery Philadelphia PA.
Section N Block 2 Lot 9

Rose and Patrick had eight children.
1 Elizabeth Rose Foley
Born October 18, 1879 – Died October 17, 1950
Buried in New Cathedral Cemetery Philadelphia PA. Section N Block 2
    Lot 9

2 Kathryn Regina Foley McCarthy
Born August 02, 1881 – Died April 12, 1954
Buried in New Cathedral Cemetery Philadelphia PA. Section N Block 2
    Lot 9
3 Joseph P. Foley
Born August 13, 1884 Philadelphia PA
Died October 21, 1931 Philadelphia PA
Died from severe burns from an explosion in a plumbing accident.
Buried Holy Cross Cemetery Philadelphia PA Section K Range 14 Lot 35

4 Thomas Foley 1886

5 Edward J. Foley April 08, 1889 – November 16, 1953
Buried Sacred Heart Cemetery Vineland NJ - Sec. H, Lot 69B

6 John Foley Born February 23, 1891 – Died June 1964

7 Rose M. Foley Born June 29,1893 – Died August 1982
Buried in New Cathedral Cemetery Philadelphia PA. Section N Block 2 Lot 9
8 Frances Foley (Male) 1897

Joseph P. Foley
Born August 13, 1884 Philadelphia PA
Died October 21, 1931 Philadelphia PA
Died from severe burns from an explosion in a plumbing accident.

Married

Elizabeth A Welsh Foley
Born July 31, 1883 - internment date January 23, 1967

They are buried in Holy Cross Cemetery Philadelphia PA Section K Range
14 Lot 35.

Joseph and Elizabeth had four children

1 Joseph P. Foley 1910 - internment date May 03, 1991
Buried Holy Cross Cemetery Philadelphia PA Section K Range 14 Lot 35

2 Mary E. Foley Born April 22, 1915 Philadelphia PA
        Died February 12, 2006 Cecil MD
        Buried Old Bohemia Cemetery
        AKA Saint Francis Xavier Shrine Cemetery
        Warwick Cecil County MD

3 John Foley Born March 8, 1917 internment date July 14, 1987
Buried Holy Cross Cemetery Philadelphia PA Section K Range 14 Lot 35

4 Margaret R. Foley Born August 22, 1921 Philadelphia PA

Printed in the United States
By Bookmasters

Printed in the United States
By Bookmasters